THE STORMS OF PROVIDENCE

*Navigating the Waters of Calvinism,
Arminianism, and Open Theism*

Michael D. Robinson

University Press of America,® Inc.
Dallas · Lanham · Boulder · New York · Oxford

For Ron and Norma Robinson
You have shown me what God must be like.

Contents

Contents   vii

Contents

Preface

If you have ever been on the ocean on a blustery day, you know how difficult it can be to stand your ground. The boat rocks and sways, as it cuts through the waves. Its passengers teeter and wobble, trying to keep their footing as they go about their business. How frightening it must be to ride out a prominent storm in all its fury! The experience is surely terrorizing and humbling. In like manner, many feel trepidation and confusion when confronting the complicated nuances of the Christian doctrine of divine providence. The prospect of finding ones way through the torrent can seem dismal indeed. Ideally, of course, the purpose of this text would be to provide smooth sailing through the troubling seas of this great Church teaching. But such a goal is beyond the paltry skills of this mariner. And so, perhaps the best I can hope for is to be a fellow-voyager who seeks (with others) to pass through the treacherous waters toward a peaceful shore. Specifically, and less metaphorically, I hope to make a case for an augmented version of traditional Arminianism—a model of providence that endorses simultaneously God's sovereignty, foreknowledge and grace along with human freedom, responsibility and intrinsic value. I suffer no fantasy that I will persuade all, or perhaps even many. But I do invite readers to join me in the journey, hoping that together we can gain insight into the Christian faith.

I hope that a variety of audiences will benefit from this text, especially those interested in Christian theology. I suspect that the book will be particularly of interest to "evangelicals" for whom discussions of Calvinism, Arminianism and Open theism have been heated. Hopefully, theology students, professors, clergy and laypersons alike will find the text interesting, challenging and beneficial.

With gratitude, I acknowledge the following persons who

have aided me in the process of producing this book. First, I thank my students for their helpful insights in class and in private conversations over some of these matters, especially Woods Nash who graciously read the first draft of the manuscript and made helpful comments throughout. Further, I thank those anonymous reviewers who read portions of this text as potential and actual journal articles, and whose comments have strengthened the work in diverse ways. Finally, I thank my colleagues at Cumberland College who helped me edit the last drafts of this text so that I might publish it with relatively few stylistic errors. Specifically, I thank Bob Dunston, Garland Young, Kirby Clark, John Powell, Jane Whitaker and Norma Dunston for their meritorious efforts.

Michael Robinson
Williamsburg, Kentucky
March 2003

Chapter 1

Plotting the Course and Gathering the Supplies

What is the relationship between God and the world? This question has puzzled sages and saints across the ages, and continues to plague us today. Are humans something like cosmic puppets and God the Grand Puppet Master? Does God not only create us, but also cause us to think what we think, will what we will, want what we want, and do what we do? Or do humans exercise a quasi-independence from God? While our origin is in the divine act of creation, has God granted us a genuine, though limited, autonomy? Can we authentically interact with God in interpersonal dialogue? Can we disappoint, even surprise God? Can we frustrate the divine intentions and plans? These are some of the questions that we will address in the coming pages, as we attempt to map-out the waters of the Christian doctrine of providence.

Plotting the Course

Over the last decade or so, controversy has raged within the evangelical Christian community concerning the nature of the divine-world relationship. This controversy has ancient roots. Three important models dominate the discussion. First, some theologians affirm what might be called the Calvinistic model of the divine-world relationship. In this view, God is conceived of as utterly sovereign over the created order. No event happens that God has not ordained. There are no surprises, no unanticipated "bumps" in the road, no unforeseen risks for God. All actions unfold according to the divine plan. Indeed, supporters of this view seem to be committed to the claim that no event happens that God does not ultimately *cause*. In turn, salvation is purely a matter of divine action. Humans play no active role in their own redemption. Rather through inner spiritual influence, God gives some humans the will, the faith and the repentance necessary to receive the benefits made available on the cross of Christ. To others, God gives no such inner spiritual gift and as a result these individuals are not saved. Further, according to this model, the future is known fully by God because he has predestined all that will happen. That is, God does not know the future by passively "observing" it; rather he knows it by deciding, in advance, what the future will be and by making sure it happens as planned.

A second noteworthy paradigm of the divine-world relationship is the Arminian model. This model also affirms divine sovereignty, insisting that God is ultimately in control of all that happens. In a certain sense, no event happens that the deity has not ordained. However, this view denies that God causes all events. Instead, God permissively wills or permissively ordains some events. Creatures cause some events. God simply foreknows (in a passive, observation-like way) what these creatures will do, and willingly permits them to perform the acts in question. The Arminian model, then, reverses the Calvinistic view of foreknowledge. Rather than asserting that God knows the future by determining it, Arminians insist that God "predetermines" the future by foreknowing it. That is, God permissively allows foreknown events to transpire. In turn, salvation involves some autonomous human effort. Arminians agree that salvation is by grace. Humans cannot atone for their own sins; thus, the cross of Christ is a uniquely divine act and is necessary for salvation. Further, left to their own devices, humans would not turn in faith to Christ; rather, divine urging is necessary for humans to exercise faith in Christ. Nevertheless, while the atonement of Christ is a divine act, acceptance of the salvation made possible through that atonement is (partially) an autonomous human act. Further, while divine aid assists humans to turn to Christ, the decision to exercise faith ultimately is a human act. It is an action that the individual may choose to enact or not.

A third key perspective on the divine-world relationship is the model presented by open theists—sometimes called freewill theism. Like the first two models, this paradigm asserts that God is sovereign over the created order. God has created all that exists and at any moment is able utterly to destroy the universe and/or manipulate world-events as they unfold. However, God chooses to limit the exercise of his power so that creatures (especially humans) may execute genuine freedom and responsibility. Like the Arminian model and unlike the Calvinistic view, open theism asserts that humans play a positive role in their salvation. While divine atonement and inner spiritual aid are necessary for salvation, the *decision* to believe in Christ and, thus, to receive the gift of salvation, is inexorably a human act. Unlike both Calvinism and Arminianism, open theism denies that God fully knows the future. This denial is made in an effort to save human freedom. Open theists believe that infallible knowledge of future events truncates the freedom of those events. After all, if it truly is *known* that tomorrow I will eat eggs for breakfast, then it seems there is no choice in the matter. I simply will eat eggs. I can do no other. Subsequently, it seems for such an event to be free, it cannot be foreknown. (We will discuss this argument more fully later).

Now the question that arises for the reader is this: Which of these three models of providence should Christians affirm? The purpose of this book is (1) to analyze these theological paradigms and the rationales that support them, (2) to evaluate the strengths and weaknesses of each, and (3) hopefully to navigate through some of the difficulties that emerge in each toward a coherent and persuasive view of the God-world relationship. The following course of study will be employed. In chapters two, three and four, I will consider respectively the basic tenets of the Calvinistic,

Arminian, and open theistic models, evaluating each as I go. In chapters five and six, I will offer first a biblical and then a philosophical defense of a modified version of the Arminian model—the perspective that I believe best resolves the issues surrounding the doctrine of providence. In chapter seven, I will present some of the practical implications of each theory, stressing what I perceive to be the advantages of the Arminian model. In the Epilogue, I will offer a brief summary of my conclusions and some closing thoughts concerning the doctrine of divine providence.

Gathering the Supplies

Before analyzing and evaluating these three models of the God-world relationship, a word is needed concerning the criteria to be used in appraising them. Also, a brief discussion is called for concerning the major themes that mutually are addressed by these theological perspectives.

Evaluative Criteria

Obviously, the criteria one uses to judge a system of thought largely determines the outcome of one's evaluation. We must be cautious, then, in choosing standards so as to avoid undue prejudice. Of course, no one nor any criterion is utterly objective. Each of us brings bias to the interpretive and adjudicatory process. Still objectivity remains an important (if often ideal) goal for any theological analysis. Three criteria seem appropriate for evaluating the paradigms that are being examined in this book. These are faithfulness to the biblical testimony, logical coherence, and compatibility with lived-experience.

Faithfulness to the Bible. The first criterion for judging these theological models is faithfulness to the biblical testimony. For Christians, the Bible is the chief authority for doctrine, faith and practice. And so, theological models must be judged according to their faithfulness to scripture. Of course, biblical interpretation is no simple matter. Huge volumes have been written defending one form of biblical hermeneutic over others and various schools of interpretation are available. Often at issue is whether authorial meaning of ancient texts can be discerned by the modern reader and what, if any, tools are available to make such interpretation possible. We cannot enter into these lengthy debates.[1] It will be assumed here that the goal of biblical interpretation is to identify the basic meaning intended by the scripture writers and that tools are available for procuring this end. This is not to say that an absolutely certain interpretation can be established, but that informed and adequate understandings of biblical texts can be formulated. Indeed, in light of historical, grammatical and literary considerations, some interpretations simply are more likely to be correct than others.[2] The method of biblical interpretation to be employed here may be described roughly as the historical-literary approach.

Even if we adopt such a method of interpreting the Bible, however, problems arise; for proponents of each of these theological models see their view as being congruent with biblical testimony. How can such diversity persist? Several explanations apply. First, biblical passages are often ambiguous and imprecise. The scriptures are not a text in systematic theology. One cannot turn to a section of the Bible and find a lengthy excursus on *the* biblical doctrine of providence.[3] The Bible was written over many centuries, by diverse individuals in differing personal/social/cultural/historical contexts. Often the chief purpose of a scriptural text is not doctrinal. Rather a variety of aims fund the work of scripture writers—including desires to generate literature for worship, exhortation, legal/moral guidance, etc. Even

---

[1] For an informative survey of contemporary discussions on biblical hermeneutics, see Grant Osborne's *The Hermeneutical Spiral: A Comprehensive Introduction to Biblical Interpretation* (Downers Grove: InterVarsity Press, 1991), especailly pp. 366-411.

[2] Ibid., pp. 406-408, 412-413.

[3] Paul Helm makes a similar point. See his *The Providence of God* (Downers Grove: InterVarsity Press, 1994), p. 27.

where doctrine is a main goal, writings are often expressed in narratives, parables, etc. While such writing is lively and has a way of drawing the reader into the worldview of the writer, it is not always precise or clear. In short, the scriptures do not attempt to articulate a clear, systematic exposition of doctrine, and as a result, multiple interpretations are often possible.

A second reason for diverse understandings of scripture is the occurrence of tradition-laden interpretations. Each reader comes to a text with assumptions about the way the world is; and such preunderstanding shapes one's interpretation of the text. For example, when we read that "God is love (1 John 4:8, NIV),"[4] our preconceived notions of both "God" and "love" condition our understanding of this sentence. Someone steeped in polytheism would interpret the term "God" somewhat differently than a person from a monotheistic heritage. In like manner, whole traditions of Christian preunderstanding evolve—like Calvinism, Arminianism, open theism, etc.—and these traditions affect the reader's understanding of scripture. Grant Osborne cites the following example of tradition-laden interpretation:

> For instance, Calvinists and Arminians often interpret 'God so loved the world' quite differently, especially in comparison to other Johannine passages (such as Jn 6:37-40; 15:1-6). Some Calvinists stress 6:37-40 and emphasize the sovereign side of divine predestination in salvation; the *world* becomes the elect. Arminians emphasize 1:4, 7, 9 and 15:1-6 and the individual responsibility in faith-decision. Every person in the "world" is given a charge to respond to God's love.[5]

---

[4]Throughout this text, the predominate number of biblical quotations will come from either *The Holy Bible: The New International Version* (New York Bible Society, 1978) (NIV) or from *The Holy Bible: Revised Standard Version*, ed. Herbert May and Bruce Metzger (New York: Oxford University Press, 1962) (RSV). Upon occasion other versions will be cited and will be noted within the text.

[5]Osborne, p. 376.

Due to diverse traditions, differing interpretations emerge.[6]
A third explanation for multiple interpretations of scripture
may be tensions, paradoxes, or even contradictions in the biblical
record. In light of the vast variety of cultural/historical contexts
from which the scriptures have come, it is not surprising that
discrepancies could materialize among the concepts and claims of
the Bible. Indeed, what often is amazing is the degree of unity
found in the overarching themes of scripture. Such tension partly
can be explained by the ambiguity or imprecision of scripture
passages. For a statement to be ambiguous means that multiple
meanings are possible. In turn, diversity of possible meanings
among several statements increases the chance for logical disagreements to exist among those statements as a group. In light of the
ambiguity and imprecision of many biblical passages, then, some
(perhaps many) tensions in scripture may be merely surface level
differences. Such problems may melt away by finding (unambigu-
ous and precise) interpretations of various statements that allow all
the claims in question to cohere. Indeed, this is often what
contrasting theological traditions have done; they have interpreted
seemingly desperate statements of the Bible so that those passages
harmonize.

However, it is not clear that all interpretational discrepancies
can be resolved in this manner. Sometimes harmonies become so
contrived as to do injustice to the authoritative text. In these cases,
it may be best simply to admit a genuine and possibly irreconcil-

---

[6]John Sanders speaks of key models or root metaphors. He notes:
"Different key models embody different theologies. Many of our
theological disputes arise because we look at the 'evidence' through
different lenses. When we read the Scripture through the lenses of certain
models, we tend to interpret Scripture from that perspective. Thus it is not
surprising that someone affirming God as the immutable king would view
the biblical texts on divine repentance as anthropomorphisms so that God
never actually changes his mind." John Sanders, *The God Who Risks: A
Theology of Providence* (Downers Grove: InterVarsity Press, 1998).

able "tension" in the biblical testimony; and leave it at that.[7] Authentic paradoxes or contradictions may exist between various authors or schools of writing within the Bible. Indeed, such tensions may exist within individual authors.[8] In short, multiple interpretations of scripture may result from genuine tensions, paradoxes, or even contradictions in the text itself.

Of course, many biblical interpreters and most "evangelicals" are reticent to claim that scriptures are contradictory. The preferred nomenclature is to speak of alleged discrepancies or paradoxes or hard sayings within scripture. Admittedly, I am reluctant to ascribe logical contradiction to scripture. Still one must acknowledge, along with many commentators—both conservative and otherwise—that there are logical tensions in the Bible. And such tensions ultimately *may be* irreconcilable.

In light of these possible explanations for variant interpretations, it will be helpful to lay down some basic methodological principles for approaching scripture and for addressing interpretational variations. First, where possible, we will look for unity, for logical consistency, of biblical doctrine. While admitting that irreconcilable discrepancies are possible within the biblical record,

---

[7]This seems to be the position taken by G. C. Berkouwer concerning the logical tension that exists between human freedom and divine governance. See his *The Providence of God* (Grand Rapids: Wm. B. Eerdmans Publishing Company, 1952), pp. 125-160.

[8]A single writer (or school of writers) may affirm views that under critical analysis simply cannot be reconciled. An example *might be* the statement in Acts 2:23, where we read: "This man [Jesus] was handed over to you by God's set purpose and foreknowledge; and you, with the help of wicked men, put him to death by nailing him to the cross (NIV)." Here we find what some perceive to be statements whose implications contradict one another. On the one hand, the writer declares that God has foreknown and planned the death of Jesus; on the other hand, the author seems to assume that his audience and particular "wicked men" were responsible for the event in question. But for many readers, such assumptions logically clash. If so, it may be that the author simply held views (tacitly or explicitly) that ultimately cannot be reconciled.

such incongruities are not necessary or inevitable. When rightly interpreted, the Bible may be quite congruent. Only where the hermeneutical evidence is overwhelming should we admit an inconsistency or even a paradox in the scriptural teaching.

Second, while acknowledging the unavoidable influence of preunderstanding and tradition for comprehending a text, we will assume and uphold as a working maxim that scripture informs tradition and modern readers. Interpretation is not a one-way street. On the one hand, the text does not "speak" independently of the reader's interpretive categories and capacities. The biblical message must be filtered through the conceptual schema of the interpreter. On the other hand, the interpreter does not utterly dominate the text. The reader reads the text, using conceptual categories available to her, but the reader does not write or wholly create the text. Rather, the interpreter and the text interact in synergistic, cybernetic interplay. And because of this, the text influences/alters the reader's understanding. By employing these basic principles, as well as other standard hermeneutical techniques, we will attempt to use faithfulness to the biblical testimony as a criterion for judging the theological models being examined in this book.

Logical coherence. A second criterion for evaluating these theological models is logical coherence. Logically inconsistent beliefs are hard to live with. Although none of us has a completely consistent view of reality, few of us are particularly happy about it. The reason for this is simple: Logic dictates that two contradictory beliefs cannot both be true. And since most of us want to affirm beliefs and systems of beliefs that are true, it does us no good to affirm contradictory beliefs. For this reason, as noted above, most Christians are uncomfortable with the idea that there could be genuine logical contradictions in the Bible. As a hermenteutical principle, we seek for logical consistency in biblical doctrine. In like manner, we appropriately expect logical consistency within post-biblical theological models. Although anomalies occur in nearly every system of thought, an overabundance of such aberrations eventually calls a system into question.

Some will perhaps protest this second criterion, alleging that scripture alone should be the norm for formulating theological positions. Two comments are warranted in the face of such protest. First, scripture itself cannot be understood without appeal to logical coherence. In interpreting a statement in a biblical passage or book, it is common to assume that the author or authors do not contradict themselves. Some interpretations of a biblical statement are deemed unlikely precisely because such renderings would contradict other statements within the passage or book as a whole. Thus, appeal to the authority of scripture usually assumes an interpretative process that implicitly endorses the principle of non-contradiction. Second, each theological system examined in this book invokes reason at key points to make a case for its interpretation of Christian doctrine. In view of this implicit and sometimes explicit affirmation of the principle of logical coherence, it is legitimate to judge these systems by such a standard.

Logical consistency applies both to isolated concepts or statements, and to groups of concepts or statements. Sometimes the ideas entailed in a singular concept do not cohere. For example, consider the notions of a "married bachelor" or a "square circle." Such conceptualizations simply do not make sense; and as a result, they are dismissed as unintelligible. On the other hand, sometimes *sets* of concepts or statements are mutually contradictory. For example, the claims that the sky is blue in a certain respect and that the sky is not blue in the same respect are contradictory statements. While each statement is coherent in itself, the two together are mutually exclusive. The affirmation of both of these statements is unintelligible. As we examine our theological models, we will watch for logical contradictions both of singular concepts or statements and of sets of concepts or statements.

Compatibility with lived-experience. A third criterion for evaluating these theological programs is to consider their practical implications for daily life. Words and ideologies do not exist in a vacuum. They live within the context of human lives and communities. In light of this, it is appropriate to demand that a theological system conform (at least in some sense) to the modes of thought through which most of us conduct our lives.

Major Themes

In addition to considering the criteria to be used in appraising these three theological models, it will be helpful to discuss some of the major themes mutually addressed by them. Because each of these theological perspectives attempts to articulate an explicitly Christian conceptualization of the divine-world relationship, each shares with the others many of the same fundamental beliefs. For example, each (explicitly or tacitly) endorses the divine creation of the universe, the atoning work of Christ, the evangelistic mission of the Church, etc. Of course, there is not perfect agreement between these models concerning such doctrines. Indeed, there is not complete concordance on such matters among those who endorse a single model. Rather, a general agreement exists concerning many of the rudimentary doctrines of the Christian faith. By the same token, even where considerable differences exist, because each model is forthrightly Christian, each finds itself compelled to address similar concerns. The remainder of this chapter is devoted to canvassing the cardinal issues that mutually arise for and are tackled by these three theological programs.

The nature of God. A central concern for these models is the nature of God. While concepts of God vary widely, two basic models vie for acceptance among our three theological paradigms. These are the static view versus the dynamic view of God. Some understand God to be an utterly static, unchanging being. Whatever God is, he is without alteration. To put it in Aristotelian and Thomistic terms, the deity is fully actual; he is pure act. There is no potential in the divine being. Usually tied to this notion of God is the claim that he is atemporal—outside of time. God does not experience temporal duration. Instead, all temporal moments—past, present, future—are present to God in a singular, unchanging eternal moment. Further, God is unaffected by human actions. If God is unchanging, with no potential, then there seems to be no window through which changing human actions can affect him. Whatever God knows about us, he always knows. Whatever

God does in "response" to human actions, he always has done (or always is doing in the singular eternal moment). God reacts to no one; he simply acts. The second view of God conceives of the deity as a dynamic being, capable of change. While his basic moral character remains unaltered, God experiences some change. God has no temporal beginning or end, but he does endure *through* time, experiencing time as it unfolds from moment to moment. Thus, God knows what time it is now, knows what events are now in the past, and what events (potentially and/or actually) are still in the future. Further, God is affected by human activity. God is able to respond to human actions. When someone prays, God "hears" that prayer and is able to answer it. When someone sins, God becomes aware of it and can react to it—condemning, punishing or forgiving the transgression. In short, both God's knowledge and actions are affected by human events.[9]

---

[9]One might debate whether a temporal God's *knowledge* must be affected by creaturely events at particular temporal moments. Proponents of open theism deny that God knows the future; and so, for them God's knowledge of some events is bound to the temporal moment at which those events occur. In other words, God does not know of some events until they happen in time. But Arminians (even of the temporalist ilk) affirm divine foreknowledge. And such an affirmation may suggest to some that God's knowledge need not depend on a particular moment in time. Rather, God knows all events of all times at every instant of the divine (temporal) existence. It seems to me, however, that even if a temporal God has complete foreknowledge, there is an important sense in which the divine knowledge would be temporally affected. Even if a temporal God fully knows the future, such a being would not know that an event is occurring *now* until that event in fact presently is transpiring. Indeed, at any given moment there will be some events that are now in the past, some that are now future, and some that are now occurring; and God will only know these truths now, at this particular moment in time. A temporal God's knowledge would be temporally impacted. For a discussion of divine knowledge of temporally indexed truth claims, see A. N. Prior "The Formalities of Omniscience," *Philosophy* 37 (1962): 114-

The static view of God is most closely tied to the Calvinistic model of the divine-world relationship. The dynamic view best represents the affirmations of open theism. Arminianism tends to offer an interesting hybrid of these two models. However, as we will see, various amalgamated positions are possible and sometimes are endorsed by differing members of these three theistic camps.

The nature of humans. A second major theme addressed by our three models of the divine-world relationship is the nature of humans—in particular, the nature of human freedom and bondage to sin. The Bible assumes that humans are morally responsible for their actions, that humans are capable of receiving moral commands. It also presumes that failure to conform to ethical demands is morally reprehensible and that human beings are culpable for such failure. All of this suggests some modicum of human freedom. But what kind of freedom do humans possess? Again, two broad options are found among our three theological models. The first is indeterministic freedom—also called libertarian freedom. This picture of freedom insists that freedom is the ability to do otherwise. If asked to perform some task, humans are able either to do the action or refrain from doing it. The free individual is not compelled by any external or internal (mental, emotional, neurological, physio-chemical) conditions to choose one action over the other. Either action is possible. This is not to say that there are no contributing conditions (external or internal) that make one action more likely than another; but it is to say that neither option is necessitated or forced by those prior conditions. The human agent is able to perform the action or refrain from it.

The second view of freedom is deterministic freedom—also called compatibilist freedom. According to this conceptualization, freedom is the ability to do what one is already disposed to do. If asked to perform some task, freedom is the ability to do what one wants to do. No conditions external to the person force that

---

129.

individual to perform the action in question. Rather, conditions within the individual—beliefs, desires, previous life-experiences—urge the person to perform the act and the individual is able to act upon that urge. This view of freedom is called deterministic and compatibilistic because it is a freedom that allegedly is compatible with determinism.[10] The first of these notions of freedom—indeterministic freedom— is endorsed by open theism and by Arminianism. The second–determinism—usually is affirmed by Calvinism. As we will see, each notion of freedom is philosophically and possibly theologically problematic.

Closely linked to the notion of human freedom and a major concern for our three theological models is the traditional Christian claim that humans are in bondage to sin, that humans have a sinful nature. A corollary of this affirmation is the belief that, in some sense, humans cannot help but sin. But precisely what is meant by such a belief? Does this mean that it is logically necessary that humans sin—in the same way that it is necessary that a glass of water is H_2O? Or does this mean that it is ontologically necessary that humans sin? That is, are humans so constituted that it metaphysically is impossible for them not to commit sins? Sin naturally flows from them.[11] Or does this mean that while humans possibly could avoid sin, it is highly probable, perhaps even inevitable, that they will? Given enough time, they are almost

---

[10]For similar distinctions between and definitions of freedom, see Ronald Nash, *The Concept of God: An Exploration of Contemporary Difficulties with the Attributes of God* (Grand Rapids: Academie Books, Zondervan Publishing House, 1983), pp. 53-55; also see, William Hasker, "A Philosophical Perspective," *The Openness of God: A Biblical Challenge to the Traditional Understanding of God* (Downers Grove: InterVarsity Press, 1994), pp. 136-138.

[11]I must admit that the category of "ontologically necessary" is a bit obscure. However, I believe that it captures what many Calvinistic writers seem to say about the human sinful nature. I will say more about the Calvinistic view of sin in chapter two.

certain to sin. While other options are imaginable,[12] these three dominate the theological models that are examined in this book. The first two interpretations of the sinful nature seem to contradict human libertarian freedom. They suggest that given a choice between doing an evil action x or refraining from doing x (which would be good), the human can only choose x. But according to libertarian freedom, such an action would not be free. To be free with regard to x, one must be able either to do x or not do it. The third interpretation of the sinful nature may or may not be compatible with libertarian freedom. We will discuss this more fully in chapter five.[13] The first two interpretations of the sinful nature seem to work best with Calvinism and its affirmation of deterministic freedom. The last interpretation seems best fitted for open theism and Arminianism, both of which affirm libertarian freedom.

The nature of salvation. A third and final concern mutually addressed by our three models of the divine-world relationship is the nature of salvation. In particular, at issue is the degree of divine influence wielded upon the human subject and the role of human choice in salvation. The New Testament asserts that a key element of or condition for salvation is that an individual exercise faith in Jesus Christ.[14] But the dynamics of enacting this faith may be interpreted in differing ways. One way to understand the faith-act is to interpret it through the lenses of deterministic freedom and through the affirmation of a sinful nature that necessitates sinful acts. According to such a view, since humans are only free to do

---

[12]In particular, Pelagius seems to have affirmed that it is not only possible for humans not to sin but that, in fact, some do not sin. See chapter two for details on some of Pelagius' views.

[13]In chapter five, I argue, as one of several possible Arminian models of human sin, for the idea that while in principle humans can avoid sinning, they in fact inevitably do sin (at some point in life), and it is precisely for this actual sinning that they stand condemned.

[14]See as examples: John 1:12; John 3:16; Acts 16:30-31; Romans 3:22-23, 28.

what they want to do, and since humans have a sinful nature and so only want to do evil, they cannot (on their own) exercise genuine saving faith. Saving faith is a good action, and humans neither want nor can perform such an act. Instead, the fundamental nature of humans must be changed by God. They divinely must be given a nature that wants to exercise faith and that can exercise faith. In short, humans partially must be saved (created anew) in order fully to be saved (created anew). This is the view of Calvinism.

Another interpretation of the act of placing faith in Christ is seen through the spectacles of indeterministic freedom. According to this perspective, while God encourages and strengthens an individual toward faith in Christ, the decision to exercise faith is determined ultimately by the human will. Even in a sinful condition, encouraged by the Holy Spirit, the human can and occasionally does exercise faith. This occurs without God causing the human agent to desire faith. Rather, the desire for faith emerges out of the undetermined choice of the individual. In other words, the human herself changes what she wants. In turn, the human agent, then, exercises the faith that she has chosen to desire. This is the view of Arminianism and open theism.

A related topic is the following. In addition to claiming that faith is a condition for salvation, the New Testament indicates that God calls or draws persons to himself for salvation and that individuals would not come to salvation without this divine call.[15] But to what degree does God influence the individual through the divine call? Again, we face two broad options. One view insists that God's call is irresistible and utterly efficacious. If God calls the individual to faith (and subsequently to salvation), the human agent must and does exercise faith (and consequently must and does receive salvation). Obviously, this standpoint meshes best with deterministic freedom, for the central idea is that once a person's disposition/desire has been altered, he will act on that disposition/desire. The person will do as he now wants to do—namely, turn to God. This is the view of Calvinism. The

---

[15]John 6:44.

other perspective on the divine call asserts that the call is resistible and not always efficacious. There simply are some persons whom God urges toward faith in Christ and toward salvation who do not accept this inner spiritual invitation. They willfully choose not to exercise such faith, in spite of God's earnest coaxing. This is the belief of Arminians and open theists.

A further associated issue concerns divine election. Who does God call to faith and to salvation? Does the deity call everyone or only a select group? In principle, either one of these options could be endorsed by members of our three theological schools. That is, a Calvinist could affirm either that God calls all or only a select group. In turn, the same could be asserted by both Arminians and open theists. However, in practice, the tendency is for Calvinists to claim that God only calls a select group, and for Arminians and open theists to assert that God calls all persons. The key difference between these two stances is that for a Calvinist, to claim that God calls all persons entails that all people will be saved. For Arminians and open theists, to claim that God calls all persons need not indicate universal salvation. Because each of these three theological models tends to affirm that some will not be saved, Calvinists most often deny that God calls all persons; Arminians and open theists insist that God calls all persons but that not all respond positively.

The Voyage Begins . . .

We now have surveyed some of the major areas of concern that are addressed by these three theological models. Obviously, other issues are dealt with by these models and will be discussed in subsequent chapters. Further, these issues will be refined in light of further discussion. We now turn to a detailed analysis of our three paradigms of divine providence. In chapter two, we consider Calvinism.

Chapter 2

Charting the Waters of Calvinism

In chapter one we saw that the Calvinistic model of the divine-world relationship asserts that God is completely sovereign over creation. God knows the future by ordaining it and nothing happens that he has not decreed. Salvation is solely a divine act. Humans have a sinful nature which has eradicated their ability to want and to do good. Prior to divine aid, we are free to do what we want, but because we only desire evil, this is exclusively what we do. God has ordained that through faith in Christ, humans can be saved from sin and its punitive consequences. But in order for an individual to exercise such faith, the deity must alter the inner being of that person, enabling him or her to desire and to exercise faith. God irresistibly calls some to faith, and those whom he calls necessarily/certainly exercise faith and subsequently are saved. Who God calls is exclusively his decision. Some are chosen; others are not. Those whom God elects are saved; those whom he does not elect cannot and do not exercise faith, and consequently are not saved. Often (but not always) the Calvinistic model endorses a static view of God. The deity is seen as utterly unchanging and outside of time. God experiences no temporal duration. Rather, he exists in a kind of singular, eternal moment, that encompasses all times. God is pure actuality and, therefore, has no potential. Further, God is not affected by the actions of creatures.

This model of the divine-world relationship developed over many centuries and in its broad form was endorsed by a number of

theologians. In this chapter, we will examine several representatives of this model and offer a preliminary evaluation of it.

Representatives of the Calvinistic Model

Throughout history a variety of authors have endorsed the
Calvinistic model of the divine-world relationship. In this section,
we will consider several examples.

Augustine

It is anachronistic to describe the perspective examined in this
chapter as "Calvinistic," for its roots and basic contours were
developed long before John Calvin. The first clear articulation of
this position was expressed by Augustine. Augustine was bishop
of the north African city of Hippo from 395-430 C.E., and was one
of the church's most brilliant theologians. While his views
changed over time, in his maturity Augustine taught the following.
In their original state, the first humans (Adam and Eve) morally
were free—free to do either good or evil.[1] But they sinned against
God and, after this, received a corrupted, sinful, nature. In this
state, Adam and Eve could no longer choose good, but only evil.
They were free, but only free to choose between various evil
actions.[2] In turn, their progeny (which includes the whole human
race) inherited from them this same sinful nature, along with the

---

[1]Augustine, *City of God*, trans. Marcus Dods, Great Books of the
Western World, vol. 18, ed. Robert Hutchins (Chicago: Encyclopaedia
Britannica, Inc., 1952), 12.21; and 13.3.

[2]Augustine, *Against Two Letters of the Pelagians*, 1.5. Unless
otherwise noted, quotes from Augustine are from *Augustin: Anti-Pelagian
Writings*, trans. Peter Holmes and Robert Wallis, revised trans. Benjamin
Warfield, Nicene and Post-Nicene Fathers, vol. 5, ed. Philip Schaff
(Peabody, Massachusetts: Hendrickson Publishing, Inc., 1995).

inability to do what is right.[3] As a result of the sinful nature and the sinful acts that exude from it, all humans stand condemned by God. However, in mercy, God has chosen to save some from this horrific plight.

Because humans are now innately sinful and, thus, unwilling and unable to do good, salvation is solely the act of God. God has provided pardon of sin through the cross of Christ; and this pardon may be appropriated by humans through faith in Christ.[4] However, both the desire to exercise faith and the performance of such faith result from a divine action upon the human inner being. Faith is not an action self-determined by the believer. It is "the gift of God."[5] In turn, perseverance of a believer in salvation is also God's gift. God alone decides whether a person remains faithful to Christ throughout life; and not all believers persevere.[6] God alone chooses who is and is not saved. God empowers some to desire and to perform faith. Others he does not so empower and, consequently, they do not exercise faith and are not saved.[7] Augustine rejects the notion that God's choice to save is based on divine foreknowledge of the future righteous actions or faith of

---

[3]Augustine, *City of God*, 13.3 and *On Forgiveness of Sins and Baptism*, 1.9.

[4]Augustine's soteriology in fact is more complex than this. Like many early Western Christian writers, Augustine saw a close connection between not only faith and salvation, but also between participation in the sacraments of the church and salvation. For Augustine, church sacraments are the chief means through which divine grace is received. This especially is true of baptism. And so, a hidden sacramentalism underlies his doctrines of salvation and of the church, a sacramentalism rejected by later Protestant writers both Calvinistic and Arminian. For a discussion of the tension in Augustine's thought, see Jaroslav Pelikan, *The Christian Tradition: A History of the Development of Doctrine, vol. 1: The Emergence of the Catholic Tradition (100-600)* (Chicago: The University of Chicago Press, 1971), pp. 302-308.

[5]Augustine, *On the Predestination of the Saints*, 3.

[6]Augustine, *On the Gift of Perseverance*, 14.

[7]Augustine, *On the Predestination of the Saints*, 11.

persons. Instead, such future meritorious actions and faith can only be grounded in the divine decision to save those persons.[8] In light of this, Augustine distinguishes two divine calls to salvation. One calling is to all people but is not accepted by all. Another calling is to a select group and always is accepted. This latter call is offered to those who are "predestined . . . to conform to the image of His Son."[9] The other call is to all people, even those who will not believe.

Augustine's views on these matters developed in reaction to the writings of Pelagius and his followers. Pelagius was a contemporary of Augustine and a moralist. He emphasized the need for Christians to live a righteous life. He rejected the doctrine of original sin, the teaching that Adam's sinful nature is passed down to his descendants. Pelagius felt that such a view makes exhortation to holiness vain and makes God's condemnation of humans unjust. If humans are born with an inner bias to sin and cannot choose good on their own, then they cannot/should not be held responsible for their actions. Only if they are free to obey God can they be held responsible for disobeying.

Pelagius taught that humans are born in a state of innocense, free to do either good or evil. The primary influence that Adam has had on his offspring is to provide a bad example for them. Adam's guilt is not imputed upon humans by God, nor is a sinful nature passed on from one generation to the next. Each person is free to accept or reject God's commands. Indeed, Pelagius believed that humans can live a sinless life and that some have done so—including various Old Testament saints, saints of the church, and Mary the mother of Jesus.

Pelagius insisted that such a sinless life, as well as the Christian life in general, is only possible through divine grace. But by the term "grace" he meant primarily, perhaps exclusively, the natural created state of humans and certain divinely given external aids. That is, according to Pelagius, humans can live the Christian

---

[8]Ibid., 7, 36.
[9]Ibid., 32.

life because (1) God has created each person free to choose good (as well as evil) and (2) God has given certain empirical/historical aids to urge individuals toward righteousness, including the Old Testament Law and the example of Christ. Through these external aids, the human heart in its freedom is emotionally moved toward obedience; but it is not forced to obey. Pelagius rejected the idea of a divine irresistible call. God's call is extended to all, but no one necessarily accepts it. Each person is free to embrace or reject the divine offer of salvation. According to Pelagius, God predestines persons to salvation only in the sense that he foreknows who will obediently turn to him and who will not.[10]

Augustine adamantly rejected much of Pelagius' teaching for a number of reasons. First and foremost, he believed that such a view leads to works-righteousness, to salvation by merit; and this undercuts the core of Christian soteriology—namely, the commitment to salvation by grace. Augustine argues that Pelagius' commitment to grace as natural human freedom and as external aids reduces divine grace to God merely helping humans do what they could in fact do without his assistance–namely, have faith in Christ and obey the divine commands. In effect, Pelagius tacitly denies the *necessity* of grace in salvation and reinstates righteousness through the law.[11] Augustine quotes Pelagius with an eye toward condemning his position. Pelagius writes:

> Those deserve judgment and condemnation, because, although they possess free will whereby they could come to have faith and deserve God's grace, they make a bad use of the freedom which has been granted to them. But these *deserve* to be rewarded, who by the right use of free will *merit* the Lord's

---

[10]Most of Pelagius' writings are lost to us. Consequently, we primarily learn of his teachings through other sources–often sources engaged in polemics against him. For an excellent survey of Pelagius' literature see Pelagius, *The Christian Life and Other Essays*, trans. Ford Battles (Pittsburgh: Pittsburgh, 1977, 1972).

[11]Augustine, *On the Grace of Christ and on Original Sin,* 1.9, 14, 29.

grace, and keep His commandments.[12]

Augustine comments:

> Now it is clear that he [Pelagius] says grace is bestowed
> according to merit . . . . For when he speaks of those persons
> as deserving reward who make a good use of their free will, he
> asserts in fact that a debt is paid to them . . . . These men
> [Pelagians] . . . attribute faith to free will in such a way as to
> make it appear that grace is rendered to faith not as a gratuitous
> gift, but as a debt—thus ceasing to be grace any longer,
> because that is not grace which is not gratuitous.[13]

For Augustine, the Pelagian interpretation of *faith* denies salvation
by grace, asserting instead a righteousness through works.
Augustine insisted, however, that salvation only truly is by
grace—a gift from God—if God not only helps us know what is
right but also "endows and assists us to act."[14] God must give us
love, give us a good will, so that we might bear the fruits of
righteousness.[15] God must inwardly act upon us, changing our very
being. And faith itself must be a divine gift.[16]

Augustine cites several scriptural passages to support his
views on grace.[17] Romans 3:24 states that we are "justified freely
by His grace . . . ." Ephesians 1:8 asserts that "by grace are ye
saved." Augustine insisted that Pelagius' emphasis on earning
divine grace cannot be squared with these statements. Concerning
faith specifically, Augustine cites Romans 11:3 and Philippians
1:29. The former states: "According as God hath dealt to every
man the measure of faith . . ." The latter says: "Unto you it is

---

[12]Pelagius as quoted by Augustine in ibid., 1.34. Emphasis mine.
[13]Ibid. Brackets are mine.
[14]Ibid. 1. 9, 13.
[15]Ibid., 1.22.
[16]Ibid.
[17]Versions of biblical passages in this paragraph are from *On the
Grace of Christ and on Original Sin,* 1.34.

given in the behalf of Christ not only to believe in Him but also to suffer for His sake." Augustine interprets each of these as teaching that God gives faith to persons so that they can believe in Christ and be saved.[18]

A second reason Augustine rejected Pelagian doctrine is because he believed that it truncates any legitimate rationale for infant baptism. It is difficult to discern which is more fundamental for Augustine—infant baptism or the doctrine of original sin. For later writers—particularly those who deny the saving efficacy of baptism and who object to the practice of infant baptism—the priority falls on original sin. But such is not clearly the case for Augustine. He sees the two as intricately tied together.

The development of and original rationale for the rite of infant baptism in the early church is shrouded in darkness. Tertullian rejected the practice, even though he offered one of the earliest affirmations of what later would be called the doctrine of original sin. Origen denied original sin, but believed the practice of infant baptism to be grounded in apostolic teaching. By Augustine's time, infant baptism was the norm, a practice so well established that neither he nor the Pelagians thought to challenge it. Cyprian seems to be the first theologian to explicate a connection between infant baptism and the doctrine of original sin. He argued that parents ought not to wait eight days after birth to baptize a child because each day of delay places the infant in danger of eternal punishment. Children are born in a state of sinfulness and need the saving waters of baptism.[19]

Augustine endorsed Cyprian's perspective on this matter, and used Cyprian's writings as an authoritative foil against the Pelagians.[20] The Pelagians paradoxically insisted that infant

---

[18]Ibid.

[19]Cyprian, *Epistle 64*, trans. Ernest Wallis, Ante-Nicene Fathers, vol. 5, ed. Alexander Roberts and James Donaldson, revised A. Cleveland Coxe (Peabody, Massachusetts: Hendrickson Publishing, Inc., 1994).

[20]Augustine, *On the Merits and Forgiveness of Sins, and on the Baptism of Infants*, 3.10.

baptism is performed so that those babies might be ushered into Christ's Kingdom, but not so that innate sinfulness might be remitted. Augustine found this explanation of infant baptism vacuous, for whether baptism remits sin or brings a person into Christ's kingdom the result is the same: with baptism one receives salvation; without it one stands condemned. Augustine insisted that only sin keeps us from Christ's kingdom, and so if baptism brings a child into heaven it is because it effectively deals with sin. For Augustine, the most reasonable explanation for infant baptism is that infants are born in a sinful state and need baptism for the remission of sins.[21]

Augustine found evidence for the doctrine of original sin in several scriptural passages. The pivotal verse was Romans 5:12 which states that "by one man sin entered into the world, and death by sin; and so it passed upon all men, in which all have sinned." Augustine interpreted the phrase "in which all have sinned" to mean that in Adam all humans sinned. He writes: "all then sin in Adam, when in his nature, by virtue of that innate power whereby he was able to produce them, they were all as yet the one Adam . . . ; the life of the one man contained whatsoever was in his future posterity."[22] Another critical text is Psalm 51:5 which laments: "Behold, I was shapen in iniquity; and in sin did my mother conceive me." Augustine follows Ambrose in interpreting this to mean that "we men are all of us born in sin; our very origin is in sin."[23]

Augustine's connecting of original sin with infant baptism led him to conclude that infants who die without baptism are divinely condemned, in spite of the fact that they commit no "personal" sin. Augustine attempted to dilute the negative impact of this claim by insisting that the punishment of unbaptised infants is less severe

---

[21]Ibid., 1.23-25.
[22]Ibid., 3.14.
[23]Augustine, *On the Grace of Christ, and on Original Sin*, 2.47.

than that imposed on any others.[24] He also admitted that such a view is difficult to reconcile with belief in divine justice, but he appealed to God's mystery somehow to soften the horror of it all. "We must . . . bend our necks to the authority of the Holy Scriptures . . ."[25] in these matters, and confess that while inscrutable to us, God remains just in selecting some infants for salvation and others for condemnation.

A third reason Augustine repudiated Pelagian teaching is because he believed that it contradicts the scriptural teaching that all humans—except Jesus—are sinners. As noted above, Pelagians taught that it is possible for persons to live without sin and that some saints had been sinless. Augustine denied this, insisting that all humans—except Jesus—are sinners.[26] He cites several biblical verses to support his position. Particularly important is 1 John 1:8 which declares that "if we say we have no sin, we deceive ourselves, and the truth is not in us." Augustine interprets this to apply to all humans, except Jesus.[27] Other key verses are Psalm 143:2 ("for in Thy sight shall no man living be justified"), James 3:2 ("We all stumble in many ways"), Romans 3:23 ("for all have sinned and fall short of the glory of God . . ."). These passages teach that all humans sin.[28] Augustine explained biblical texts that assert that certain persons were holy or righteous as descriptions of these persons as judged by human standards of righteousness, but not by divine standards.[29] Augustine insisted that it is possible for

---

[24]Augustine, *On the Merits and Forgiveness of Sins, and on the Baptism of Infants*, 1.21, 22.

[25]Ibid., 1.29.

[26]Augustine seems to make one other exception in Mary the mother of Jesus. See *On Nature and Grace, Against Pelagius*, 42.

[27]Augustine, *On Nature and Grace, Against Pelagius*, 42. Also see *On Merits and Foregiveness of Sins, and on the Baptism of Infants*, 2.8.

[28]For these verses respectively, see *On Merits and Foregiveness of Sins, and on the Baptism of Infants*, 2.8, 3.13, and *On Nature and Grace, Against Pelagius*, 48.

[29]Augustine, *On the Grace of Christ and On Original Sin*, 1.53.

humans to be sinless, but only via divine grace.[30]

Pelagian doctrine formally was condemned by the Council of Ephesus in 431 C.E., the year following Augustine's death. Even before his demise, however, a movement similar to Pelagianism had arisen, threatening the Augustinian perspective. Writers sympathetic to Augustine's views dubbed this new movement "the remnants of the Pelagians." Sixteenth century reformers would call it Semi-Pelagianism. Augustine considered authors of this new group to be brothers in Christ and admitted that they affirmed convictions abundantly distinct from "the error of the Pelagians."[31] Nevertheless, he found several problems with their teaching. Unlike Pelagius and like Augustine, these writers affirmed the doctrine of original sin and taught that "no one can suffice to himself either for beginning or for completing any good work."[32] God's grace precedes our exercising faith in Christ, urging us to that decision; and divine grace follows our exercise of faith, increasing our faith and spiritually altering our being. Unfortunately, laments Augustine, these writers assert (as Pelagius had before them) that the exercise of faith in Christ is a human act, rather than one that God works within us. That is, they taught that "we have faith itself of ourselves, but that its increase is of God; as if faith were not given to us by Him, but were only increased in us by Him . . . ."[33] For Augustine, this was a return to the error made by Pelagius concerning faith. It made faith a merit which earned further divine assistance/grace; and this was a return to works-righteousness. Semi-Pelagianism eventually was condemned at the Council Orange in 529 C.E. However, as we will see in the next chapter, it continued to influence the medieval church.

Thus far we have examined Augustine's doctrine of the divine-world relationship from the standpoint of his soteriology. As we have seen, for Augustine, because the Bible teaches that

---

[30]Augustine, *On Man's Perfection in Righteousness*, 16.
[31]Augustine, *On the Predestination of the Saints*, 2.
[32]Ibid.
[33]Ibid., 3.

salvation is by grace, that each human is innately a sinner through Adam, and that all humans in fact sin, salvation must be solely the act of God. However, another set of beliefs influenced Augustine's understanding of the God-world relationship—namely, his doctrine of God. Here we see the considerable influence of Greek, especially Platonic, philosophy on Augustine's thought, and ultimately on the thought of Western Christianity as a whole. Plato had argued that a truly perfect being cannot change, because such change would involve either its getting better or worse. But a perfect being cannot get better; it is already perfect. And if a being is truly perfect, it would not allow itself to get worse.[34] In turn, Plato insisted that the highest form of reality cannot be physical, for physical things are subject to change, and anything subject to change cannot be perfect.[35] Further, the highest form of reality must be timeless. Since it undergoes no change, whatever it is it always is. Consequently, Plato writes: "[T]he past and future are created species of time, which we unconsciously but wrongly transfer to the eternal essence; for we say that he 'was,' he 'is,' he 'will be,' but the truth is that 'is' alone is properly attributed to him."[36] In other words, God must exist in a singular, eternal moment, not experiencing temporal duration. Plato also maintained that the highest form of reality (which he sometimes called the Idea of the Good) is the source of the being of all things, and is superior to all things.[37]

Aristotle mimicked and enhanced these ideas. According to him, God is pure actuality. There is no potential in the divine being. Whatever God is, he simply is—forever. There is no change in the deity. In turn, this implies that God is immaterial, for

[34]Plato, *Republic*, trans. G. M. A. Grube, revised C. D. C. Reeve (Indianapolis: Hackett Publishing Company, 1992), 380-381.

[35]Plato, *Timaeus*, trans. Benjamin Jowett, Great Books of the Western World, vol. 7, ed. Robert Hutchins (Chicago: Encyclopaedia Britannica, 1952), 28.

[36]Ibid., 37-38.

[37]*Republic*, 509.

matter is the principle of potentiality. That is, matter always is subject to change, capable of taking a multitude of shapes/forms. Since God cannot change, God cannot be material.[38] Ironically, however, the deity is the ultimate cause of change in other things. He is the Unmoved Mover, the primary and ultimate explanation for why things change in the universe.[39]

Augustine, more or less, adopted these views of the divine nature. He echoes Plato and anticipates Anselm when he says that God is "a nature than which nothing more excellent or more exalted exists, " and concludes that such a being cannot change.[40] In turn, Augustine insists that God cannot be corporal, for material things are subject to change.[41] Further, in words similar to Aristotle's notion of God as fully actual, Augustine writes that

> God is the only unchangeable substance or essence, to whom certainly BEING itself . . . most especially and most truly belongs. For that which is changed does not retain its own being; and that which can be changed although it be not actually changed, is able not to be that which it had been; and hence that which not only is not changed, but also cannot at all be changed, alone falls most truly . . . under the category of Being.[42]

For Augustine, then, God's essence is existence; God is fully actual, fully Being. Augustine cites Exodus 3:14 as a scriptural

---

[38]Aristotle, *Metaphysics*, trans. W. D. Ross, Great Books of the Western World, vol. 8, ed. Robert Hutchins (Chicago: Encyclopaedia Britannica, 1952), 1071b-1072a.

[39]Ibid.

[40]Augustine, *On Christian Doctrine*, trans. J. F. Shaw, Great Books of the Western World, vol.18, ed. Robert Hutchins (Chicago: Encyclopaedia Britannica, 1952), 1.7.

[41]Ibid. Also see, Augustine, *City of God*, 7.6.

[42]Augustine, *On the Trinity*, trans. Arthur Hadden, revised trans. William Shedd, Nicene and Post-Nicene Fathers, vol. 3, ed. Philip Schaff (Peabody, Massachusetts: Hendrickson Publishing, Inc., 1995), 5.3.

confirmation of this view. In this text, God's name is declared to be "I am that I am." Augustine understands this to mean that being/existing uniquely and inseparably belongs to God.[43] Augustine also asserts that God is timeless, that God does not exist through a series of temporal moments, but exists in a singular eternal moment that incorporates all times at once. All temporal moments are simultaneously present to God, in a singular eternal moment. And so, God's being and knowledge are timeless and unchanging. Concerning the timeless nature of God's being, Augustine writes:

> Thy years neither come nor go; whereas ours both come and go .... Thy years stand together, because they do stand; nor are departing thrust out by coming years, for they pass not away; but ours shall all be, when they shall no more be. Thy years are one day; and Thy day is not daily, but Today, seeing Thy Today gives not place unto tomorrow, for neither doth it replace yesterday. Thy Today is Eternity.[44]

Concerning the divine timeless knowledge, Augustine notes:

> For not in our fashion does He look forward to what is future, nor at what is present, nor back upon what is past; but in a manner quite different and far and profoundly remote from our way of thinking. For He does not pass from this to that by transition of thought, but beholds all things with absolute unchangeableness; so that of those things which emerge in time, the future, indeed, are not yet and the present are now, and the past no longer are; but all of these are by Him comprehended in His stable and eternal presence.[45]

---

[43]Ibid.

[44]Augustine, *Confessions*, trans. Edward Pusey, Great Books of the Western World, vol. 18, ed. Robert Hutchins (Chicago: Encyclopaedia Britannica, Inc., 1952), 11.16.

[45]Augustine, *City of God*, 11.21.

In turn, God's will and actions are also unchanging. God's will and actions are performed from the singular moment of timeless eternity, so that the emergence of divine events in time—including events future to us—is already certain, already eternally performed. Augustine writes: "But if we speak of that will of His [God's] which is eternal as His foreknowledge, certainly He has already done all things in heaven and on earth that He has willed—not only past and present things, but even things still future."[46]

In light of these claims concerning the nature of God, it is not surprising that Augustine denies that humans causally affect God. Since God is fully actual, timeless, and unchanging, there is no way for contingent human events to impact him. According to Augustine, when humans turn to God in repentance and thus receive grace, or when humans remain in their sins and so reap divine condemnation, no change occurs in God. Only the creatures and their experiences of God change. The relationship between God and humans is analogous to the relationship between the sun and the human eye. When the eye is healthy, the light of the sun is pleasant, but when the eye is injured, the light is painful. In each case, the sun remains unchanged. Only the eye and its experience of the sun change.[47] God's eternal being, will, and action remain what they have always been.

A consequence of Augustine's view of the nature of God

---

[46]Ibid., 22.2. Brackets are mine.

[47]Ibid. Also see, *On the Trinity*, 5.16. It must be admitted that portions of Augustine's writings suggest that human actions causally affect God, especially God's knowledge. And so, Augustine speaks of divine timeless knowledge as a "spiritual vision," which suggests a passive reception of knowledge based on what humans in fact do. *City of God.*, 11.21. In turn, Augustine insists that the first humans freely chose to sin, and that God anticipated this based on his eternal foreknowledge. Ibid., 14.11. Again such language insinuates that certain human actions causally influence the divine knowledge of them. However, the predominant view expressed by Augustine is that human actions do not causally impact God.

seems to be that God determines what humans do. The following argument is implicit in his system: Since God is fully actual, there is no potentiality in God. Since there is no potentiality in God, the deity cannot be causally affected by creatures. Since God cannot be causally affected by creatures, divine knowledge of creatures cannot be grounded in the creatures themselves, nor in any other source independent of God. That is, God's knowledge of an event is not caused by the event itself. And so, God's knowledge of creatures must be grounded in the divine being itself. But mere knowledge of the divine being alone would not give God knowledge of the *specific acts* of humans, for it was possible for humans not to exist at all and, thus, not to act at all. And so, the simplest explanation of God's knowledge of specific creaturely actions is that God knows what creatures will do because he knows what he wants them to do. That is, God knows what creatures will do because from eternity he has chosen (willed, determined) what they will do.

Augustine does not spell out this argument fully, but rather hints at it. For example, he comments that there is a sure causal sequence of events in the created order and that God's will is the ultimate effecting cause of that sequence. Included in this causal ordering are human wills. Thus, "whatever power they have, they have it within most certain limits; and whatever they are to do, they are most assuredly to do . . . ."[48] In short, humans choose what God has determined that they will choose. In another place, Augustine interprets Philippians 2:13—which states that "it is God who works in you to will and to act according to his good purpose" (NIV)—to mean that God causes the righteous will of believers. Indeed, ironically, God causes believers to will some things which, ultimately, he does not want to occur. And so, believers "pray in a pious and holy manner—but what they request He [God] does not perform, though He Himself by His own Holy Spirit has wrought in them this will to pray."[49] Again, such language suggests divine

---

[48]Ibid., 5.9.
[49]Ibid., 22.2. Brackets are mine.

causal determinism—at least, determinism of the good wills of believers.

We see, then, that Augustine's view of the divine-world relationship essentially is what we have called "Calvinistic." He insists that after the fall of Adam and Eve, humans received a sinful nature that precludes them from desiring or performing righteousness. Consequently, salvation is solely the act of God. In order for an individual to exercise saving faith in Christ, God must alter the inner being of that person, enabling her to desire and to perform faith. God irresistibly calls some to faith, and those whom he calls certainly exercise faith and subsequently are saved. Those the deity does not call do not exercise faith and, thus, are damned. Whom God calls is exclusively his decision.

Concerning the nature of God, Augustine endorses the static model of divinity. God is fully actual, with no potential. He is utterly unchanging and atemporal, experiencing all temporal moments simultaneously in a singular eternal moment. Further, the deity is unaffected by human actions. Created beings utterly depend upon God but in no way does the divinity depend on them. Whatever God knows about the created order, he always knows. Whatever God does in "response" to creaturely actions, he always does (or always is doing) in the singular eternal moment.

In turn, Augustine appears to subscribe to a determinist (compatibilist) interpretation of freedom, especially concerning post-fall human beings. Such a view is implied in his claim that unregenerate humans can choose only between sinful actions and cannot choose righteous acts. Augustine's understanding of freedom prior to the fall is less clear. At first glance, he seems to endorse an indeterminist (libertarian) model of freedom, for he claims that before the fall humans could have chosen either good or evil. However, even here, ambiguity fogs the horizon. Augustine's assertion that God is the ultimate cause of an inescapable causal order in creation suggests that even the original fall of humans may have been determined by God.

In closing, we may note that Augustine's position on the divine-world relationship seems to be grounded in two axiomatic rationales—namely, (1) his doctrine of salvation by grace and (2) his doctrine of the static nature of God. Reasoning from the doctrine of salvation, Augustine concludes that because the Bible teaches that salvation is by grace, that each human is innately a sinner through Adam, and that all humans in fact sin, salvation must be solely the act of God. Reasoning from the doctrine of God as perfect being, Augustine assumes that God cannot be affected by human actions and, thus, that divine knowledge of such actions must be grounded in the very being of God—or more specifically, in the will and power of God. The deity knows what will happen because God ordains it. As we will see, to greater or lesser degrees, these two foundations underlie the thoughts of most who espouse the Calvinistic model of the God-world relationship.

Between Augustine and Calvin

Augustinian predestinarian themes resounded in various writers throughout the middle ages and into the Reformation period. An exhaustive study of such authors is well beyond the scope of this book. But two premier examples warrant a brief examination. First, we may consider the views of Thomas Aquinas (1224-1274). Aquinas was a Dominican monk and eventually became the primary authoritative theologian of the Roman Catholic Church. Much like Augustine, Aquinas greatly was influenced by the Greek-philosophical representation of deity and, subsequently, accepted a static model of God. For Aquinas, God's existence can be established by rationally reflecting on the nature of the physical world. The universe needs an explanation and God is the best answer. God is the unmoved mover, the first efficient cause, the necessary source of contingent things, the perfection that is implied in a gradation of imperfect beings, and the intelligent designer of an orderly and goal-oriented universe.[50] As such a being, some of

---

[50]Thomas Aquinas, *Summa theologica*, trans. Fathers of the English Dominican Province, revised Daniel J. Sullivan, Great Books of the Western World, vol. 19, ed. Robert Hutchins (Chicago: Encyclopaedia Britannica, Inc., 1952), 1.2.3.

God's attributes rationally can be demonstrated. God is simple (without parts and identical to the divine essence), fully actual (with no potentiality), noncorporal, perfect, immutable, omniscient, and atemporal.[51] God's knowledge, will and actions are atemporal and unchanging. Whatever God knows, wills, and does he always (timelessly) knows, wills and does in the singular instance of timeless eternity. As a fully actual being, God cannot be affected by creaturely actions; there is no potential in the divine being. And so, God cannot be causally influenced by creatures. The causal influence is strictly one way: from God to creatures.[52] In turn, God's will is utterly effectual. That which God wills is certain to happen, and God's will pertains to all events. Aquinas insists that God's plan includes all happenings and that the deity often uses creatures as secondary causes to bring about the events that he has planned.[53] Aquinas denies, however, that God's effectual providence curtails human freedom. Rather, in willing certain events, the deity also wills the causes of such events, including some contingent/free causes. In other words, God decrees that some creatures *freely* perform specific actions.[54]

Concerning predestination, Aquinas admits that God predestines some to salvation and others to reprobation. However, his position is more nuanced than Augustine's. According to Aquinas,

---

[51]Ibid., 1.3-10.

[52]Ibid., 1.3.6, 1.23.7. Interestingly, Aristotle had claimed that since God is fully actual and immutable, the deity cannot know of the changing events of cosmic history. While agreeing with Aristotle that God is fully actual and thus immutable, Aquinas denied that God is ignorant of creaturely actions. Instead, he claimed that all perfections that exist in the created order pre-exist in the divine nature; and so, in knowing the divine self, God also knows all creaturely events. Ibid., 1.14.5. For a criticism of such a view, see Michael Robinson, *Eternity and Freedom: A Critical Analysis of Divine Timelessness as a Solution to the Foreknowledge-Free Will Debate* (Lanham, New York: University Press of America, Inc., 1995), pp. 50-61.

[53]Aquinas, *Summa theologica*, 1.19.6, 1.22.3.

[54]Ibid., 1.22.4.

predestination to salvation involves a fully causal divine will. The deity imposes upon some humans the desire for and ability to exercise saving faith. Thus, salvation is passively received by humans as a pre-ordained gift from God. Those who are predestined to salvation certainly are saved. Reprobation, on the other hand, involves divine permissive will. God wills to *permit* some humans freely to fall into and remain in sin; and as a result, God condemns them for their freely chosen status as sinners.[55] Nevertheless, as noted above, Aquinas believes that such freely chosen sins are certain to obtain, for somehow God is able to ensure that some creatures freely perform specific acts, including sins.

Aquinas' view of freedom is complex and, perhaps in the end, incongruent. On the one hand, he endorses something like indeterminate freedom. He writes:

"The will does not desire of necessity whatever it desires."

"The will is mistress of its own act, and to it belongs to will and not to will."

"[T]he will is an active principle, not determined to one thing, but having an indifferent relation to many things."

"Free choice is the cause of its own movement, because by his free choice man moves himself to act."

"Man has free choice. Otherwise counsels, exhortations, commands, prohibitions, rewards and punishments would be in vain . . . . [R]eason in contingent matters may follow opposite courses . . . . Now particular operations are contingent, and therefore in such matters the judgment of reason may follow opposite courses, and is not determined to one. And since man

---

[55]Aquinas writes: "as predestination includes the [divine] will to confer grace and glory, so also reprobation includes the will to permit a person to fall into sin, and to impose the punishment of damnation on account of that sin." Ibid., 1.23.3. Brackets are mine.

is rational man must have free choice."[56]

In short, Aquinas affirms indeterministic freedom, that the human will is able to choose between contrary options. On the other hand, as we have seen above, Aquinas also contends that God can and does determine with certainty what a free creature will do. But this seems to imply deterministic freedom, that in fact humans have only one choice to make, namely the choice that God has preordained. It is not clear that Aquinas' views on freedom are coherent. (We will discuss this matter more fully later in this chapter).

We see then that Aquinas affirms many of the teaching expressed by Augustine. He affirms a static model of God and a strong view of God's sovereign grace. A second thinker to consider is Martin Luther (1483-1546). Luther was the fountainhead of the Protestant Reformation, especially in Germany. As an Augustinian monk, Luther was overwhelmed by a sense of guilt due to sin and could find no sense of forgiveness in the sacramental system of the Roman Catholic Church. Eventually, through intense inner examination and investigation of the scriptures, Luther experienced a divinely given inner peace and became convinced that salvation is through grace alone. Salvation through faith alone and through grace alone became the clarion calls of both Luther's theology and of the theology of the Protestant Reformation in general.

As with Augustine, for Luther the doctrine of salvation by grace disallows human effort or merit as sources of salvation. Not even faith is an autonomous human act. Rather, only those whom the Holy Spirit spiritually changes can desire and exercise saving faith. Those whom the Spirit does not change, do not want faith nor enact it; and subsequently, they are doomed to eternal damnation. In an often quoted analogy, Luther explains the utter inability of the human will autonomously to act either for good or for ill. The will is ever subject to forces greater than itself, namely, to God

---

[56]Ibid., 1.82.2, 1 of 2.9.3, 1 of 2.10.4, and 1.83.1.

or to Satan. Luther writes:

> So man's will is like a beast standing between two riders. If God rides, it wills and goes where God wills . . . . If Satan rides, it wills and goes where Satan wills. Nor may it choose to which rider it will run, or which it will seek; but the riders themselves fight to decide who shall have and hold it.[57]

Luther explicitly endorses deterministic freedom. The evil will is able to do what it wants, namely, evil. It does not do what it does not want, namely, righteousness. And so, contends Luther, the will is not compelled. Its actions are spontaneous and voluntary, even though it can in no way perform godly righteousness. Further, Luther insists that ultimately God's will is the cause of all creaturely events. And so, Luther writes:

> What I assert and maintain is this: that where God works apart from the grace of His Spirit, He works all things in all men, even in the ungodly; for He alone moves, makes to act, and impels by the motion of His omnipotence, all those things which He alone created; they can neither avoid nor alter this movement, but necessarily follow and obey it, each thing according to the measure of its God-given power.[58]

Again, Luther notes:

> Since God moves and works all in all, He moves and works of necessity even in Satan and the ungodly. But He works according to what they are, and what He finds them to be: which means, since they are evil and perverted themselves, that when they are impelled to actions by this movement of Divine omnipotence they do only that which is perverted and evil.[59]

---

[57]Martin Luther, *The Bondage of the Will*, trans. J. I. Packer and O. R. Johnston (Grand Rapids, Michigan: Revell, Baker Bookhouse Co., 1957), pp. 103-104.

[58]Ibid., p. 267

[59]Ibid., p. 204.

Yet again, Luther states:

> [A]ll we do, however it may appear to us to be done mutably
> and contingently, is in reality done necessarily and immutably
> in respect of God's will. For the will of God is effective and
> cannot be impeded, since power belongs to God's nature; and
> His wisdom is such that He cannot be deceived.[60]

Luther was well aware that from the standpoint of reason his
position seemed unfair. One naturally is inclined to ask why God
"does not remove or change this fault of will in every man . . . or
why He lays this fault to the charge of the will, when man cannot
avoid it . . . .?"[61] But in the end, Luther insists that such questions
simply are inappropriate, indeed "unlawful." God's will ultimately
is hidden in the divine Being, and is not subject to human inquiry
or judgment. Luther distinguishes between "God preached" and
"God hidden," insisting that

> God preached works to the end that sin and death may be taken
> away, and we may be saved . . . . But God hidden in Majesty
> neither deplores nor takes away death, but works life, and
> death, and all in all; nor has He set bounds to Himself by His
> Word, but has kept Himself free over all things . . . . Thus, He
> does not will the death of a sinner—that is, in His Word; but
> He wills it by His inscrutable will.[62]

To those who complain that the appeal to divine hiddenness is
simply a dodge, Luther insists that such an invocation is not his
own invention but is the very command issued by the apostle Paul
when confronted with similar issues. In short, the appeal to divine
hiddenness in these matters is supported by scripture.[63]

In Luther, as in Aquinas, we hear the continuing echoes of

---

[60]Ibid., pp. 80-81,
[61]Ibid., p. 171.
[62]Ibid., p. 170.
[63]Ibid., p. 177.

Augustinian predestinarian thought. While Aquinas emphasizes the static nature of God and Luther accentuates salvation by grace alone, both Augustinian themes reverberate in each writer. We turn now to the thought of John Calvin.

Calvin

Not surprisingly, John Calvin offers another principle example of what we have called the Calvinistic model of the divine-world relationship. Calvin (1509-1564) was a key leader of the Protestant Reformation in Geneva Switzerland, and one of the first truly systematic theologians of that movement. In many ways, Calvin reiterates the doctrines expressed by Augustine. However, his justification of these teachings relies almost exclusively on the doctrine of salvation by grace, rather than on the doctrine of God per se.

Calvin insists that God created the first humans, Adam and Eve, with free will—with the power to serve God in righteousness. In this state, they could have obtained eternal life by their own actions. But in an act of rebellion, this couple freely sinned against God and, thus, received a corrupted sinful nature. This nature made it impossible for them to do good or even to want to do good. In turn, this corrupted state was passed down from them to their descendants, so that now each human is born with a propensity to sin and with the inability to desire good or to do it.[64] The only "freedom" that humans have, in this state, is the ability to choose between evil options. Consequently, the whole human race, from Adam onward, stands condemned by God.

Mercifully, God did not want all humankind to remain in this desperate situation. And so, the deity chose to save some through the atoning work of Jesus Christ. The benefits of this work are received by faith; but faith is not an autonomous human act. Rather, God must give saving faith to persons so that they might

---

[64]John Calvin, *Institutes of the Christian Religion*, trans. Ford Lewis Battles, ed. John T. McNeill (Philadelphia: Westminster, 1960), 1.15.8. Also, see 2.1.5-8.

believe in Christ.[65] Those to whom God gives faith most certainly believe and are saved. Those to whom God does not give faith cannot believe and are doomed to eternal punishment. The choice of who is saved and who is damned is solely God's. Calvin explicitly rejects the notion that God might predestine by foreseeing the faith or good works of various individuals. Rather, faith occurs only because God gives it, and foreknowledge is grounded in the divine decree that certain events will happen.[66] Further, persons only persevere in their faith if God chooses to empower them.[67] Like Augustine, Calvin recognizes two types of divine call—a general call to all people and an effective call only to those whom God has chosen to save.[68]

Calvin's view on the "freedom" of the original human couple must be interpreted in light of his doctrines of divine predestination and providential rule. Calvin contends that when considering the original human nature per se, one can declare that Adam and Eve were free to sin or not sin. They could have attained eternal life by freely living righteously.[69] However, when appraising these events in the light of divine predestination and providence, the fall of humankind was necessary. It was necessary because God decreed it.[70] Indeed, according to Calvin, all events of the created order occur as God specifically and precisely decrees them to be. No event occurs that God has not willed.[71] This includes all human thoughts, volitions, and actions.[72]

The Geneva reformer, likewise, affirms the doctrine of total depravity. He proclaims that only damnable thoughts, volitions, and actions come from unregenerated sinners. Humans can in no

---

[65]Ibid., 2.2.10-12, 20-21, 27; 2.3.
[66]Ibid., 3.23.7
[67]Ibid., 2.3.9.
[68]Ibid., 3.21.7.
[69]Ibid., 1.15.8.
[70]Ibid., 3.23.7-8.
[71]Ibid., 1.16.1-8.
[72]Ibid., 1.17.4; 1.18.1-2.

way desire good nor do it. Calvin admits that in every age unbelievers have done noble deeds. But he denies that this counts against his claim that humans are totally evil. He explains that such noble actions result from an unseen divine restraint upon such persons. God exercises grace upon them, not sufficient to save them, but enough to hold back the full flood of their evil nature.[73]

Calvin's affirmation of the predestination of some to salvation and some to damnation seems to flow from four major considerations: (1) that post-fall humans are inherently sinful (indeed, totally depraved) and, subsequently, unable either to want or to do good, or to exercise saving faith; (2) that salvation is exclusively by God's grace; (3) that some persons are not saved; and (4) that only what God has willed happens. One (1) and two (2) imply that humans cannot choose to exercise faith unto salvation and, consequently, that only God can give this to them.[74] One (1), two (2) and three (3) together insinuate that God does not choose to give faith or salvation to all, but only to some.[75] Three (3) and four (4) entail that the salvation and the damnation of various persons are equally willed by God.[76]

Calvin admits that God's justice is hard to comprehend in matters such as the divine decree of the fall of mankind or the predestination of reprobates (including infants) to damnation. Indeed, he confesses that such decrees are "horrible."[77] Nevertheless, in each case, the reformer appeals to divine mystery to justify God's actions. He maintains that these doctrines are clearly taught in scripture; and so, while we cannot penetrate God's counsel, we

---

[73]Ibid., 2.3.1-4.

[74]Ibid., 2.2.6, 10-11, 20, 27; 2.3.6-14.

[75]Ibid., 3.21.1-7. Calvin believed that the claim that some are not saved (and thus not chosen) was supported not only by scripture, but also by simple observation. It simply is the case that the gospel is not preached to all persons nor received by all who hear it. Calvin concluded that God's call to salvation is not given to all. Ibid., 3.21.1.

[76]Ibid., 1.18.1-4; 2.4.6-7.

[77]Ibid., 3.23.8.

must affirm that God is righteous and that such events are somehow just.[78]

Calvin's doctrine of God is less plainly affected by Platonic philosophy than was Augustine's. Calvin preferred to use biblical categories to describe the divine being. Still aspects of the Greek static view of deity surface in his writings. For example, he asserts that God's essence is simple and undivided, and that the divine is infinite and incomprehensible.[79] Because of this, scripture often depicts God not as he essentially is, but as he is experienced by humans.[80] In the holy writ, God speaks to us as a nurse lisps to a child, accommodating to our inabilities to comprehend.[81] In light of this, when repentance or even emotions (like anger) are ascribed to the deity in the Bible, such claims are not to be taken literally. God's inner experience, will, and plan do not genuinely change. Rather, humans simply experience different phases of God's eternally decreed plan temporally unfolding.[82]

Calvin cites a number of biblical passages to support his teachings. Concerning the transfer of the sinful nature from parent to child, he alludes to Psalm 51:5 and Job 14:4. The former states that one is "begotten in iniquities, and conceived by his mother in sin." The latter proclaims: "For who can bring a clean thing from an unclean? There is not one." Calvin interprets these to mean that "all of us, who have descended from impure seed, are born infected with the contagion of sin."[83] He also evokes Romans 5:12, 17 and 1 Corinthians 15:22. Calvin interprets these as teaching that through Adam the sinful nature is transferred to all humanity and with it the penalty of death.[84]

---

[78]Ibid. See also, 1.15.8, 1.17.2.
[79]Ibid., 1.13.1-2.
[80]Ibid., 1.10.2.
[81]Ibid., 1.13.1.
[82]Ibid., 1.17.12-13.
[83]Ibid., 2.1.5. The immediately preceding versions of biblical passages are from Calvin's text.
[84]Ibid., 2.1.6.

Regarding total depravity, Calvin especially advances Romans 3:10-16. Here, citing various Old Testament passages, the apostle Paul asserts:

> "No one is righteous, no one understands, no one seeks God. All have turned aside, together they have become unprofitable; no one does good, not even one" [Ps. 14:1-3; 53:1-3]. "Their throat is an open grave, they use they tongues deceitfully" [Ps. 140:3]. "The venom of asps is under their lips" [Ps. 140:3]. "Their mouth is full of cursing and bitterness" [Ps. 10:7]. "Their feet are swift to shed blood; in their paths are ruin and misery" [Isa. 59:7].[85]

Calvin understands these words to apply to all humans. He concludes that all human beings are "utterly devoid of all good."[86] Other verses with the same implications are 2 Corinthian 3:5, Genesis 8:21, John 8:34, and Jeremiah 17:9.

For Calvin, the claim that God controls all events is supported by passages like Psalm 8:2, Leviticus 26:3-4, Deuteronomy 11:13-14, Isaiah 28:2, and Matthew 10:29. Each verse accredits God with performing some natural event. Regarding divine control of human thoughts, volitions, and actions, Calvin appeals to scriptures such as Proverbs 21:1 (where it states that God turns the heart of the king wherever he wills) and Exodus 8:15, 32 (where it speaks of God hardening the heart of Pharaoh). Other passage evoked as foundations for this perspective are Ezekiel 7:26, Psalm 106:40, 107:40, 1 Samuel 26:12, and Acts 2:23, 4:28.

In support of the doctrine of double predestination, the Geneva theologian cites numerous passages, including Ephesians 1:4, 5 and 2 Timothy 1:9. According to Calvin, these verses teach that God chose some humans for the purpose of making them holy; God did not choose them because he *foresaw* their holiness. Indeed, these passages explicitly assign God's will (and not human

---

[85]Ibid., 2.3.2. Romans 3:10-16, as quoted by Calvin.
[86]Ibid.

effort) as the cause of the divine election. Other verses cited include John 6:37, 39, 44 which assert that no one can come to Christ unless the Father draws them and that those whom God has given to Christ will come to him and will not be driven away. In like manner, John 15:16 indicates that believers do not choose Christ, but that Christ chooses them.

Clearly, then, Calvin affirms what we have called the Calvinistic model of the God-world relationship. He maintains that after the fall of the first humans, mankind has become innately sinful—unwilling and unable to do good or exercise saving faith. In light of this, God alone can provide salvation. God chooses to save some and condemn others. Those whom the deity chooses to save are given saving faith and, subsequently, given spiritual power to live for God and inevitably receive salvation. Those whom God chooses to damn, do not receive saving faith and, therefore, are not saved.

Calvin offers minimal discussion of the static nature of God; however, as we have seen, elements of this perspective are found in his writing. While Calvin does not clearly draw out the implications of these elements, they are consistent with the affirmation of God's total determining of natural events, including human actions. Concerning freedom, Calvin endorses the determinist (compatibilist) theory. He argues that unregenerate humans are innately sinful and cannot desire or do good. Indeed, more explicitly than Augustine, Calvin insists that while sinful humans necessarily sin and cannot do good, they act voluntarily; they act according to their own inner desires and characters. And so, their actions are necessary, but allegedly also free.[87]

After Calvin

Calvinism continued to develop after John Calvin, taking slightly different forms but echoing most of the themes found in Augustine, Calvin and other similar earlier writers. The details of

---

[87]Ibid., 2.3.5.

this historical progression need not concern us. Suffice it to say that after Calvin's death, a variety of issues and controversies arose which forced Calvinists to articulate more fully and precisely their doctrine. From these disputes a general doctrinal consensus emerged.

Today, the acrostic TULIP is widely used as a tool to summarize the central commitments of Calvinism.[88] This mnemonic device outlines the five principal teachings of the Synod of Dort (1619), which was a Calvinistic repudiation of Arminian theology.[89] TULIP stands for the affirmations of total depravity, unconditional predestination, limited atonement, irresistible grace, and perseverance of the saints. That is, Calvinists insist that (1) unregenerate humans are unable to desire or to perform righteous acts or saving faith; (2) God predestines human beings either to glory or to hell without regard for their actions or merits; (3) Christ's death on the cross (while it could have atoned for the sins of all persons) in fact only atones for the sins of the elect; (4) God's call to salvation is completely effective, ensuring that those who receive it respond and obtain salvation; and (5) those whom God has elected certainly persevere in their faith and, consequently, attain salvation. With the possible exception of limited atonement,[90] each of these precepts is well grounded in Calvin's writings, and often the rationales offered by later Calvinists for supporting these teachings repeat argumentation found in Calvin and/or Augustine. These five principles continue to serve as fundamental elements of the Calvinistic model.

---

[88] Millard Erickson, *Christian Theology* (Grand Rapids: Baker Book House, 1988), pp. 914-915.

[89] See "The Canons of the Synod of Dort," in Philip Schaff, *Creeds of Christendom*, vol. 3 (New York: Harper & Brothers, 1877), pp. 581-597.

[90] Augustus Strong contends that while Calvin affirmed limited atonement in his *Institutes of the Christian Religion* (3.21.5; 3.23.1), he later endorsed unlimited atonement in his commentary on 1 John. Strong, *Systematic Theology* (Valley Forge: Judson Press, 1907), p. 778.

Calvinism is not monolithic. Several discrepancies persist. An important distinction among Calvinists is that between supralapsarianism and infralapsarianism. These distinctions emerged germinally in the first few decades following Calvin's death, in the writings of theologians such as Jerome Zanchi (1516-1590), Theodore Beza (1519-1605), and Francois Turretin (1623-1687). At issue was the logical order of the divine decrees. According to supralapsarianism (endorsed by Beza), God's decree to save some and damn others is logically prior to the divine determination to create humans, to permit (or cause) the fall into sin, and to provide salvation for the elect. According to infralapsarianism (as expressed by Turretin), the divine ordaining of creation and of the fall logically precede the decree to save some and damn others, which in turn logically is followed by the decree to provide salvation for the elect alone.[91]   Official creeds of the Reformed church have tended to favor an infralapsarian interpretation of these matters. However, general tolerance has been given for each position.[92]

Other differences among Calvinists have surfaced as well. For example, there are disputes concerning how the sinful nature is transferred from Adam to other humans, conflicts over whether God's decree of the fall and of other sins is causal or merely "permissive,"[93] deviations regarding the static versus the dynamic

---

[91]Erickson, p. 918; also see Justo González, *A History of Christian Thought*, vol. 3, *From the Protestant Reformation to the Twentieth Century* (Nashville: Abingdon Press, 1975), pp. 245-253.

[92]Louis Berkhof, *Systematic Theology* (Grand Rapids: Wm. B. Eerdmans Publishing Company, 1939, 1962), p. 123.

[93]Gordon Clark affirms a direct divine causing of all events, including sin, whereas Augustus Strong and Louis Berkhof speak of God's permissive decree of the fall and of sin.   See Clark, *Biblical Predestination* (Nutley: Presbyterian and Reformed, 1969), p. 53; Strong, *Systematic Theology*, p. 365; Berkhof, pp. 107-108.

nature of God,[94] and even discrepancies about whether the atonement is limited or unlimited.[95] Still, even with these disagreements, there is an over-arching accord among Calvinists concerning the divine-world relationship.

Evaluating the Calvinistic Model

What are we to make of the Calvinistic model of the divine-world relationship? Positively, first we may commend this theory for its strong endorsement of divine sovereignty. Numerous biblical passages allude to the all-pervasive and efficacious nature of God's plan and rulership. We will discuss many of these in chapter 5. A second positive element of the Calvinistic model is that it takes seriously divine grace. There can be little doubt that progenitors of this theory fully accept the Pauline claim that ". . . it is by grace you have been saved, through faith—and this not from yourselves, it is the gift of God—not by works, so that no one can boast (Ephesians 2:8-9, NIV)." The Calvinistic model leaves no room for human effort in the reception of salvation, which comes exclusively by God's grace and activities. A third positive aspect of the Calvinistic model is that it fully acknowledges the ensnaring power of sin in human lives. For Calvinists, sin is a horrendous problem, unsolvable by human efforts. Sin makes pleasing God by self-effort impossible. If sin is to be eliminated, divine intervention is required. Human effort alone will not suffice. This seems to fit well with key scriptural passages, including the one cited immediately above.

---

[94]Ronald Nash appears to make room for some change in God, while still affirming that God's plan and essential character are unchanging. Ronald Nash, *The Concept of God: An Exploration of Contemporary Difficulties with the Attributes of God* (Grand Rapids: Zondervan Publishing House, 1983), pp. 99-105.

[95]Strong, *Systematic Theology*, p. 778.

The Problem of Human Responsibility

In spite of these positive elements, a multitude of problems haunt the Calvinist viewpoint. A chief difficulty is that the type of freedom affirmed by Calvinism (deterministic freedom) does not clearly allow moral responsibility. A common assumption in ethical and legal parlance is that a person cannot be held responsible for an event that he is "forced" by another to perform. For example, if a group of persons overpower a man, place a gun in his hand, and physically force his finger to press against the trigger, consequently firing the weapon at an innocent by-stander, no jury would hold responsible the man whose finger tripped the trigger. In a similar manner, many see the Calvinist model to be asserting that God forces persons to do whatever they do in life. God decrees that a person will perform a particular action and then forces/causes that person to perform the deed in question.

A typical Calvinistic response to such reasoning is to argue that it confuses compulsion with voluntary (though determined) action. The man in the scenario above was externally compelled, *against his will*, to pull the trigger. Thus, his actions were involuntary and for this reason he was not culpable. However, in the divine-human scenario, humans act voluntarily, according to their own (divinely given) desires, without external compulsion. As a result, humans are held responsible.

Such a rejoinder fails to recognize the legitimacy of another form of compulsion—namely, *internal* or *psychological* compulsion. This notion is commonly recognized in ethical/legal argumentation. Consider the following examples: A person attempts to kill someone because she has been hypnotized to believe falsely that the victim is an evil monster or some sort of game animal. In such a case, most jurors would consider the individual who commits the crime to be innocent, precisely because her actions were internally compelled. Or again, imagine technology that would allow an individual's actions to be determined by someone else sending electrical charges to the brain. Should a person perform a crime under such conditions, most would judge the individual to be innocent of his actions. Again, this is because the subject's activities were internally compelled. Or yet again, consider a future where genetic engineering allowed scientists to generate infants with an overwhelming (absolutely compelling) desire to perform some evil act; in turn, suppose later in life these children deliberately are placed in situations where they have the opportunity to commit such crimes and in fact do. Under such circumstances, jurors likely would not blame the children, but rather would condemn the scientists who engineered it all. Indeed, jurors who seriously might consider blaming the children likely would do so because they doubted that the youngsters really were inwardly compelled. If the jurors truly believed that the children were engineered so that they could *only choose* the evil act, they would not hold them responsible. In a similar manner, many feel that the God-human relationship envisioned by the Calvinistic model involves God in psychologically manipulating human beings in such a way that their actions are internally compelled and, consequently, not morally culpable. God creates beings with specific characteristics such that they always act in certain ways under particular circumstances. In turn, God deliberately places those entities in circumstances so as to ensure that they respond in divinely calculated ways. But all of this smacks of internal compulsion, and under such conditions, responsibility seems to evaporate.

Some Calvinists respond to the claim that deterministic freedom is incompatible with moral responsibility by asserting that the indeterminist view of freedom does not allow moral responsibility either. McGregor Wright argues that the only alternative to deterministic freedom is to contend that human choices are uncaused, random events. In this case, he argues, humans still could not be held responsible for their "choices." Such events would not be acts of an agent, but merely inexplicable, uncaused occurrences.[96]

---

[96]R. K. McGregor Wright, *No Place for Sovereignty: What's Wrong with Freewill Theism?* (Downers Grove: InterVarsity Press, 1996), pp. 48-53.

Wright's argument may be criticized at two points. First, he may present a false dilemma. The options concerning freedom may be broader than merely that between determined events and uncaused events. Many libertarian authors contend for an alternative between these two.[97] (We will discuss these issues further in chapter three.) Second, Wright's argument does not rebut the central claim being asserted, namely that deterministic freedom is not compatible with responsibility. Even if an indeterminist view of freedom were not in harmony with human responsibility, it would hardly demonstrate that the determinist interpretation is congruous with such accountability. Each perspective may be problematic. Nevertheless, assuming that responsibility is a valuable concept for Christian theism (not to mention society in general), such a conclusion should goad us toward further investigation of the notion of freedom rather than merely opting for one bad notion over another.

Another Calvinistic retort to the claim that deterministic freedom is incompatible with moral responsibility is to reject the assertion that God's decrees imply internal coercion. Some Calvinists agree that if human actions were internally coerced, genuine responsibility would be eradicated. And so, they deny that divinely decreed human actions are internally forced. Augustus Strong argues that free agency is not simply the power to choose what one already desires to do; it is the capacity to choose between differing desires. Strong explicitly disagrees with those writers who believe that freedom is the ability to act on one's strongest motives. For Strong, experientially we are aware of some "actions by which character is changed, rather than expressed, and in which the man acts according to a motive different from that which he previously had."[98] In such cases, "God's decrees are not executed by laying compulsion upon the free wills of men."[99] According to

---

[97]For example, see William Hasker, *Metaphysics: Constructing a World View* (Downers Grove: InterVarsity Press, 1983), pp. 44-50.

[98]Strong, pp. 360, 512.

[99]Ibid., p. 361.

Strong, genuinely free actions are not necessary.

At first glace, Strong seems to endorse libertarian freedom; and perhaps formally he does. But Strong quickly complicates matters when he declares that while free actions are not necessary, they are certain. They are certain because God has decreed them.[100] According to Strong, God decrees that some creatures *freely* perform specific actions; and so, allegedly, freedom itself is secured and established by the divine decree.[101] Other Calvinistic writers make similar pronouncements.[102] William Shedd and Louis Berkhof contend that God's decrees make the actions of free agents certain, though not necessary or forced.[103] Millard Erickson attempts to explain these distinctions by writing:

> The key to unlocking the problem is the distinction between rendering something certain and rendering it necessary. The former is a matter of God's decision that something *will* happen; the latter is a matter of his decreeing that it *must* occur. In the former case, the human being will not act in a way contrary to the course of action which God has chosen; in that latter case, the human being cannot act in a way contrary to what God has chosen. What we are saying is that God renders it certain that a person who could act (or could have acted) differently does in fact act in a particular way (the way that God wills).[104]

For many, such distinctions simply are incoherent. If an agent certainly will act in a given way, then in what sense can that being act in a contrary way? Can a being fail to do what it certainly will do? No! And if such an agent cannot act in a contrary way, how

---

[100]Ibid., p. 362.

[101]Ibid., p. 360.

[102]As we have seen, Aquinas, makes such claims. See *Summa theologica*, 1.22.4.

[103]William Shedd, *Dogmatic Theology* (Grand Rapids: Zondervan, 1969, 1888), 1.413 and Berkhof, p. 106.

[104]Erickson, p. 357. Erickson's emphasis.

does this differ from Erickson's definition of an event that *must* happen? The answer is that it does not differ. If an event certainly will happen, then it appears that it must happen. Erickson's (as well as Strong's, Shedd's, and Berkhof's) contrasts are vacuous. Equally puzzling is the question of how God might make events certain, if he does not also make them necessary. A close examination of Erickson's own explanation of how the deity makes events of free creatures certain demonstrates a tacit commitment to what I have called internal compulsion.[105] Similar reproaches may be offered against Aquinas' and Strong's proposal that God determines that some creatures freely enact specific deeds. Such an assertion merely begs the question. Without further and clear argumentation, it is not obvious that anyone can *certainly* determine that someone else *freely* (in the libertarian sense) will enact some specific effect. I conclude that attempts to deny that God's decrees imply internal coercion fail.

In turn, I conclude and reiterate that it is not clear that the Calvinistic understanding of freedom allows for genuine moral responsibility. Since responsibility for sins is a key assumption of the biblical literature, the failure of the Calvistic system to deal adequately with this notion is theologically troublesome.

The Problem of Divine Justice

A second problem faced by the Calvinistic model of the divine-world relationship is that it makes it difficult to affirm divine justice. This follows from the incompatibility between deterministic freedom and responsibility, and from the affirmation that God punishes the wicked. Clearly, if humans are not responsible for the actions that they perform, it makes little sense for the deity to hold them responsible and/or to punish them for their actions. Again, an analogy or two may be helpful. If a parent should command a child not to walk out into the street, and then should externally force her to step into the roadway, it would be

---

[105]Ibid., pp. 357-360.

irrational (indeed, unfair and cruel) for that adult to punish the youngster for violating the parental mandate. Or again, if a scientist should probe a portion of a patient's brain that is known to activate a given bodily reaction, it would make little sense for the scientist to be angry with the patient when the patient's body reacted. In a similar way, it makes little sense for God to punish or hold responsible creatures who are internally compelled to act in certain ways. Indeed, not only is it irrational; it flatly is wrong. As James Arminius observes, the Calvinistic system implies that God "imparts to the creature what does not belong to it . . . ," namely, responsibility for and punishment of sin. (192) The Calvinist theory implies divine injustice.

Calvinists are not without rejoinder in these matters. Most wish to claim that humans, in fact, get what they deserve when punished by God; and so, God is not unjust in punishing them. But this line of reasoning is defeated by the argumentation made above that concludes that the Calvinist system does not allow for genuine moral responsibility.[106]

---

[106]Many Calvinists accept Augustine's and Calvin's claim that the first humans (Adam and Eve) were genuinely free and, thus, were culpable for their initial sinful choices. Further, somehow their progeny were "in" them when they sinned and, therefore, all humans sinned when the first couple sinned. The difficulties with this line of reasoning are readily recognizable. One problem is that it is not clear how all humans can be held accountable for the sins of the first humans. It is one thing to assert that from the originating couple all humans inherit a propensity to sin; it is another to claim that humans are *responsible* either for the first ancestral sin or for the propensity to sin that came with it. Most people, Calvinists included, would be aghast to hear of a tribe that held responsible and was seeking to annihilate all the members of another tribe because in years past a key ancestor of the latter tribe had killed a forerunner of the former tribe. Such actions would be deemed ungodly, evil, unjust. But this is precisely the picture of human responsibility and divine punishment envisioned by the Calvinistic theory. Another problem with this line of reasoning is that, as noted in the previous section, it is unclear that the Calvinist system allows for genuine freedom, even for the first humans. It is not obvious

Another Calvinist reply is to appeal to divine mystery. As we have seen, Augustine, Luther and Calvin assert that ultimately God's will in these matters cannot be penetrated. For Augustine, it cannot be discerned why God damns unbaptised infants. For Calvin, it is beyond comprehension how God imputes the sins of the first humans upon all humans or how he *justly* condemns some to damnation *before* they have acted. For Luther, it is unclear why God does not save all men or how the deity can *justly* condemn persons who cannot do other than sin. Each author insists that God's actions in these matters are somehow just, but none can explain how.

The benefit of such a maneuver is that it is unassailable. If some truth is beyond human reason's ability to grasp it, then one cannot demonstrate via reasoning that the position is false. The proponents of the claim always can say that it is true, even though humans cannot understand how it can be true. The deficiency of the appeal to mystery is that it is rationally unsupportable. It presents seemingly logically contrary statements—such as "God is just," "it is not just to punish someone for an act he or she is forced to perform," and "God punishes persons whom he has forced to sin"—and then demands that one accept each claim without explaining how each can be true. A further problem with the appeal to mystery is that it undermines the use of reason in other contexts. It is due to the force of reason that Calvin and others draw the conclusions that they do concerning divine predestination. For example, in endorsing the propositions that (1) "God's will is always done" and (2) "some humans are damned," the Calvinist seems compelled by reason to conclude that (3) "God wills that some be damned." But if appeal to mystery is easily evoked, there seems to be no clear reason why an Arminian could not simply proclaim that it is *not* the case that "God wills that some be damned," even though propositions (1) and (2) are true. When asked how this is rationally possible, the Arminian might declare

---

that anyone, God included, can *determine* that an agent will *freely* perform a specific act.

that it is a divine mystery. In other words, appeal to divine mystery cuts both ways; it undermines the argumentation of Calvinists and Arminians alike. In any case, we may conclude that it is not clear that the Calvinist system rationally can affirm that God is just.

The Problem of Divine Responsibility

A third difficulty found in the Calvinistic model is that it seems to incriminate God as the author of sin. If humans are not responsible for their actions because they are internally coerced by God, then who is responsible? For the Calvinist system, the logically consistent answer is God. Again, an analogy is helpful. In the case of the scientist who sends electrical charges to someone's brain, knowing that a certain bodily action will occur, the patient whose body acts would not be held accountable; rather the manipulative scientist would be culpable. Even if such electrical charges caused not only external bodily reactions but also the desire within the patient to do such outward acts, the patient would not be held responsible for the desires or the acts. Instead, the doctor controlling the brain-tampering would be blameworthy, especially if she knew what the results of her actions would be. The same holds for the God envisioned by Calvinism. God knowingly creates beings with necessitating propensities to act in certain ways in specific circumstances. In turn, God manipulates the environment of those beings so as to guarantee the divinely intended results. This implies that God is the ultimate cause of creaturely actions, including sin.

Calvinists offer a variety of replies to such reasoning, none of which particularly is convincing. Perhaps the dominant response is to appeal to the notion of divine permissive will versus necessitating or causally determining will. Berkhof insists that God does not effectively/positively cause evil, but only *permits* free agents to perform evil acts.[107] Such a declaration could easily be made by Arminians and open theists. Unfortunately, Berkhof quickly adds

---

[107]Berkhof, pp. 105-107.

that God's permissive decree "does not imply a passive permission of something which is not under the control of the divine will. It is a decree which renders the future sinful act absolutely certain . . . ."[108] This reasoning is duplicated by other Calvinists, including Aquinas. As we have seen, however, the distinction between necessary and certain events is foggy at best, incoherent at worst. It is unclear how any being could render an event certain, without likewise necessitating the event. Or again, it is not obvious that one *certainly* could cause another agent *freely* to choose only one alternative. The appeal to divine permissive will, as interpreted by Calvinists, seems to fail.

Another response to the claim that the Calvinist model makes God the author of sin is to assert that God's causality is of a different kind, at a different level, than that of creatures, and that because of this, creatures genuinely are responsible for their actions, including sin. Defenders of the Calvinistic paradigm commonly distinguish between primary and secondary causation (or they make similar distinctions). God is the primary cause of events; humans (and other creatures) are secondary causes of events. Secondary causation is a bona fide form of self-determining causation; consequently, humans (and other creatures) are authentic authors of their actions. Unfortunately, the precise meaning of primary and secondary causation often is shrouded in obscurity and frequently the way this distinction solves the dilemma of the divine authorship of sin likewise is left unspecified.

Sometimes Calvinistic writers speak of primary and secondary causation as if these were different causes within a linear *series of causes*, each previous event causing the next. In this case, divine primary causation is the first cause in a chain of successive causes, and creaturely secondary causes are the intermediate causes in the series. Calvin describes God's causation as the ultimate cause and

---

[108]Ibid., p. 105.

human causation as "proximate" causes of creaturely events.[109] In like manner, Augustine speaks of an order of efficient causes, God's will being the originating cause of the sequence.[110] If this is the basic meaning of primary and secondary causation, however, such distinctions hardly exempt God from being the author of sin. According to the Calvinist model, as the first cause, God *determines* the outcome of all subsequent events. But as Cottrell comments, in such a series of events, "it would seem that the first or ultimate cause of a thing should bear the real . . . responsibility for it, while the proximate cause (itself caused) should be relieved of the blame."[111]

Another way of interpreting primary and secondary causation, however, is available—a way that avoids the problem cited immediately above, but in the end one that does not resolve the difficulty of the divine authorship of sin. In this interpretation, divine and human causes are not understood respectively as the first cause and the intermediate causes in a linear series of events. Rather, creaturely events are seen as a series of mutually effecting causes that are unfolding through time, and divine causation is conceived of as that which *gives being to* the various creaturely events as they evolve. In short, God *sustains* creatures in their existence, but the creatures themselves, through their divinely given "being," cause/determine their own particular actions, including sin. Various Calvinistic writers affirm this view of divine and human causation. Berkhof insists that the divine

decree . . . makes God the author of free moral beings, who are themselves the authors of sin. God decrees to sustain their free agency, to regulate the circumstances of their life, and to permit

[109]John Calvin, "A Defense of the Secret Providence of God," *Calvin's Calvinism*, trans. Henry Cole (Grand Rapids: Eerdmans, 1956), p. 209. Cited by Jack Cottrell, *What the Bible Says About God the Ruler* (Joplin, Missouri: College Press Publishing Company, 1984), p. 80.
[110]Augustine, *City of God*, 5.9.
[111]Cottrell, p. 80.

that free agency to exert itself in a multitude of acts, of which some are sinful."[112]

Strong notes that the divine decrees "make God, not the author of sin, but the author of free beings who are themselves the authors of sin. God does not decree efficiently to work evil desires or choices in men. He decrees sin only in the sense of decreeing to create and preserve those who will sin."[113]   Aquinas, Luther, and possibly Augustine each make similar claims concerning divine and human causality.[114]

The chief difficulty with this second rendition of divine and human causation is that the Calvinist system demands and most of these writers explicitly or implicitly affirm not only that God is the cause of the *power* of creaturely choice or of the *existence* of the human will, but also that God determines the *specific choices* that those wills make. In other words, God not only gives being to the authors of sin and to their choices, but also *determines* what choices these authors make. Again, Arminians and open theists readily might agree that God sustains creatures in their existence, but they would deny that God determines the actual choices that those beings make. In order for such choices to be free, arguably it is necessary that they be generated exclusively by the human authors themselves.[115]   The Calvinist system does not exonerate

---

[112]Berkhof, p. 108.

[113]Strong, p. 365.

[114]See Thomas Aquinas, *Summa theologica*, 1.22.2, Martin Luther, *The Bondage of the Will*, p. 204, and Augustine, *City of God*, 5.9. Other writers who interpret divine and human causation in this way are Etienne Gilson, *The Christian Philosophy of St. Thomas Aquinas* (New York: Random House, 1956), p. 246; James Ross, "Creation" in *Journal of Philosophy* 77 (1980): 614-629; and "Creation II," *The Existence and Nature of God*, ed. Alfred Freddoso (Notre Dame: University of Notre Dame Press, 1983; John Yates, *The Timelessness of God* (Lanham: University Press of America, 1990), pp. 146-147.

[115]For a fuller discussion of these matters, see Robinson,, pp. 59-61, 145-157.

God from the charge of being author of sin.

The Problem of Divine-Human Interpersonal Relationships

A fourth problem facing the Calvinistic model of the divine-world relationship is that it does not allow for a genuine interpersonal relationship between God and humans. A running assumption of many (perhaps most) Christians—Calvinists included—is that God is personal and that the deity's design for humans is that we enter into personal fellowship with him. For example, moderate Calvinist Millard Erickson declares that God is personal and that salvation involves God bringing humans into a personal and righteous relationship with him.[116] Now for many, a central element of personhood and of a truly interpersonal relationship is the ability to choose freely ones own actions and one's relationships with others. A primary aspect of love and of moral choice is the ability to choose between options. C. S. Lewis articulates this perspective well in his discussion of God's rationale for creating moral beings that are capable of evil. He notes:

> God created things which had free will . . . . If a thing is free to be good it is also free to be bad . . . . Why, then, did God give them free will? Because free will, though it makes evil possible, is also the only thing that makes possible any love or goodness or joy worth having. A world of automata—of creatures that worked like machines—would hardly be worth creating. The happiness which God designs for His higher creatures is the happiness of being freely, voluntarily united to Him and to each other in an ecstasy of love and delight . . . . And for that they must be free.[117]

All of this becomes problematic, however, when we note that

---

[116]Erickson, pp. 268-271, 904-905.
[117]C. S. Lewis, *Mere Christianity* (New York: The MacMillan Company, 1960), pp. 37-38.

the Calvinistic model denies to humans the freedom to do otherwise. God seems internally to coerce the actions of humans. The God-human relationship that is pictured in the Calvinistic paradigm, then, is very much like the view which Lewis rejects, namely, one where humans are automata, who act precisely as they have been programmed to act by God. As John Sanders complains, in the Calvinist model "a genuine give-and-take interpersonal relationship between God and humanity is denied."[118] Instead, we have one person (God) acting upon instrument-like beings (humans). God ensures that some of these instruments act nicely and that others do not. The Calvinist model does not make room for an interpersonal relationship between God and humans.

Divine Atemporality, Immutability, and Personhood

As we have seen, many representatives of the Calvinist theory affirm that God is timeless and utterly unchanging. But a whole range of problems arise in the face of such claims. A full discussion of these difficulties is beyond the reach of this chapter; however, we may mention two in passing. Some religious philosophers argue that the alleged relationship between temporal events and divine timelessness does not make sense. According to the theory of divine timelessness, God "sees" all temporal moments as present in the singular moment of eternity. But this seems to imply that all temporal moments are simultaneous with one another. If E (eternity) is simultaneous with t1 (yesterday) and with t2 (tomorrow), then it appears that t1 (yesterday) is simultaneous with t2 (tomorrow). If E = t1, and E = t2, then t1 = t2. But this does not make sense. Subsequently, the theory of divine timelessness is unintelligible.[119] Other philosophers insist that

---

[118]John Sanders, *The God Who Risks: A Theodicy of Providence* (Downers Grove: InterVarsity Press, 1998), p. 174.

[119]Richard Swinburne, *The Coherence of Theism* (Oxford: Clarendon Press, 1977, 1993), p. 228.

divine timelessness and immutability are incompatible with the claim that God is personal. Robert Coburn comments:

> Surely it is a necessary condition of anything's being a person that it should be capable (logically) of, among other things, doing at least some of the following: remembering, anticipating, reflecting, deliberating, deciding, intending, and acting intentionally. To see that this is so, one need only ask oneself whether anything which necessarily lacked all of these capabilities noted would, under any conceivable circumstances, count as a person. But now an eternal being would necessarily lack all of these capacities inasmuch as their exercise by a being clearly requires that the being exist in time.[120]

We will discuss these difficulties more fully in chapter six.

The Problem of Evil

A final problem faced by the Calvinistic model concerns the existence of evil. Why does a perfectly good and omnipotent God allow evil and sin to exist? Among Christian theists, the most common explanation of God's tolerance of evil is that he does so for the sake of human freedom. God wants creatures that can love, make moral choices, and enter into personal relationships. But in order for this to be possible, evil also must be possible. Humans must be free to choose between love and not love, between good and not good. And so, God was willing to allow evil for the sake of generating free creatures, creatures who could love, act morally and enter into personal relationships.

Unfortunately, such an explanation is not available to Calvinists, for their theory denies that humans are free in the sense required by the above argument. The Calvinist system denies that in order to love one must be free not to love, or that in order to be

---

[120]Robert Coburn, "Professor Malcolm on God," *Australasian Journal of Philosophy* 40-1 (1962-3), quoted by Nelson Pike, *God and Timelessness* (New York: Schocken Books, 1970), p. 121.

good one must be able to do evil. Instead, proponents of this theory maintain that God easily could have created beings that always choose to love, always choose good, always choose a personal relationship with him, and that this would not have negatively impacted human moral significance. And so, God's tolerance of evil cannot be explained by appealing to human (libertarian) freedom. But why then does God allow evil?

Calvinists offer some interesting answers. Some insist that through the existence of evil, a certain aspect of God's nature is revealed, namely, divine justice. God's punishment of evil demonstrates his righteous intolerance of evil.[121] This explanation faces two difficulties. First, it *may* make God dependent upon the created order. Consider the following dilemma: Could God's justice be demonstrated in no other way? If so, the question remains, why does God tolerate evil? If not, then, perhaps God needs to demonstrate his justice and in turn needs to create evil creatures upon whom to exercise and manifest such justice.[122] Second, as argued above, it is doubtful that genuine justice is shown in a system where God punishes beings that are internally coerced to sin.

Another Calvinist answer to the problem of evil is to assert that perhaps God needed some evil in order to generate higher goods. Aquinas argues that conceivably some forms of evil contribute to the good of the whole cosmos.[123] Augustine suggests

---

[121] Augustine, *City of God*, 21.12; John Calvin, *Institutes of the Christian Religion*, 3.23.11. Augustine and Calvin, in fact, are addressing the question, why does God not save all persons. But the question of why God tolerates evil is closely related to this, for according to the Calvinist paradigm, God has the power to make humans so that they never would have sinned. And so, the question remains: why did God not create a universe free of evil?

[122] This is perhaps part of John Sanders point when he comments: "If God must express his justice in the damnation of certain people, then God is *dependent* on the damned . . . for the fulfillment of his nature." Sanders, pp. 241-242.

[123] Aquinas, *Summa theologica*, 1.22.2.

that maybe some evil is permitted "for the sake of demonstrating how the most righteous foresight of God can make a good use even of them . . . ."[124] Such an explanation faces two difficulties. First, it seems to imply that evil is necessary for good to exist, a position that Augustine himself rejects.[125] Second, within the Calvinist system, this explanation appears to entail that every evil event leads to some higher good. But it is not clear that every evil event does lead to a higher good. The Calvinist model seems to assume that when God ordains an event there is some good reason for ordaining it. And so, if God decrees that an evil event will occur it can only be so that some higher good will eventuate. But do all evil events lead to higher ones? Obviously, we cannot answer this question definitively, but prima facie there seem to be numerous evil occurrences that do not lead to good consequences. And even if each does lead to some higher consequence, it is not evident that some other means of obtaining such an end were not available. And so, it is not at all clear that the Calvinist model allows one to appeal to higher goods as an explanation for the divine toler-ance/decreeing of evil.[126]

A final Calvinist explanation for God's tolerance of evil is that it is simply a divine mystery. Calvin asserts that, from a rational perspective, it would have been better if God had created creatures that could not and would not sin. But God has done

---

[124] Augustine, *The City of God*, 14.12.

[125] Ibid.

[126] Aquinas' and Augustine's comments are not far removed from the insights found in the free will defense, which we briefly described above. To assert that God tolerates evil for the sake of human freedom—for the sake of possible loving, morally good, interrelating persons—is to maintain that there is a higher good for which God is willing to tolerate some evil. But unlike the Calvinist system, the standard free will defense allows one to explain God's tolerance of evil *in a general way*, without having to explain why every specific evil event occurs. God tolerates evil in general for the sake of human freedom in general. But God need not ordain every evil event for the sake of some specific higher goods.

otherwise, and we simply do not know why.[127]   As pointed out above, however, the appeal to divine mystery is problematic in various ways. I will conclude then that the Calvinist system has an unusually difficult time explaining the existence of evil in the world. (We will discuss the problem of evil in more detail in chapter seven).

Preliminary Conclusion

The Calvinistic model of the divine-world relationship is complex and intriguing. Some of the greatest minds of the Christian era have endorsed some form of this system. However, the model faces numerous difficulties, many of which have been discussed here. Specifically, this system cannot elucidate why God permits evil, nor how the deity justly blames humans, nor why God is not responsible for sin. Calvinism offers no substantial rebuttal to any of these complications. Furthermore, versions of this theological model find it hard to demonstrate that the notion of divine timelessness is coherent or that a timeless God can be personal or interpersonal. In light of these problems, it is not surprising that other theories have been proposed in Christian literature. In the next chapter, we will examine one of these paradigms—namely, the Arminian model.

---

[127]Calvin, *Institutes of the Christian Religion*, 1.15.8.

Chapter 3

Charting the Waters of Arminianism

The Arminian model of the divine-world relationship offers a different perspective than that of Calvinism. Arminianism embraces divine sovereignty, contending that God is finally in control of all that happens. However, unlike Calvinism, this view denies that God causally determines all events. Rather, the deity grants to some creatures the ability to generate and to self-determine some of their own actions. God still controls these events in the sense that he permissively allows free creature to act as they do. At any moment, he can revoke his permission and so prevent the actions from occurring. Thus, God predestines all events, but in the case of some occurrences his predestining only involves permissively allowing creatures to act as they choose. The Arminian model reverses the Calvinistic view of foreknowledge and foreordination, at least for some incidents. In the case of events generated by free creatures, God foresees that these events will occur and permissively lets them take place.[1] And so, while agreeing with Calvinists that salvation is by grace and that humans cannot atone for their own sins or even turn to God on their own initiative, Arminians insist that the decision to exercise faith in Christ and subsequently to receive salvation is an autonomous human choice. God graciously helps humans turn to Christ in

---

[1]As we will see, claiming that God permits that which he foresees is a problematic stance. Certainly not all Arminians affirm such a view, but some do.

faith, but the decision to employ faith ultimately is a human act. Humans are free to believe in Christ or to reject him. God's grace is not irresistible. Obviously, then, Arminians affirm an indeterministic or libertarian interpretation of freedom. More surprisingly, Arminians traditionally have endorsed a static view of God. In the following pages, we will examine some of the key progenitors of this view and offer a brief critique of the model.

Representatives of the Arminian Model

The Arminian model has been endorsed by a number thinkers down through the ages. Let us look at some chief examples.

Patristic Writers

Like the Calvinistic model, the Arminian theory has rich roots in patristic theology. Indeed, prior to Augustine, the general consensus of orthodox Christian writers seems to have been that humans are free to do good or evil, and that God's election to salvation or to damnation is based on the divine knowledge of future creaturely choices. Justin Martyr (110-165) insisted that unless humans "have the power of avoiding evil and choosing good by free choice, they are not accountable for their actions . . . ."[2] And so, while scriptural prophecy demonstrates divine knowledge of the future, this does not mean that future human actions are fated or divinely ordained. Instead God conditionally has decreed "that the future actions of men shall all be recompensed according to their several values."[3] Justin admitted that God's foreknowledge

---

[2] Justin Martyr, *First Apology,* 43. Quotes in the following section from the patristic writers Justin Martyr, Tertullian, Clement of Alexandria, and Origen are from the series Ante-Nicene Fathers, vols. 1-5, ed. Alexander Roberts and James Donaldson, revised A. Cleveland Coxe (Peabody, Massachusetts: Hendrickson Publishing, Inc., 1994).

[3] Ibid., 44.

entails that future creaturely events are sure to occur, but denied that this nullifies the freedom of such events.[4]

In like manner, Tertullian (155-225) asserted that freedom is a defining element of and evidence for the image of God in humans.[5] "Man was given freedom with regards to both good and evil;"[6] and without such freedom, humans could not be held responsible for disobeying divine commands.[7] In granting freedom to humans, God often does not prevent them from enacting sinful events, even though he does not want such actions to occur. He does this apparently because he honors the freedom that he has granted.[8] Such freedom explains the fall of humans into sin, in spite of God's goodness and prescience. God foreknew that humans would sin, could have prevented it, but choose to allow it for the sake of human freedom.[9] Tertullian did not clearly spell out his views on predestination, but he did note that "it is not the mark of a good God to condemn beforehand persons who have not yet deserved condemnation," and that God "dispenses reward according to the deserts of each case with a most unwavering and provident decision."[10]

Clement of Alexandria (150-215) explicitly denied that God causes evil events. Rather, "such things happen without the prevention of God."[11] While nothing happens in the universe that God has not willed, many things transpire because God *permissively wills* them. According to Clement, only in this way can both divine providence and divine goodness be preserved.[12] Origen (185-230), a student of Clement, likewise affirmed the power of

---

[4]Justine Martyr, *Dialogue with Typho*, 141.
[5]Tertullian, *Against Marcion*, 2.5.
[6]Ibid., 2.6.
[7]Ibid., 2.5.
[8]Ibid., 2.7.
[9]Ibid., 2.5.
[10]Ibid., 2.23.
[11]Clement of Alexandria, *Stromata*, 4.12.
[12]Ibid.

humans to do good or evil, insisting that this is an essential component of being rational. Without such an ability we could not be praised for doing good or condemned for doing evil.[13] Origen was aware of various Bible verses that suggest that we are divinely "fated," but he denied the validity of such interpretations, offering instead his own (often strained) exposition of the meaning of these texts.[14] Indeed, Origen proposed a thoroughly unorthodox explanation of God's election of Jacob over Esau, insisting that each man's soul must have existed prior to birth and, thus, God's choice was still based on the merits of their (preexistent) lives.[15] Origen admitted that divine foreknowledge requires that those events divinely known certainly will occur, but insisted that God's knowledge does not causally determine those happenings. Indeed, the causal relationship is just the opposite. Future events cause God's foreknowledge of them.[16] Other patristic writers held similar views.

Interestingly, these patristic theologians also usually endorsed a static model of God. According to many of them, God is utterly immutable, atemporal, simple, and impassible.[17] Later in this chapter, we will examine the tension that such affirmations create for the Arminian view. In passing, we may note also that each of these writers tended to speak of God's acceptance of humans and consequently of human salvation in terms of divinely foreseen *merited actions,* and less in terms of divinely foreseen *faith* in Christ. As we have seen, this same proclivity is found in Augustine and serves as a seedbed for later medieval theology's turn toward sacramentalism. Not surprisingly, such a tendency did not gel well with later Protestant Arminian doctrine which emphasized

---

[13]Origen, *De Principiis,* 3.1.3.

[14]Ibid., 3. 1. 1-18

[15]Ibid., 2.9.7.

[16]Origen, *Contra Celsum,* 2.18-20.

[17]See Justin Martyr, *First Apology* 13, and *Hortatory Address to the Greeks,* 21; also see Clement of Alexandria, *Stromata,* 1.16, 4.23 and Origen, *De Principiis,* 1.1.5-6.

salvation through faith alone.

Semi-Pelagians and Medieval Catholic Theology

As pointed out in chapter two, just before Augustine's death and for several years following, a movement arose that challenged his views, particularly concerning the human exercise of saving faith. Similar to Augustine and unlike Pelagius, these authors maintained that humans have a sinful nature and cannot do good or obtain salvation on their own. Divine grace must antecede the human act of faith, inwardly helping a person believe. Further, God graciously must continue giving humans inner aid to do good, throughout the Christian life, so that ultimate salvation might be attained. Nevertheless, for these thinkers, the initial act of saving faith is a human choice, one that God does not cause in the person, but one freely enacted by the individual. For Augustine, such claims were a repeat of the basic mistakes made by Pelagius concerning faith. It made faith a merit that earned God's grace and salvation. These Semi-Pelagian views were condemned at the Council of Orange in 529 C.E. In particular the notion that humans execute the initial act of faith was rejected.[18] However, a close examination of the documents of this council show that even in its denial of Semi-Pelagianism, the conference did not fully endorse Augustine's program. Specifically, they rejected the notion of predestination to sin and to damnation.[19] Further, the documents did not explicitly deny divine predestination by means of fore-knowledge, nor positively affirm God's irresistible grace. These subtle shifts of the Council of Orange away from portions of Augustine's doctrine anticipated later medieval Catholic theology's move toward a more "Semi-Pelagian" perspective. Further,

---

[18]"The Council of Orange," 5, *Creeds of the Churches: A Reader in Christian Doctrine from the Bible to the Present*, 3rd edition, ed. John Leith (Atlanta, Georgia: John Knox Press, 1982).

[19]Ibid., 23, and Conclusion.

a continuing growth of sacramentalism also is evidenced in the canons of the Council of Orange. Similar to Augustine, the council insisted that God's grace is received through baptism.[20]

The swerve toward Semi-Pelagianism and sacramentalism, whispered in the Council of Orange, became more pronounced in the writings of medieval Catholicism. Pope Gregory I (Gregory the Great, Bishop of Rome 590-604) set the tone when he wrote that God predestines to salvation those whom he foreknows "will persevere in faith and in good works,"[21] and when he contended that God justifies humans through their obedience to the divine commands. In turn, Gregory's emphasis on baptism as the means of pardon for original sin and on penance as a way of rendering satisfaction to God after baptism further advanced the growing legalism of the medieval Church.[22] By the 9th century, many Catholic leaders were appalled when the monk Gottschalk of Orbais resurrected Augustine's doctrine of double predestination and openly denied that God predestines based on foreknowledge of future human actions. Unknowingly, opponents of Gottschalk endorsed a semi-pelagian perspective. A controversy ensued, with assorted church leaders taking different sides. In the end, an ambiguous compromise was derived at the Council of Toucy (860). There it was declared that God predestines some to eternal life, that Christ died for all sinners, and that human free will was damaged by the fall into sin, but not utterly destroyed.[23] Left unclear was whether God predestines to damnation and whether grace is irresistible.

The migration toward works-righteousness continued

---

[20]Ibid., 8, 15.

[21]Gregory the Great, *Ezekiel*, as quoted by Justo González, *A History of Christian Thought, vol. 2, From Augustine to the Eve of the Reformation* (Nashville: Abingdon Press, 1971), p. 71.

[22]O. W. Heick, "The Theology of Gregory the Great," J. L. Neve and O. W. Heick, *A History of Christian Thought*, vol. 1 (Philadelphia: Fortress Press, 1946), p. 174.

[23]Neve and Heick, *A History of Christian Thought*, p. 179.

throughout the middle ages. By the time of Peter Lombard (d. 1160), the Church recognized seven sacraments, which in turn were officially endorsed by the Council of Florence in 1439. Through these sacred rites, participants were thought to be restored to their original righteousness and to receive the redemptive merits of Christ. Further, via these sacraments, persons were enabled to live a moral life as a means to eternal life. Failure to live virtuously could be absolved through the sacrament of penance, whereby individuals could render satisfaction to God and, consequently, be freed from the threat of purgatory and/or hell. Eventually, monetary payments (indulgences) were accepted in the place of acts of penance. The end result of these practices, particularly the operation of penance, was a paradoxical mixture of both works-righteousness and easy grace. To receive salvation one needed to submit to and enact key consecrated rituals and then live a moral life, but too easily the formal performing of the rites became a replacement for a life of genuine virtue.[24]

The semi-pelagianism and moralism of the medieval Church continued evolving into the late middle ages and is observed in the writings of the 16th century Catholic Reformer, Erasmus. Erasmus (1466-1536) became a major critic of the Church of his day, particularly decrying the moral abuses of the ecclesiastical leadership. Like Luther he was disgusted with the flagrant materialism and psychological manipulation exhibited in the Church's use of indulgences. Initially, it appeared that Erasmus and Luther would be allies in their respective calls for reformation in the Church. But whereas Erasmus was content to protest the moral decay of the Church, Luther also found the Church's theology wanting. Out of this difference emerged a considerable ideological antagonism between the two thinkers. Luther's writings quickly revealed his commitment to the Augustinian doctrines of double predestination and irresistible grace, tenets that did not set well with the prevailing "semi-pelagian" Catholic doctrine of the time. In 1524, encouraged by friends and Church

---

[24]Ibid., pp. 203-205.

leaders, Erasmus offered a criticism of Luther's views in a small book entitled *Discourse on Free Will*. He submitted sundry arguments against Luther's doctrine. Erasmus' positive teaching reflected the Church's theology of his day, as well as the tensions within that theology.

Erasmus defined free will as "the power of the human will whereby man can apply to or turn away from that which leads unto eternal salvation."[25] He distinguished between four types of grace. First is a grace that resides in all humans. It is not added by a special divine act, but is a natural aspect of being human. It is given in God's work of creating humans. Through this grace one is free to do some good acts and, thus, is capable of preparing oneself for the reception of a more direct and extraordinary form of divine grace. The second type of grace is one where God directly "moves the undeserving sinner to contrition."[26] Here the person does not yet receive the infusion of "ultimate grace which can eliminate . . . sin."[27] But one is "displeased with himself,"[28] and subsequently is moved to acts of penitence, such as alms-giving and prayer. This level of grace Erasmus names operative grace or prevenient grace.[29] Such grace also is given to all, "for God offers everyone favorable opportunities for repentance."[30] This grace is an invitation to seek further aid from God, but it does not compel one to choose God. The third form of grace is cooperative grace, wherein God promotes righteousness in the person through the internal working of the Spirit. It is a grace that "assists those who strive until they have received their goal."[31] Apparently, it is the grace that is active throughout the Christian life. But even

---

[25]Erasmus, *Discourse on Free Will*, trans. Ernst Winter (New York: Continuum Publishing Company, 1961), 2.13.

[26]Ibid., 2.20.

[27]Ibid.

[28]Ibid.

[29]Ibid., 2.19.

[30]Ibid., 2.20.

[31]Ibid., 2.19.

here, the human will is working with God in attaining righteousness, and is not internally forced to act righteously. The fourth
type of grace leads to the final goal, the elimination of sin.
In these teachings, Erasmus iterates the view of justification
and of merit common in the Scholasticism of his day. J. I. Packer
and O. R. Johnston explain:

> . . . Erasmus echoes the Scholastic theory of a distinction
> between *congruent* merit (*meritum de congruo*) and *condign*
> merit (*meritum de condigno*). The first of these, according to
> the theory, was that which a man attained by what he did in his
> own strength (*ex puris naturalibus*) in applying himself to
> spiritual concerns. Its effect was to make him a fit subject for
> the gift of internal grace. It did not positively oblige God to
> give internal grace (from this point of view, it was meritorious
> only in a loose and improper sense); it merely removed the
> barrier which had hitherto stood in the way of God's giving it;
> however, it was held to be a certain fact that God in mercy
> gives internal grace to all who have made themselves fit
> subjects for it. Grace (i.e. supernatural spiritual energy) having
> thus been given, its recipient could use to do works of a quality
> of goodness previously out of his reach, works which God was
> necessarily bound, as a matter of justice, to reward with further
> supplies of grace and, ultimately, with heavenly glory. The
> merit which these works secured (*condign* merit) was meritori-
> ous in the strict sense, and put the Creator under a real obliga-
> tion. The purpose of the whole theory was to hold together, on
> the one hand, the reality of God's freedom in giving salvation
> and, on the other, the reality of man's merit in earning it: to
> show that God really becomes man's debtor (because He is
> under obligation to reward man's merit) while yet at the same
> time remaining sovereign in salvation (because He gives the
> grace which creates the merit freely and without obligation).[32]

---

[32]J. I. Packer and O. R. Johnston, "Historical and Theological
Introduction," forward to Martin Luther, *The Bondage of the Will*, trans.
Packer and Johnston (Grand Rapids: Fleming H. Revell, 1957), pp. 48-49.

In short, for Erasmus and Scholastic theology, God justifies sinners by giving them a grace that makes them factually righteous, that is, that enables them gradually to perform acts of righteousness and so become righteous. In turn, because of their righteousness, devotees are rewarded with eternal life. As Timothy George notes, in such a system "one was declared righteous because he had already been made righteous, to some degree at least, by the infusion of a supernatural quality."[33] Obviously, the sacraments played a critical role in the human reception of this supernatural empowerment.

In sum, medieval Roman Catholicism drifted toward a semi-pelagian interpretation of the God-World relationship. Like their patristic predecessors, medieval theologians (including the Semi-Pelagians proper) recognized the need for human libertarian freedom so as to ensure human moral responsibility and to protect God from being the author of sin. Admittedly, later authors did this in the context of formally affirming Augustine's doctrine of original sin and its claim that humans are unable to want or to do good without divine grace. Still there was an ever-present attempt to safe-guard human responsibility by interpreting divine grace as being compatible with some degree of creaturely libertarian freedom. In these affirmations—of human sinfulness, of humanity's inability to do good without divine grace, and of the need for human libertarian freedom—the pre-Reformation Catholic theologians were in considerable concordance with their post-Reformation Arminian siblings. However, as we are about to see, there were substantial differences between these groups, particularly in their understanding of the means to salvation. Like other Protestants, the Reformation Arminians fully endorsed Luther's conceptualization of justification as a forensic declaration by God of the righteousness of persons who in fact remain sinners. Pre-Reformation medieval Catholics, on the other hand, tended to see

---

[33]Timothy George, *Theology of the Reformers* (Nashville: Broadman Press, 1988), p. 64.

justification more as the divine act of generating genu-inely/factually righteous people.

Not surprisingly, like Augustine and patristic theologians before them, Catholic authors of the middle ages endorsed a static model of the divine nature. So that, for example, Erasmus could proclaim that change does not occur in the divine being and that Biblical statements to the contrary are mere accommodations to our "weakmindedness and dullness."[34] Such sentiments were the norm of the middle ages.

James Arminius

As suggested in the last section, a hallmark of the Protestant Reformation was its reinterpretation of the doctrine of justification, away from the patristic and medieval understanding of this principle, back to (according to Protestants) a genuinely Biblical perspective. Luther's infamous insecurity concerning his own salvation while under the tutelage of the medieval Roman Catholic system of sacraments, penance and merits, echoed the uneasiness felt by many who faced the daunting possibility of personal moral failure within this network, and the subsequent eternal damnation that it could bring. Luther's resolution of this frightening prospect was to discern in the writings of the apostle Paul an understanding of justification that circumvented the need for the actual obtaining of righteousness, either by moral effort or by participation in Church sacraments. For Luther, justification essentially was a legal status of a human sinner before the court of a gracious God. Christ had atoned for human sin on the cross, and now through faith alone, one could appropriate this righteousness into one's life. Such righteousness was not literally infused into the believer, nor factually lived out by the Christian; rather, it graciously was imputed to or declared to belong to the believer.[35] Such an interpretation of justification by faith alone marked a radical

---

[34]Erasmus, 1.7.
[35]George, pp. 67-70.

departure from pre-Reformation theology, including the doctrine of Augustine. In spite of his emphasis on divine grace, like other ancient and medieval Christian thinkers, Augustine tended to see justification as the factual infusing and/or practicing of righteousness in the believer's life. But Luther and early Protestant Reformers denied this, opting for a more forensic interpretation of divine justification. Of course, as we have seen, Luther and Calvin contended that the faith through which one appropriates this forensic justification is itself a gift from God and does not originate in the will of humans. And so, in regards to predestination these writers were thoroughly Augustinian; but concerning their view of justification, these Reformers detour notably from Augustine's teachings.

It is in the light of these considerations that we can best understand the teachings of James Arminius (1560-1609). On the one hand, he thoroughly endorsed the views of Luther and Calvin concerning the doctrine of justification.[36] On the other hand, he rejected their proclamations about unconditional divine predestination and irresistible grace. Arminius was a Reformed pastor and scholar from the Netherlands, who initially endorsed Calvin's doctrine of unconditional predestination and irresistible grace. However, around 1599 this Dutch theologian was asked to refute the teachings of a layperson named Dirck Koornhert who denied these Calvinistic tenets. Upon studying the issues, Arminius became convinced that Koornhert essentially was correct and began espousing similar views. In 1603, Arminius was appointed as a professor of theology at the University of Leyden which quickly led to controversy between himself and other members of the faculty—particularly with a supralapsarian named Franciscus Gomarus. The details of the conflict need not concern us.

Arminius rejected both supra- and infra- lapsarianism. As

---

[36] James Ariminius, "A Declaration of the Sentiments of Arminius," *The Works of James Arminius*, vol. 1, trans. James Nichols, The Master Christian Library, version 6 [CD-ROM] (Albany, Oregon: AGES Software, 1997), pp. 226-228.

noted in chapter two, these theories declare that God unconditionally and eternally decreed that some humans would be saved and others would be damned, that the fall into sin would happen (permissively or otherwise), and that a set of means would be provided for bringing the elect to salvation and the reprobate to damnation. These models differ from each other in how they perceive the logical sequencing of the decrees. Arminius renounced each of these paradigms, insisting that they lead to a denial of genuine moral responsibility in humans, and that they make God unjust and the author of sin.[37] He also complained that these theories fail to ground salvation in its true foundation as revealed in scripture, namely in Christ and the Gospel. Instead, each attempts to base salvation on an alleged hidden will of God.[38] Arminius offered an amusing parody of how he believed supralapsarians must interpret John 3:16: "God so loved those whom he had absolutely elected to eternal life, as to give his son to them alone, and by an irresistible force produce within them faith in him."[39] But this, argued Arminius, is hardly what the passage says and the passage cannot be reconciled with the strict Calvinistic formula.

In the place of the unconditional decrees envisioned by supra- and infra-lapsarians, Arminius advocated the following order and content of the divine decrees:

1. The first absolute decree of God concerning the salvation of man, is that by which he decreed to appoint his Son, Jesus Christ, for a Mediator, Redeemer, Savior, Priest and King, who might destroy sin by his own death, might by obedience obtain the salvation which had been lost, and might communicate it by his own virtue.

2. The second precise and absolute decree of God, is that in which he decreed to receive into favor those who repent and believe, and,

---

[37]Ibid., pp. 191-197.
[38]Ibid., pp. 187-188, 198-199.
[39]Ibid., p. 200.

in Christ for his sake and through Him, to effect the salvation of such penitents and believers as persevered to the end; but to leave in sin, and under wrath, all impenitent persons and unbelievers, and to damn them as aliens from Christ.

3. The third Divine decree is that by which God decreed to administer in a sufficient and efficacious manner the means which were necessary for repentance and faith . . . .

4. To these succeeds the fourth decree, by which God decreed to save and damn certain particular persons. This decree has its foundation in the foreknowledge of God, by which he knew from all eternity those individuals who would, through his preventing grace, believe, and, through his subsequent grace would persevere, according to the before described administration of those means which are suitable and proper for conversion and faith; and, by which foreknowledge, he likewise knew those who would not believe and persevere.[40]

Clearly, then, Arminius saw God's decree to salvation as provisional, conditioned by the human choice for or against Christ. In the second decree this ordination is general; it concerns all who might choose Christ (and might persevere). The fourth decree is particular. Through divine foreknowledge, God knows which individuals in fact will choose Christ (and will persevere), and through this decree the deity declares that these specific persons will be saved. Concerning the third decree, Arminius notes that the mechanisms that God uses to draw persons to salvation are in accord with divine wisdom and justice, so that the means used to bring persons to salvation is consistent with their freedom. No one is internally compelled to believe. The first decree reflects Arminius' thesis that the ultimate grounding of the Christian faith and of salvation is Christ and his Gospel, and not some hidden will of God.

In light of his interpretation of the decrees, it is not surprising

---

[40]Ibid., pp. 213-214.

that Arminius denied the limited atonement of the cross. Christ died for all and his death was sufficient for the salvation of all.[41] Further, regarding the perseverance of the saints, Arminius left open the possibility that some, through their own negligence, might "desert the commitment of their existence in Christ"[42] and so render God's grace ineffectual in their lives. For Arminius, assurance of salvation is grounded on this simple syllogism: "'they who believe, shall be saved;' I believe, therefore, I shall be saved."[43] More profoundly, it also is grounded in the testimony of the Holy Sprit in the Christian's life.[44]

To the charge that his views deny that salvation is by divine grace and that he teaches that humans are the final arbiters of their own salvation, Arminius argued that his position affirms grace but denies irresistible grace. He writes:

> I ascribe to grace the commencement, the continuance and the consummation of all good, and to such an extent do I carry its influence, that a man, though already regenerate, can neither conceive, will, nor do any good at all, nor resist any evil temptation without this preventing and exciting, this following and co-operating grace. From this statement it will clearly appear, that I by no means do injustice to grace, by attributing, as it is reported of me, too much to man's free-will. For the whole controversy reduces itself to the solution of this question, "is the grace of God a certain irresistible force?" That is, the controversy does not relate to those actions or operations which may be ascribed to grace, (for I acknowledge and inculcate as many of these actions or operations as any man ever did,) but it relates solely to the mode of operation, whether it be irresistible or not. With respect to which, I believe, according to scriptures, that many persons resist the Holy Spirit and reject the grace that is offered. [45]

---

[41]Ibid., *The Works of James Arminius*, vol. 3, pp. 403-404.
[42]Ibid., "A Declaration of the Sentiments of Arminius," p. 219.
[43]Ibid., p. 187.
[44]Ibid., p. 220.
[45]Ibid., p. 219.

In other words, all along the path toward salvation, God's grace is required in order for humans to want or to do good. Nevertheless, all along the way, humans also have the freedom to reject this same grace. Humans can "resist the Holy Spirit and reject the grace that is offered."[46] For Ariminius the issue is not whether he affirms divine grace (which he does), but whether he affirms irresistible divine grace (which he does not).

Arminius distinguished between two forms of divine grace—preventing grace and subsequent or cooperating grace. The former is a grace offered to all humans so that they freely may choose for or against Christ and, thus, for or against salvation. Without this grace, no one could choose Christ or be saved.[47] The latter is a grace which follows after one's initial faith in Christ. It is a

> perpetual assistance and continued aid of the Holy Spirit, according to which he acts upon and excites to good the man who has been already renewed, by infusing into him salutary cogitations, and by inspiring him with good desires, that he may thus actually will whatever is good; and according to which God may then will and work together with man, that man may perform whatever he wills.[48]

At each level of grace, human free will is active.

Underlying Arminius' teachings on grace was a commitment to the doctrine of original sin. As a result of Adam's sin, all humans are innately sinful and unable to do good. Without divine "preventing" grace, no human could long for or exercise faith in Christ, and none could desire or do good. However, unlike progenitors of the "Calvinistic" model who assert that God only grants to a few the grace that enables them to trust Christ, Arminius believed that this grace is available to all people, and that all

---

[46]Ibid.
[47]Ibid., "The Apology," pp. 315-316.
[48]Ibid., "A Declaration of the Sentiments of Arminius," p. 219.

who receive it freely may either exercise its power to believe or not exercise it.[49] Arminius also contended that humans are only condemned for the actual sins they commit and that unbaptised infants that die receive salvation.[50]

In spite of the conditional quality of the divine decrees, Arminius insisted that his system fully endorses divine sovereignty. Nothing happens that God has not willed; however, evil events are only permissively willed by the deity.[51] Further, in knowing the future, God foresees what will happen and he is free either to let future events happen or not. Therefore, the deity remains sovereign. He freely chooses to allow certain future events to unfold, but is not compelled to do so. Like other Christian writers of his era, Arminius also affirmed a static model of the divine nature. God is simple, infinite, eternal, immeasurable, unchangeable, impassable, and incorruptible. God knows all things through his awareness of the divine nature, including future contingent events.[52]

Obviously, Arminius endorsed the central elements of what we have called the Arminian model of the divine-world relationship. According to him, after the fall of Adam, all humans became sinful—prone to sin and unable to do what is right.[53] Because this sinful nature leads to actual sins, all adult humans in fact sin and consequently stand condemned by God. But God has decreed a means whereby sinners might be saved, namely, through Jesus Christ and his death. Through faith in Christ, a person may be declared righteous and be saved. Further, in spite of their sinful nature, God has sent a prevenient grace down upon all humans so that they are able to believe in Christ if they so choose. Because God knows the future, he knows who freely will exercise faith in

---

[49]Ibid., p. 218.

[50]Ibid., "The Apology," pp. 274-277.

[51]Ibid., "A Declaration of the Sentiments of Arminius," p. 217.

[52]Ibid., "Private Disputations," *The Works of James Arminius*, vol. 2, pp. 32-36.

[53]Ibid., "A Declaration of the Sentiments of Arminius," p. 218.

Christ and who will not, who will persevere in that faith and who will not. Consequently, God knows who will and who will not be saved. In the decision to create the universe, knowing the results that would follow, the deity has predestined some to salvation and others to damnation. But this predestining involves a permissive granting of the choices humans make for or against their own salvation. God does not cause persons to believe or not to believe. The deity remains utterly in control of the process, however, for he did not have to create at all, nor did he have to make creatures that had free will. But God freely chose this world-scenario. Obviously, Arminius subscribes to an indetermistic interpretation of human freedom. Further, like so many other Western theistic writers, he also supports a static view of the divine nature.

Arminius' untimely death in 1609 did not end the controversy that his writings fostered. The following year, a company of forty-six Reformed pastors signed a document, entitled the Remonstrance, which approved of the central teachings of Arminius. This work denies the doctrine of an unconditional divine decree unto salvation and damnation, and rejects irresistible divine grace. Grace is required for sinful humans to turn to God, but humans are not inwardly forced to believe through that grace. The Remonstrance also affirms the unlimited atonement of Christ's death and leaves open for further discussion the possibility that regenerate believers could fall from grace and, thus, lose their salvation. The formal rebuttal of this work came in the declarations of the Synod of Dort (1619), which we mentioned in chapter two.

John Wesley

Arminius was hardly the first or only Protestant to affirm free will. From the earliest days of the Reformation, Anabaptists and other "radical" reformers, such as Conrad Grebel (1498-1526) and Menno Simons (1496-1561), advocated human freedom and rejected strict predestination. Likewise, Philip Melanchthon and other Lutheran scholars migrated away from Luther's strong views on deterministic freedom.[54] In turn, writers sympathetic to the Arminian perspective multiplied throughout the 17th and 18th centuries. The first large group of Baptists in England, eventually known as General Baptists, endorsed the unlimited atonement of Christ's death, affirmed human indeterministic free will, and maintained that a believer could renounce her faith in Christ and, accordingly, lose salvation.[55]

Of all the Protestant thinkers influenced by Arminian thought perhaps none had greater impact than John Wesley (1703-1791), the founder of the Methodists. Wesley was a priest in the Anglican Church and formally endorsed its creeds throughout his life. He was deeply influenced by the pietist movement, following its pattern of establishing societies for enriching Christian spirituality. Wesley endorsed the basic contours of Arminian doctrine. He believed that the central decree of God was to save those who will one day express faith in Jesus Christ and to reject those who will refuse to believe.[56] For Wesley, God predestines to salvation or to damnation only in the sense that he acquiesces to the divinely foreknown decisions of human beings. To those who will believe, God grants eternal life. To those who will reject Christ, damnation is ordained. In knowing what humans will do prior to their existence, God's choice to create them is a kind of predestining unto salvation or damnation. It is a decision to allow the unfolding of what God foresees humans will do. Wesley explicitly invoked the notion of divine timelessness as a way of explaining God's knowledge of the future. For God, all events—past, present and future—are occurring in a singular present eternal moment.

---

[54]Justo González, *A History of Christian Thought*, vol. 3, *From the Protestant Reformation to the Twentieth Century* (Nashville: Abingdon Press, 1975), pp. 79-88, 96-97.

[55]H. Leon McBeth, *The Baptist Heritage: Four Centuries of Baptist Witness* (Nashville: Broadman Press, 1987), pp. 32-39.

[56]John Wesley, "On Predestination," *The Complete Works of John Wesley*, 3d ed. (1872), vol. 6, The Master Christian Library, version 6 [CD-ROM] (Albany, Oregon: AGES Software, 1997), p. 245.

Echoing Origen, Wesley insisted that while divine foreknowledge indicates that future events are certain, it does not cause such events and, consequently, does not take away human freedom. He argues:

> We must not think they [future events] are because he knows them. No; he knows them because they are. Just a I . . . now know the sun shines: Yet the sun does not shine because I know it, but I know it because it shines. My knowledge supposes the sun to shine; but does not in anywise cause it. In like manner, God knows that man sins; for he knows all things: Yet we do not sin because he knows it, but he knows it because we sin.[57]

Wesley also endorsed the doctrine of original sin. Because of Adam's sin, all humans possess a sinful nature. All are prone to sin and, indeed, none can want or do good on his own.[58] Like Arminius, Wesley insisted that grace is necessary for salvation. Humans could not turn to God without divine aid. However, God has given to all humans a prevenient grace that allows them freely to choose Christ or remain in sin. This grace is required for salvation, but it is not irresistible.[59] Further, like Arminius, Wesley

---

[57]Ibid., pp. 244-245. Brackets are mine.

[58]Ibid., "Justification by Faith," *The Complete Works of John Wesley*, vol. 5, pp. 114-115.

[59]It is not quite accurate to say that Wesley affirms that prevenient grace enables a person to exercise *saving faith*, for he insists that genuine faith is a gift from God. Rather, Wesley contends that prevenient grace allows a person to become aware of his sinful and helpless condition and, in turn, this awareness or despair allows God to give the gift of faith to the individual. Wesley maintains, however, that this prevenient grace does not irresistibly force one to admit his sinfulness. Rather, the individual freely can refuse to acknowledge his sinful and dire state and, thus, can be left unable to receive the gift of faith from God. And so, even though prevenient grace does not enable the person freely to exercise saving grace, the end result is that human freedom still plays an essential role in the reception of salvation. It allows a person freely to see his sinful condition and need for God, and to (in some sense) turn toward the deity.

left room for the salvation of unbaptized infants who die and never have the opportunity to express personal faith in Christ.[60] Wesley accepted the fundamental interpretation of justification set down by Luther and other early Reformers. Justification essentially is divine forgiveness of sins, made possible through the atoning death of Jesus. It is the act of being declared righteous by God, in spite of our sins. Only sinners are justified, for the truly righteous need no forgiveness. Of course, since all persons sin, all need this imputation of righteousness by God. In turn, justification comes only through faith in Christ. And this faith, while a gift from God and while aided by divine prevenient grace, ultimately is freely chosen.[61]

Wesley affirmed the on-going work of the Holy Spirit in the life of the believer; God leads individuals to a sanctified life-style. Indeed, Wesley taught that it is possible in this life for believers to avoid conscious sins against God. Humans always remain prone to sin, and may well perpetually be engaged unconsciously in various moral breaches before God. But it is possible for some to reach a level of consecration to and love for God that they avoid willfully disobeying divine precepts.[62] In a similar manner, Wesley's commitment to libertarian freedom, led him to conclude that it also is possible for believers to fall from grace, to turn from

---

See Charles Rogers, *The Concept of Prevenient Grace in the Theology of John Wesley* (Ph.D. dissertation, Duke University, 1967), pp. 215-242. Also see Mark Royster, *John Wesley's Doctrine of Prevenient Grace in Missiological Perspective* (D.Miss. dissertation, Asbury Theological Seminary, 1989), pp. 90-91.

[60]Wesley, "A Treatise on Baptism," *The Complete Works of John Wesley*, vol. 10, p. 217. Wesley, however, does insist that Baptism is the standard means by which righteousness is imputed to those who are guilty of original sin, namely, all humanity.

[61]Ibid., "Justification by Faith," pp. 114-122.

[62]Ibid., "On Perfection," *The Complete Works of John Wesley*, vol. 6, pp. 437-451.

their original faith in Christ and, accordingly, lose their salvation.[63] Wesley maintained that God is fully in control of the world. Nothing happens that he has not willed. Obviously many events God permissively wills, granting humans freedom to make choices, including evil ones. The deity does this so that humans can make genuine moral decisions. God could truncate such freedom, but this would contradict his own will; for he has desired to make humans in the divine image, so that they might be morally responsible. Such self-limitation is not a sign of weakness in the deity but demonstrates "the depth of the wisdom of God . . . ."[64] Obviously, Wesley supported an indetermistic understanding of freedom. Likewise, as is evidenced by his comments on divine timeless knowledge, Wesley (perhaps tacitly) affirmed a static view of God's nature.

Contemporary Arminians

The broad contours of Arminianism are found in a variety of contemporary theologies. Obviously, these teachings are reflected in recent conservative Protestant writers who see themselves as keepers of the Arminian/Wesleyan tradition, such as H. Orton Wiley, Paul Culbertson,[65] Henry Thiessen,[66] and more recently

---

[63]Ibid., "Serious Thoughts on the Perseverance of the Saints," *The Complete Works of John Wesley*, vol. 10, pp. 321-337.

[64]Ibid., "On Divine Providence," *The Complete Works of John Wesley*, vol. 6, p. 340.

[65]Orton Wiley and Paul Culbertson, *Introduction to Christian Theology* (Kansas City, Missouri: Beacon Hill Press, 1957).

[66]Henry Thiessen, *Lectures in Systematic Theology* (Grand Rapids, Michigan: Wm. B. Eerdmans Publishing Company, 1949).

Jack Cottrell,[67] Michael Peterson,[68] and Bruce Reichenbach.[69] These perspectives also appear in the writings of orthodox Roman Catholicism, where the doctrine of justification continues to be interpreted as a state of receiving infused righteousness/merit and where non-determinative divine foreknowledge is still endorsed.[70] The central elements of the Arminian model also are found in Neo-Orthodox writer Emil Brunner who affirms human libertarian freedom and yet also divine knowledge of a contingent future.[71] Further, it perhaps is safe to say that for the majority of contemporary Christians, the Arminian model represents their own, often precritical, intuitions concerning the divine-world relationship. Most wish to affirm that humans are free to choose or reject Christ as Savior, are responsible for their sins, and that God somehow knows the future without negating human freedom.

Evaluating the Arminian Model

The Arminian model has much to commend it. Its commitment to human responsibility and culpability reflect central claims of the Biblical tradition; and conceivably, its endorsement of human indeterminisitic freedom is better equiped to make sense of such claims than is its Calvinistic counterpart. In turn, the

---

[67]Jack Cottrell, *What the Bible Says about God the Ruler* (Joplin, Missouri: College Press Publishing Company, 1984).

[68]Michael Peterson, *Evil and the Christian God* (Grand Rapids: Baker Book House, 1982).

[69]Bruce Reichenbach, "God Limits His Power," *Predestination & Free Will: Four Views of Divine Sovereignty & Human Freedom,* ed. David and Randall Basinger (Downers Grove: InterVarsity Press, 1986), pp. 101-124.

[70]G. M. Van Doornik, et. al., *A Handbook of the Catholic Faith: The Triptych of the Kingdom* (Garden City, New York: Image Books, 1956).

[71]Emil Brunner, *Dogmatics, vol. 1: The Christian Doctrine of God,* trans. Olive Wyon (Philadelphia: The Westminster Press, 1949).

Arminian model is able to avoid some of the more debilitating problems faced by Calvinism, namely the problems of divine justice, divine authorship of sin, and divine tolerance of evil. Because humans determine their own actions and, thus, are responsible for their deeds, God is just in condemning them for their moral failures. Further, since God does not inwardly coerce humans to act, the deity is not the author of creaturely sins. Further still, the Arminian theory better explains God's tolerance of evil. Unlike the Calvinist perspective, the Arminian view can assert that God allows evil for the sake of human indeterministic freedom, which in turn is necessary in order for humans truly to love God and others. Despite these positive features, however, the Arminian model faces a number of challenges.

Incompatible with Divine Sovereignty

Calvinistic writers often charge that the Arminian emphasis on human free will is not compatible with divine sovereignty. For example, Louis Berkhof rejects the Arminian idea that God merely preserves the existence of humans, while creatures themselves generate their own decisions and actions. He repudiates such a notion because "if this were the situation, it would be in the power of man to frustrate the plan of God, and the First Cause would become subservient to the second. Man would be in control, and there would be no divine providence."[72]   More flamboyantly, Gordon Clark asserts that "the idea that man's will is free . . . is totally unbiblical and unchristian. As a clear denial of omnipotence, it dethrones God and takes man out of God's control."[73]

Neither of these writers spells out precisely how creaturely freedom negates divine control. However, the following scenario may demonstrate their point. Suppose that God wants some event E to occur. But the actualization of this event depends on the free

---

[72]Berkhof, *Systematic Theology*, (Grand Rapids: Wm. B. Eerdmans Publishing Company, 1939, 1962), p. 172.

[73]Gordon Clark, *Biblical Predestination* (Nutley: Presbyterian and Reformed, 1969), p. 125.

choice of a human to perform some other action A. If A happens, then E occurs. If A does not happen, then E does not eventuate. Because the human is free, she can either do A or refrain from it. It is fairly clear, then, that if the human choice remains free, God cannot ensure that event E will transpire, since God cannot (or at least does not) make certain that the free creature enacts A. An Arminian might propose that in this special case God could force the creature to enact A so as to ensure E. But this dodges the issue, because the point is that *free will* negates divine sovereignty. Obviously, if the deity takes away free will (even momentarily), God can control human choices and the subsequent unfolding of causally connected events. An explicit example may be helpful. Let us suppose that God wants Mary to bear the infant Jesus. But also assume that the deity wishes to honor the free will of Mary and to let her choose whether she will carry the child or not. If God cannot (or at least does not) make certain that Mary will say yes to this proposed responsibility, God cannot guarantee that Jesus will be born to her. In turn, God cannot assure the salvation of the world through the "child of Mary." When such a scenario is multiplied by the vast number of humans whose free will God might want to "honor," God's control apparently is greatly diminished.

Arminians are quick to reply that there is ambiguity in the Calvinist's case at this point. The problem revolves around the meaning of the term "control," and ultimately around the meaning of sovereignty. Berkhof says that human self-determinism implies that creatures are in control and that there is no divine providence; Clark asserts that free will takes humans out of the deity's control. But what does it mean to say that humans with free will are out of divine control? According to Arminians, it cannot mean that creatures are *ultimately* out of God's control. In the Arminian system whatever lack of control the deity might suffer due to human freedom is a *divinely self-imposed* limitation. God does not have to grant freedom to creatures. Humans are free only because God in the past willingly granted it to them and in the present continues to grant it. God retains the power to rescind this gift at any moment and, indeed, at times perhaps does rescind it. And so, in a strong sense, God remains utterly in control. Only those events occur that God permissively grants.[74]

Calvinists counter-reply that such a notion of divine sovereignty is insufficient. They offer a multiple rationale. First, such an interpretation allegedly does not allow God to construct an unchanging, all-inclusive plan for the world, and such a plan is implied by various scriptures. Commenting on Isaiah 46:10, Clark writes:

> When . . . God says, My counsel shall stand, he asserts omniscient and omnipotent control . . . . He did not merely look ahead and see what would happen independently of him. Nothing is independent of him . . . . Thus the course of history from the past on to the things that are not yet done are parts of God's plan; and God, declaring the end from the beginning, says, my counsel, my plan, my decree shall stand, and I shall do all my pleasure.[75]

For Clark, God's plan is meticulous—dealing with every event that occurs through time—and it is unchanging. But if (as Arminians claim) God's plan is subject to the self-determining actions of creatures, it cannot be all-inclusive and unchanging. It must be open to the ever-altering free actions of creatures.

It is not abundantly clear, however, that Clark's conclusion follows. As Cottrell points out, such a criticism fails to take into account the Arminian affirmation of divine foreknowledge as an essential element of divine providence. According to Cottrell, divine foreknowledge

> enables God to maintain complete control of his world despite the freedom of his creatures. God *knows* the future; it is not open or indefinite for him. This gives God the genuine option of either permitting or preventing men's planned choices, and

---

[74]Cottrell, pp. 187-228.
[75]Clark, p. 51.

prevention is the ultimate control . . . . In addition to permitting and preventing, God's foreknowledge also enables him to plan his own responses to and uses of man's choices even before they are made, even in eternity.[76]

For Cottrell, because God's foreknowledge is all-inclusive, the divine plan is also all-inclusive and unchanging. In spite of genuine human freedom, God eternally knows what will happen, what he will do, and how he will accomplish the divine purposes.[77]

Cottrell is perhaps correct in declaring that divine foreknowledge allows God's plan to be both all-inclusive and unchanging. And so, his response deflects some of the force of Clark's conclusions. Given the Arminian assertion that God knows the future, it seems possible that the deity also could construct a comprehensive and unchanging plan. As we will see below, however, it is less certain that foreknowledge grants divine control over the future.

A second reason Calvinists reject the Arminian view of divine sovereignty is that it does not take into account those Biblical passages that implicitly teach that God *causes* all things and not merely that God allows some events. This seems to be Calvin's complaint against the notion of divine permissive will. Citing as one example the claim that Job 1 teaches that God merely permissively allowed Satan to test Job, Calvin notes that the text also states concerning this episode that "the Lord gave, and the Lord has taken away; as it pleased the Lord, so it has been done." From this Calvin infers that "God was the author of that trial of which Satan and wicked robbers were merely the instruments."[78] That is,

---

[76]Cottrell, pp. 214-215. Cottrell's emphasis.

[77]Indeed, Cottrell insists that divine foreknowledge allows one to affirm both that divine election unto salvation is an election of specific individuals and is conditional upon the response of those persons. For in knowing the future, God knows who will in fact exercise faith in Christ and, subsequently, will be saved. Ibid., pp. 338-345.

[78]John Calvin, *The Institutes of the Christian Religion*, trans. Ford Lewis Battles, ed. John T. McNeill (Philadelphia: Westminster, 1960), 1.18.1, 2.4.3.

God is the ultimate cause of the events surrounding Job. In a similar vein, Clark believes that some scriptures plainly teach or imply that God causes all events.[79]   We will reserve judgment concerning the validity of these Calvinistic interpretations of scripture for chapter five. For now, let us admit that numerous Biblical passages seem to affirm the direct divine causation of various cosmic and human events.

For many Calvinists, a third difficulty with the Arminian understanding of divine sovereignty is that it makes God dependent upon creatures and allegedly this is not possible or appropriate. Berkhof says that if creatures were self-determining it would make the "First Cause [God] subservient to the second [creatures]."[80] Clark notes that to claim that God merely permissively wills some creaturely events "supposes that there is some force in the universe independent of God,"[81] a view that Clark rejects. Underlying these Calvinistic objections seems to be the presumption that God cannot be conditioned in any way by creatures. Often the precise rationale for this assumption is not expressed. But for several it seems to be grounded in an explicit or tacit endorsement of the static model of God and, in turn, this model is founded upon an intuition concerning divine perfection. As we saw in chapter two, Plato taught that a perfect being cannot change. Aristotle insisted that the highest being is fully actual, with no potential for alteration. Augustine believed that God is the most excellent being possible and, as such, must be immutable. Aquinas taught that since the deity is unchanging and is the source of all other things, God cannot be influenced by created beings. Even God's knowledge is unaffected by creatures. Whatever the deity knows about others, he knows through an awareness of the divine essence.

These ideas are repeated by various contemporary Calvinistic writers. For example, Berkhof declares that as an absolutely perfect being, God must be immutable because in a perfect being

---

[79]Clark, pp. 49-65.
[80]Berkhof, p. 172. Brackets are mine.
[81]Clark, p. 53.

"improvement and deterioration are both equally impossible."[82] For this reason, Berkhof rejects the Arminian affirmation of a divine foreknowledge that is conditioned by future human actions since this implies that "God is subject to change, not in His Being, but in His knowledge and will, so that His decisions are to a great extent dependent on the actions of man."[83] In a similar manner, Clark contends that "God's knowledge is not empirical. He does not discover the truth. He always has the truth . . . . He does not learn from things: his knowledge depends on himself alone and is as eternal as he is."[84]

Notice that for these writers the issue is not only God's immutability, but also the divine non-conditionality. God cannot be affected by, conditioned by, creaturely events. Subsequently, Cottrell's (and other Arminians') appeal to divine foreknowledge as a means of securing an unchanging divine plan is not helpful, for the issue is not simply that God's plan and knowledge cannot change, but that they cannot be *causally affected* by creatures. Here we find a fundamental parting of the ways among theologians. For some it seems intuitively obvious that a perfect being cannot be affected by any other. For others such conditionality is not only acceptable but desirable. We will have to reserve further comments on these matters for chapter six.

Proneness Toward Works-Righteousness

Another Calvinistic objection to the Arminian model of divine providence is that it is not compatible with divine grace. As we have seen, this was Augustine's accusation against both the Pelagians and the Semi-Pelagians. According to Augustine, Peligius had made salvation a reward granted by God to humans for their meritorious efforts; the Semi-Pelagians had made initial faith in Christ a human work that God rewards with further grace and ultimately with salvation. In each case, claims Augustine,

---

[82]Berkhof, p. 61.
[83]Ibid., p. 62.
[84]Clark, pp. 39-40.

salvation is no longer by grace; it (partly) is earned. Luther essentially alleges the same indictment against Erasmus and medieval Roman Catholic soteriology. In this system, God's grace aids a person toward expressing faith in Christ, but the choice ultimately is decided by the human believer. And so, salvation is partly the result of a human effort. Further, according to the Catholic system, after initial faith in Christ, God's grace continues working in the Christian, urging the believer toward a life of actual and infused righteousness. If the believer cooperates with this divine urging, everlasting life is rewarded. But such cooperation unto righteousness is not guaranteed. Humans can and sometimes do resist God's goading and, thus, fail to receive eternal life. For Luther, such a position makes salvation partly a human accomplishment and, thus, not truly an event achieved by divine grace alone.

Arminians often are puzzled by these accusations, insisting that even though their doctrine affirms that humans freely exercise faith and, thus, that the *reception* of salvation is up to creatures, it hardly means that salvation is not by divine grace or even that the reception of salvation is totally a human affair. God remains the initiator of salvation. Without the divine sacrifice on Calvary and the subsequent offer of salvation through faith in Christ, there would be no chance for the human sinner to enter into eternal life. God remains the primary causal factor in the dynamic of human salvation.[85]

But for Calvinists such a view of divine grace is unacceptable. Two rationales undergird this rejection of the Arminian model of grace. One is the belief that the human heart is totally depraved and, thus, utterly unable to want or to do any good. If humans are so despicable that they cannot desire good at all, then they can only respond to God in faith if the deity first spiritually changes them. And so, for Augustine God must grant faith itself as a spiritual gift. And for many Protestant Calvinists, God must regenerate the

---

[85]See John Sanders' comments in *The God Who Risks: A Theology of Providence* (Downers Grove: InterVarsity Press, 1998), pp. 247-248.

human heart *before* it can exercise faith.[86]

The chief Arminian response to this Calvinistic line of reasoning is to assert that the human sinful condition is partially neutralized by a divine grace bestowed upon *all humans*. Through this grace the controlling effect of the sinful nature is sufficiently overcome that persons may freely choose to believe or disbelieve in Christ. This rejoinder is found in both Catholic and Protestant "Arminian" writers. Erasmas speaks of an operative grace which is given to all persons so that they might freely perform acts of contrition and turn to God. Arminius and Wesley respectively mention a preventing or prevenient grace that God confers on all people so that the determining effects of original sin might be subdued and individuals might freely choose for or against faith in Christ. Calvinists retort that there is little scriptural evidence for such an all-pervasive "prevenient" grace. Arminians return by insisting that there is some scriptural warrant for such claims and that this doctrine is a natural implication of the overall testimony of scripture. We will consider these issues more fully in chapter five.

Another rationale undergirding the Calvinistic charge that the Arminian system is incompatible with salvation by grace is the assumption that God can in no way be conditioned by humans. As noted above in our discussion of divine sovereignty, a tacit supposition of many Calvinists is that as a perfect being, God cannot be causally influenced by creatures. If this is the case, then salvation cannot be conditioned by self-generated human faith. All creaturely events, including faith, ultimately must be caused by the divine being, by the effectuating will of God. As pointed out earlier, however, it is debatable whether a notion of God as static and unassailable is necessary or even desirable for Christian theology. For some, such a conceptualization of divinity is required; for others, it is not. Cottrell complains that, despite Calvinistic claims to the contrary, "to say that election is of grace does not mean that it is unconditional; it simply means that it is not

---

[86]Berkhof, pp. 491-492.

conditioned on works."[87] For Cottrell, as for other Arminians, salvation is conditioned by our response of faith to God's gracious offer.

As with the debate over sovereignty, we will reserve a fuller discussion of the issues revolving around salvation by grace for chapter five. In passing, we may note that there are substantial differences between the "Arminian model" as expressed in traditional Roman Catholic thought and that of typical Protestant Arminianism. In following the broad contours of Martin Luther's insights concerning the justification of sinners by faith, Protestant Arminian writers tend to be less susceptible to the Calvinistic charge that they teach salvation by works-righteousness. For like Luther and unlike Catholic theology, these authors tend to see justification as a forensic declaration by God of the righteousness of one who in fact is still a sinner, rather than as the actual obtaining of righteousness. In turn, salvation is seen not as the reward of eternal life that one receives because of one's actual righteousness, but as a gift freely given in spite of one's unrighteousness; and faith is understood to be the reception of this gift.

The Problem of Indeterministic Freedom

A third difficulty faced by the Arminian model of divine providence concerns its conceptualization of freedom. Various writers contend that the notion of indeterministic freedom simply is incoherent, unintelligible. The 18th century pastor and theologian Jonathan Edwards complained that indeterministic freedom requires that one affirm the emergence of events in the universe out of nothing, without cause. For Edwards, such an assertion is unintelligible for it contradicts our basic intuitions concerning causation and the need for explanation. It implies that some events ultimately cannot be explained, that reality (in part) is absurd. Further, all of this threatens the unique role of God as Creator and

---

[87]Cottrell, p. 350.

Sovereign Ruler. If there are events that come into being without cause, not only are they absurd; they are independent of God as the primary cause of all.[88]

Other writers maintain that indeterministic freedom is incompatible with human responsibility. As we saw in chapter two, McGregor Wright insists that indeterministic freedom implies that human choices are uncaused, random events, and that such happenings disallow human responsibility. Wright bids us imagine an unrepentant sinner, standing before the throne of God, complaining that he cannot be held responsible for his actions because they were mere chance events, deeds over which he had no control. Such a defense before God would be possible, claims Wright, if libertarian freedom obtained.[89]

The principle Arminian (indeterminist) reply to such reasoning is two-fold. First, one may question Edward's axiom that all cosmic events must have a cause, must be explainable. Such a principle is not clearly demonstrable or verifiable. It is more akin to a basic intuition than to a provable theorem; and not all share this intuition. Further, there is some reason to believe that at least on the atomic level there are some events whose occurrence are not directly caused by prior states, whose happenings genuinely are random and thus unintelligible.[90]

Second, and perhaps more importantly, the Arminian may deny that libertarian freedom entails that human choices are merely random, uncaused events. For libertarians, there is a cause for humans choices, namely the human person (agent) herself. The critical claim of the libertarian here is that while the human agent

---

[88]Jonathan Edwards, *Freedom of the Will*, ed. Paul Ramsey (New Haven: Yale University Press, 1966, 1957), pp. 180-185.

[89]Indeed, Wright tastelessly goes so far as to name this particular "sinner," whom he apparently is confident is hell-bound! R. K. McGregor Wright, *No Place for Sovereignty: What's Wrong with Freewill Theism?* (Downers Grove: InterVarsity Press, 1996), p. 48.

[90]William Hasker, *Metaphysics: Constructing a World View* (Downers Grove: InterVarsity Press, 1983), pp. 38-44.

is the cause of her own free actions, those actions do not flow necessarily from the agent's character. Rather, in cases of free choice, the agent is able to transcend and to act contrary to whatever her general predispositions might be.[91] This differs from the determinist view which asserts that actions of an agent flow necessarily from the preexisting character of the agent.

A typical rejoinder of the determinist, at this point, is to ask why the agent chooses what she chooses and to insist that there must be some set of pre-existing conditions within the agent that bring about the choice that she makes. Otherwise, again, the act is unintelligible. Libertarians counter this stratagem, however, by insisting that in using it the determinist is begging the question. The demand that there always be an explanation beyond the agent's actual choice "is equivalent to asserting determinism as an *a priori* requirement of successful explanation."[92] And it is not clear that the libertarian must accept such an *a priori* maxim. Further, the libertarian denies that an agent's free actions emerge from some set of constituent parts of the agent, but rather insists that such actions are produced by the agent as an integrated whole. And so, it is inappropriate to demand that an action flow from a set of conditions *within the agent* rather than from the agent herself.[93]

When asked for evidence for his views on freedom, the libertarian offers a number of comments. One is to question the determinist's assumption that all events have a cause or explanation. Such a claim is not unambiguously verified in empirical observations of various natural and human phenomena, and seems

---

[91]So argue the following writers: C. A. Campbell, "Libertarianism," Raziel Abelson, et. al., *Ethics for Modern Life*, 4th edition (New York: St. Martin's Press, 1991), pp. 93-95; Richard Taylor, "Libertarianism: Defense of Free Will," Louis Pojman, *Introduction to Philosophy: Classical and Contemporary Readings*, 2nd edition, (United States: Wadsworth, 2000), pp. 492-494; William Hasker, *The Emergent Self* (Ithaca: Cornell University Press, 1999), pp. 99-109.

[92]Hasker, *The Emergent Self*, p. 104.

[93]Ibid.

to be contradicted by standard interpretations of quantum physics. Further, the request for a cause of every event seems logically to require an infinite regress of causes and, thus, offers no ultimate explanation for any event.[94] A second libertarian tactic for grounding belief in indeterministic freedom is to appeal to the human experience of freedom in daily life. In numerous cases we are aware of our own ability to choose one option over another, and feel that whatever choice we in fact make, we could have made another. When combined with our intuitions concerning the need for libertarian freedom in establishing human moral responsibility, these insights serve as powerful data for affirming indeterministic freedom. The libertarian admits that our experience of freedom could be an illusion, but insists that such experience it is strong enough for us to demand considerable evidence to the contrary before giving up belief in indeterministic freedom; and such evidence allegedly is not available.[95]

The debate over libertarian versus deterministic freedom is perennial. This brief discussion will hardly satisfy either side of the discussion. At best we may claim that the Calvinist charges against indetermistic freedom are unresolved. In the end, one's conclusions on these matters may boil down to personal intuitions. While one may argue over them, argument may never resolve the issues.

Divine Atemporality, Immutability and Personhood

A fourth problem faced by the Arminian model of the divine-world relationship emerges from its traditional affirmation of

---

[94]Taylor, pp. 486-487.

[95]Campbell, p. 98; Peter Bertocci writes: "[O]ne does not have to know how will is possible even as one does not have to know how it is possible for a red sensation to be red, or a pleasant feeling to be pleasant. Willing is an ultimate activity of experience with its own peculiar psychic tone. All I can do is point to it." *Free Will, Responsibility and Grace* (New York: Abingdon Press, 1957), pp. 38-39.

divine atemporality and immutability. As we have seen in this chapter, progenitors of the traditional Arminian model endorse divine timelessness and changelessness. But as noted in chapter two (when considering similar claims by Calvinistic writers), it is not clear that such divine attributes are compatible with divine personhood or even that the alleged relationship between time and timelessness is coherent. Because the problems mentioned in chapter two are essentially the same as those faced by Arminians on this score, we need make no further comment—except that if these difficulty are not countered, the Arminian model of divine providence is untenable.[96] We will consider these issues more fully in chapters four and six.

The Incompatibility of Freedom and Divine Foreknowledge

One of the more critical impediments faced by the Arminian model is its endorsement of both human libertarian freedom and divine foreknowledge. Since ancient times, a logical tension has been detected between these traditional theistic claims. Augustine expresses the dilemma well when he writes:

> I have a deep desire to know how it can be that God knows all things beforehand and that, nevertheless, we do not sin by necessity. Whoever says that anything can happen otherwise than as God has foreknown it, is attempting to destroy the divine foreknowledge with the most insensate impiety . . . . Since God foreknew that man would sin, that which God foreknew must necessarily come to pass. How then is the will

---

[96]The affirmations of atemporality and immutability create other problems for the Arminian model–quandaries not as pertinent to the Calvinistic system. Specifically, some writers contend that divine timelessness and immutability are incompatible with libertarian freedom–a position that we will examine in chapter six.

free when there is apparently this unavoidable necessity?[97]

We will discuss this conundrum more fully in the next two chapters. Let us note now, however, that if this challenge is not met, the Arminian system collapses. For it either destroys the Arminian view of freedom or it annuls the key tool by which the model attempts to sustain a meticulous divine providence, namely divine foreknowledge.

The Utility of Foreknowledge for Providential Control

A final obstacle for the Arminian model concerns its appeal to divine foreknowledge as an instrument through which God generates a meticulous and unchanging providential plan. As noted earlier, Cottrell appeals to God's knowledge of the future as a means whereby the deity can construct an exact, unchanging, and exhaustive plan for the created order. Allegedly, by knowing the future in every detail, God can providentially grant or deny such a future (in every detail). Unfortunately, vigorous philosophical challenges have been offered against such contentions. In brief, one may wonder what possible aid a passive foreknowledge might give to the deity's control of the future. It seems that if God knows now what the future will be, there is no way for God to change it or control it. It simply is (or will be) as God now sees it. There is no opportunity for God to operate providential control upon it. And so, one may argue that while Cottrell is correct in claiming that God's "plan" can be exhaustive and meticulous because of foreknowledge, one cannot maintain that the divine plan is a form of control. Rather, it seems more like a kind of acquiescing to the inevitable. We will consider these challenges more fully in the next chapter.

---

[97]Augustine, *On Free Will, Augustine: Earlier Writings*, vol. 6, trans. J. H. S. Burleigh (Philadelphia: The Westminster Press, 1953), 2.2.4.

Preliminary Conclusion

Like Calvinism, Arminianism is an intricate and vigorous theological system and one that faces its own set of theoretical problems. Philosophically and theologically, the following questions are particularly troublesome for Arminianism: (1) Can God in any way depend on creatures?, (2) Does the Bible teach that God is the direct cause of all things?, (3) Does the Bible allow for belief in prevenient grace?, (4) Can a personal and interpersonal God be timeless and immutable?, (5) Are foreknowledge and freedom compatible?, and (6) Is foreknowledge useful to divine providence?. Questions (1) and (2) stem from the Calvinistic concern over divine sovereignty. Questions (1) and (3) emerge out of disquiet over divine grace and works-righteousness. In chapter five, we will discuss questions (2) and (3). In chapter six, we will ponder conundrums (1), (4)-(6). Before contemplating these issues, however, it will be helpful to consider a third model of divine providence, namely, open theism. In many ways, open theism is a form of Arminianism that negatively answers the last three questions above. It insists that a personal and interpersonal God cannot be timeless and immutable, that foreknowledge and freedom are incompatible, and that divine foreknowledge cannot aid providence. In the next chapter, we analyze this theological model.

Chapter 4

Charting the Waters of Open Theism

We now turn to the open theist's model of divine providence. Like Calvinism and traditional Arminianism, open theism teaches that God is sovereign over the creation. God has created the universe and at any moment is able utterly to destroy it or to control events within it. Nevertheless, God freely chooses to limit the exercise of the divine power so that creatures (especially humans) truly may be free and accountable. Like the Arminian model, but unlike Calvinism, open theism insists that humans actively participate in their salvation. While Christ's atonement for sin and the work of the Holy Spirit upon the human heart are necessary for salvation, the *decision* to believe in Christ and, subsequently, to receive salvation is a human act. Unlike both Calvinism and traditional Arminianism, open theism denies that God fully knows the future, because allegedly sure divine knowledge of future events negates the freedom of those occurrence. Rather, God has complete knowledge of the past and the present, and has conjectural knowledge about some aspects of the future.

Like Arminianism, open theism endorses a libertarian or indeterministic view of human freedom. An action is free if a person can perform that act or refrain from performing it, and if that person is not externally or internally compelled to make the choice in question. Open theism also affirms the dynamic model of God's nature, conceptualizing the deity as a temporal being who undergoes some change. While God's basic moral character does not alter, the divine experience undergoes some change. God has no temporal beginning or end, but persist *through* all times, experiencing temporal events as they emerge. Further, God is affected by human actions and is able to react to them. When someone prays, God becomes aware of the prayer and can answer it. When someone sins, God comes to know this and is able to react to it.

In this chapter, we explore the major themes of open theism's model of the divine-world relationship, and provide a brief critique of the system. Because open theism is a relatively recent movement in theology, it will not be necessary to examine the writings of its various progenitors on an individual basis. Rather, we will examine the overarching themes of this school of thought before offering some criticisms.

Basic Themes of Open Theism

Open theism is endorsed by a number of contemporary writers, including Richard Rice, Clark Pinnock, William Hasker, John Sanders, and David Basinger. Two fundamental commitments undergird this theological model: (1) the affirmation of human libertarian freedom and (2) the endorsement of divine-human interpersonal relationships. That is, open theists believe that a human being must be free to perform or refrain from performing an act, if that person is to be responsible for the action in question. And since God holds humans responsible for many of their actions, humanity must be free in the libertarian sense with regard to these events. Further, open theists insist that there is genuine divine-human personal interaction. Humans affect God and God affects humans. The openning lines of a text co-written by the authors named immediately above demonstrates their commitment to these two key ideas. They write that

> God, in grace, grants humans significant freedom to cooperate with or work against God's will for their lives, and he enters into dynamic, give-and-take relationships with us. The Christian life involves a genuine interaction between God and

human beings. We respond to God's gracious invitation and God responds to our responses . . . and on it goes. . . . God does not control everything that happens. Rather, he is open to receiving input from his creatures. In loving dialogue, God invites us to participate with him to bring the future into being.[1]

Because of its commitment to freedom and to divine-human interchange, open theism rejects two teachings of traditional Christian theism, namely, (1) divine foreknowledge (of future contingent events) and (2) the static (timeless, immutable) nature of God. According to open theists, these conventional doctrines are incompatible with freedom and with divine-human personal interaction. Let us consider the open theist's case against each of these tenets.

Rejection of Divine Foreknowledge

The case against the compatibility of divine foreknowledge and freedom is well-rehearsed historically, finding expression in numerous ancient, medieval and contemporary writers. Various versions of the argument have been produced. Perhaps the most powerful and ingenious rendering is expounded by the Calvinistic writer, Jonathan Edwards. Edwards argues:

> 1. I observed before, in explaining the nature of necessity, that in things which are past, their past existence is now necessary: having already made sure of existence, 'tis too late for any possibility of alteration in that respect: 'tis now impossible, that it should be otherwise than true, that that thing has existed.
> 2. If there be any such thing as a divine foreknowledge of the volitions of free agents, that foreknowledge, by the supposition, is a thing which already has, and long ago had existence; and so, now its existence is necessary; it is now utterly impossi-

---

[1]Clark Pinnock, et. al., *The Openness of God: A Biblical Challenge to the Traditional Understanding of God* (Downers Grove, Illinois: InterVarsity Press, 1994), p. 7.

ble to be otherwise, than that this foreknowledge should be, or should have been.

3. 'Tis also very manifest, that those things which are indissolubly connected with other things that are necessary, are themselves necessary. As that proposition whose truth is necessarily connected with another proposition, which is necessarily true, is itself necessarily true. To say otherwise, would be a contradiction; it would be in effect to say, that the connection was indissoluble, and yet was not so, but might be broken. If that, whose existence is indissolubly connected with something whose existence is now necessary, is itself not necessary, then it may possibly not exist, notwithstanding that indissoluble connection of its existence. Whether the absurdity ben't glaring, let the reader judge.

4. 'Tis no less evident, that if there be a full, certain and infallible foreknowledge of the future existence of the volitions of moral agents, then there is a certain infallible and indissoluble connection between those events and that foreknowledge; and that therefore, by the preceding observations, those events are necessary events; being infallibly and indissolubly connected with that whose existence already is, and so is now necessary, and can't but have been.[2]

Edwards makes four principal points. First, he notes that the past is unalterable. Once a past event has occurred, it is necessary; it cannot be changed. The unchanging nature of the past is sometimes referred to as *accidental necessity.* Before an event happens it may well be contingent, capable of either being or not being. But once it occurs, it cannot now have not happened. Its occurrence is now necessary per the "accident" or condition that it has indeed happened. Second, Edwards declares that foreknowledge is an event (Edwards says it is a "thing") in the past. Subsequently, God's knowledge of the future seems to be an occurrence that is now necessary; it is accidentally necessary

---

[2]Jonathan Edwards, *The Works of Jonathan Edwards*, vol. 1, *Freedom of the Will*, ed. Paul Ramsey (New Haven: Yale University Press, 1957), pp. 257-258.

because it already has happened. Third, Edwards maintains that statements that are entailed in a necessary proposition are themselves, also, necessary. In other words, the statement "necessarily, if p then q" apparently entails that if "necessarily p" then "necessarily q." Finally, Edwards concludes, that if there are happenings that are necessarily connected with divine foreknowledge, then these events are necessary because divine foreknowledge itself presently is necessary. Divine foreknowledge is necessary because it is an event in the past.

Edwards' argument formally may be restated as follows. Based on the assumption that to know something is to know something that is the case, one may assert that

(1) Necessarily, if God knows that I will do A, then I will do A.[3]

Based on the traditional theistic claim that God knows the future and that such knowledge is now in the past (and therefore, accidentally necessary), one may claim that

(2) (Accidentally) necessarily, God knows that I will do A.

Assuming that necessity transfers from necessary propositions to propositions that are entailed by those necessary propositions, then it seems to follow that

(3) Therefore, (accidentally) necessarily, I will do A.

To show that such a conclusion is not compatible with human

---

[3]Edwards notes: "To say, the foreknowledge is certain and infallible, and yet the connection of the event with that foreknowledge is not indissoluble, but dissoluble and fallible, is very absurd. To affirm it, would be the same thing as to affirm, that there is no necessary connection between a proposition being infallibly known to be true, and its being true indeed." Ibid., p. 258.

freedom, one need only add the premise that

(4) If necessarily I will do A, then I will not do A freely.

And from (3) and (4), it follows that

(5) I will not do A freely.

Edwards' argument is valid. If its premises are true, the argument seems to establish that divine foreknowledge and human freedom are contradictory. Similar arguments are found among an assortments of writer, including open theists such as William Hasker.[4] Indeed, most open theists endorse (explicitly or implicitly) some form of the incompatibility argument.

Not surprisingly, open theists reject attempts to reconcile divine foreknowledge and human freedom. For example, they disavow divine timelessness as a solution to the foreknowledge-free will dilemma. Long ago, Boethius argued that God exists outside of time in a static eternal moment. And so, the deity experiences all events of all times at once, in a singular, unchanging, moment. Thus, God does not know events as they are going to happen in the future, but knows them as they are happening in the divine timeless perspective. According to Boethius, since human knowledge of currently occurring events does not causally necessitate current events, neither does God's timeless knowledge of future events causally necessitate them. Boethius concluded that divine foreknowledge (interpreted as timeless knowledge) does not truncate human freedom.[5]

Open theists reject divine timelessness for a variety of reasons. Many argue that the alleged ontological relationship

---

[4]William Hasker, *God, Time, and Knowledge* (Ithaca: Cornell University Press, 1989), pp. 64-74.

[5]Boethius, *The Consolation of Philosophy*, The Loeb Classical Library, trans. I. T., revised H. F. Stewart (Cambridge Massachusetts: Harvard University Press, 1918), 5.6.

between time and timeless eternity is incoherent. It simply makes no sense to say that events of the past are somehow eternally simultaneous with events of the future.[6] Others contend that divine timelessness contradicts the pivotal theistic belief that God is personal and interpersonal. If God is timeless, he cannot react to or interpersonally relate with creatures.[7] Still others deny that appeal to divine timelessness solves the free will dilemma, alleging that divine timelessness leads to its own form of determinism.[8] (We will discuss some of these issues in chapter six.)

In light of these difficulties with divine timelessness, open theists affirm the temporality of God. For these writers, the divine eternity must be understood as a beginningless, endless temporal duration and not as a static, unchanging, singular eternal moment. In this view, God endures process. The past has been experienced by God and is now held in the divine memory, which is ever growing. The present is that which is immediately experienced by the deity. The future has not yet been experienced and the future is ever open before God. There is no singular future, but rather a

---

[6]This point was forcefully made by Anthony Kenny, "Divine Foreknowledge and Human Freedom," *Aquinas: A Collection of Critical Essays*, ed. A. Kenny (New York: Doubleday, 1969), pp. 255-270. Similar observations have been made by Richard Swinburne, *The Coherence of Theism* (Oxford: Clarendon Press, 1977, 1995), p. 228.

[7]Nicholas Wolterstorff, "God Everlasting," *God and the Good*, ed. Clifton Orlebeke and Lewis Smedes (Grand Rapids: Eerdmans, 1975), pp. 181-203.

[8]While Alvin Plantinga is not properly among them, many freewill theists would agree with his claim that even if God's knowledge of all times is not in time, true sentences about the future may be constructed in time based on God's eternal knowledge, and these temporally bound true statements about the future are incompatible with libertarian freedom. See Plantinga, "On Ockham's Way Out," *Faith and Philosophy* 3 (July 1986), 239-240.

multitude of possibilities that could be actualized.[9]

Many open theists claim that because God is temporal, it is no great surprise that the deity does not know the future, since the future is non-existent. There is literally nothing for God to know. Clark Pinnock is most clear on this point when he says that "God is omniscient in the sense that he knows everything which can be known . . . . But free actions are not entities which can be known ahead of time. They literally do not yet exist to be known."[10]

Open theists also discard divine middle knowledge as a possible cure for the incompatibility between libertarian freedom and divine foreknowledge. Advocates of middle knowledge insist that God knows counterfactuals of freedom. He knows not only what could be (possibilities) or what will be (actualities), but also what *would be if* a given set of counterfactual conditions were to occur. Thus, the deity knows what any given created being *freely* would do in any given set of circumstances. This knowledge is called middle knowledge because it lies between knowledge of possibilities and actualities. In turn, middle knowledge coupled with knowledge of divine intentions allows God to know the future. William Craig explains:

> By his middle knowledge God knows all the various possible worlds which he could create and what every free creature would do in all the various circumstances of those possible worlds . . . . By a free decision of his will, God then chose to create one of those possible worlds. Knowing both every possible world he could create and his decision to create one of them, God foreknows exactly what will happen, that is to say,

---

[9]For examples of these views, see Hasker, *God, Time, and Knowledge*, pp. 177-205 and Swinburne, *The Coherence of Theism*, pp. 217-229.

[10]Clark Pinnock, "God Limits His Knowledge," *Predestination and Free Will: Four Views of Divine Sovereignty and Human Freedom*, ed. David and Randal Basinger (Downers Grove: InterVarsity Press, 1986), p. 157.

he has foreknowledge.[11]

Open theists reject middle knowledge on a number of grounds. One major difficulty involves how counterfactuals might be known. It simply is not clear that there can be any ontological grounding for truly free counterfactual propositions. William Hasker argues that if counterfactuals are true, they cannot be counterfactuals *of freedom*, for in order to be true a counterfactual statement must be necessary. On the other hand, if an agent genuinely is free there can be no true counterfactual propositions about what that agent will do.[12]

Many open theists also reject the Ockhamist solution to the foreknowledge-free will dilemma. Ockhamism insists that while God is temporal, he somehow knows the future by presently experiencing future events. Thus, Ockhamism seems to be committed to the retroactive causal impact of future events on God's past beliefs. But open theists argue that reverse temporal causation is impossible and, thus, cannot explain divine foreknowledge.[13]

Finally, open theists adamantly deny the Calvinist claim that God knows the future by predetermining it. As we have seen, Calvin believed that God "foresees future events only by reason of

---

[11]William Lane Craig, *The Only Wise God: The Compatibility of Divine Foreknowledge and Human Freedom* (Grand Rapids: Baker Book House, 1987), p. 133.

[12]Hasker, *God, Time, and Knowledge*, p. 52.

[13]Ockhamism derives from the writings of medieval theologian William of Ockham; see his *Predestination, God's Foreknowledge, and Future Contingents*, 2nd ed., trans. Marilyn McCord Adams and Norman Kretzmann (Indianapolis: Hackett, 1983). A number of open theists explicitly reject the Ockhamist solution. See William Hasker, *God, Time, and Knowledge*, pp. 75-143 and Richard Swinburne, *The Christian God* (Oxford: Clarendon Press, 1994), p. 132.

the fact that he decreed that they take place . . . ."[14] In other words, the deity knows the future by determining it. Such a view contradicts the open theist's affirmation of libertarian freedom and, thus, is rejected by them. In sum, open theists contend that divine foreknowledge and human freedom are incompatible; subsequently, they reject divine foreknowledge (of future contingent events) for the sake of human freedom.

Rejection of the Static Model of God

Open theists also spurn the traditional static model of the divine nature. According to this paradigm, God is timeless and utterly unchanging. There is no potential in the divine being, and so God cannot be affected by the created order. Open theists reject this notion of divinity for multiple reasons. Richard Rice insists that such a perspective implies absolute divine foreknowledge and this cancels human freedom. Rice reasons that "if a changeless God has infallible knowledge of reality, then His knowledge must also be changeless. It cannot increase or decrease."[15] Whatever God knows, he always know, including future events. Since infallible foreknowledge negates freedom, such a view must be disavowed.

William Hasker criticizes the static view of God, among other reasons, because it is based on a false dichotomy. As we saw in chapter two, Plato reasoned that a perfect being could not change because this would require that it either get better or worse. But it is impossible for a perfect being to do either. And so, as a perfect being, God cannot change. Hasker complains, however, that such

---

[14]John Calvin, *Institutes of the Christian Religion*, trans. Ford Lewis Battles, ed. John T. McNeill (Philadelphia: Westminster, 1960), 3, 23, 6. For a recent defense of this perspective see John Feinberg's "God Ordains All Things," *Predestination and Free Will: Four Views of Divine Sovereignty and Human Freedom*, ed. David and Randal Basinger, pp. 19-43.

[15]Richard Rice, *God's Foreknowlege & Man's Free Will* (Minneapolis: Bethany House Publishers, 1980, 1985), p. 17.

reasoning fails to recognize a third option. It is quite possible for a change to be neutral, neither for the better nor for the worse. And this is precisely what the open theist wishes to claim. The kinds of changes in the divine being that are endorsed by open theists are neutral changes. While God's knowledge and experience increase, God's basic moral character does not. Indeed, the changes in the divine being that are envisioned by open theists may be necessary for claiming that God truly is perfect. Hasker offers the anlogy of a watch. It is precisely because a watch changes that it is able to keep "perfect time." In like manner, there may be changes in God that are "consistent with and/or required by a constant state of excellence."[16]

Yet another reason for rejecting the static model of divinity is offered by John Sanders. He maintains that such an understanding prevents the deity from entering into personal relationships with humans. As noted above, the static model denies that God is affected by the created order. But Sanders argues that "God's project involves the creation of significant others who are ontologically distinct from himself and upon whom he showers his caring love in the expectation that they will response in love."[17] The problem with perfect being (static being) theology is that it disallows "a genuine give-and-take interpersonal relationship between God and humanity."[18]

The Divine Nature and Knowledge

In light of their rejection of divine foreknowledge and the static model of deity, open theists endorse the following perspective on God's nature and knowledge. First, as we have seen, God is temporal and dynamic. He endures through time and is able to interact with creatures. The deity's experiences and activities

---

[16]William Hasker, "A Philosophical Perspective," *The Openness of God*, pp. 132-133.
[17]John Sanders, *The God Who Risks: A Theology of Providence* (Downers Grove: InterVarsity Press, 1998), p. 169.
[18]Ibid., p. 174.

change as he relates to and responds to creatures. This is the case even though the divine essence and moral nature do not change. Second, God is loving and personal. Indeed, these attributes are more fundamental than and provide the grounding for the divine temporality and dynamism. It is precisely because the Bible teaches that God is loving and personal that he also must be understood as temporal and dynamic. God enters into interpersonal and loving relations with creatures, and such relationships are central to the divine plan. Third, the deity is everlasting. While God endures through time and undergoes some change, his existence is never threatened. God has no beginning and no end. He exists always, through all temporal moments. Fourth, the deity is perfectly good. God does not do evil.

A fifth divine attribute is omnipotence. The deity can do all that is logically possible. God has created the universe out of nothing and now sustains it from moment to moment. In principle, God can control/determine every event that occurs in the world. However, the deity freely limits the exercise of his power over the created order for the sake of creaturely freedom. Graciously and voluntarily, God bestows limited freedom upon humans[19] Unlike Calvinists, then, open theists deny "that God can both grant individuals freedom and control its use."[20] Rather, these writers "maintain that to the extent that God grants individual freedom, he gives up complete control over the decisions that are made."[21]

A sixth divine characteristic is omniscience.[22] However, because of its denial of divine foreknowledge, the open theist's concept of divine knowledge carefully must be conceptualized. We will examine the views of three open theists: Richard

---

[19]David Basinger, *The Case for Freewill Theism* (Downers Grove: InterVarsity Press, 1996), p.12.

[20]Ibid.

[21]Ibid., p. 33.

[22]Portions of the remainder of this section are excerpted from Michael Robinson, "Why Divine Foreknowledge?" *Religious Studies* 36 (2000), 251-275.

Swinburne, William Hasker, and Richard Rice. Swinburne denies that divine omniscience involves knowledge of all true propositions because (1) certain propositions may be known only at certain times or by certain persons[23] and (2) knowledge of future contingent actions would destroy both human and divine freedom.[24] In light of this denial, Swinburne generates the following definition of omniscience.

> A person P is omniscient at a time *t* if and only if he knows every true proposition about *t* or an earlier time and every true proposition about a time later than *t* which is true of logical necessity or which he has overriding reason to make true, which it is logically possible that he entertains then.[25]

By the phrase "which it is logically possible that he [God] entertains then," Swinburne attempts to account for the fact that some propositions can be known only at certain times or by certain persons.[26] Thus, for example, it is logically impossible for God to know at some later time t_2 that "it is now t_1." Or again it is logically impossible for God to know the truth of the proposition "I am in the hospital" when the term "I" indexes a person who is in the hospital, but who is not God.[27] Keeping this qualification in mind, Swinburne insists that his definition of omniscience allows the deity to know all true propositions about the past and about the present. It allows God to know any logically necessary propositions about the future. And it allows him to know now any future events that he currently has overriding reasons to make sure will happen (or not happen). Concerning this last category, Swinburne especially has in mind those future divine contingent events that divine omnipotence would enable God to perform but

---

[23]For example, the statement "'it is now t_1' . . . can only be known at t_1." Richard Swinburne, *The Coherence of Theism*, p. 168.
[24]Ibid., p. 177.
[25]Ibid., pp. 180-181.
[26]Ibid., p. 172.
[27]Ibid., pp. 168-172.

which the divine moral perfection would not permit—such as committing sin or suicide—or which divine moral perfection would require.[28]

On the other hand, Swinburne's definition does not allow the deity to know future freely enacted creaturely or divine events. If humans and God truly are free, God cannot know in advance what either will do freely.[29] Admittedly, this lack of divine foreknowledge implies a universe that may "contain the occasional surprise for God."[30] But Swinburne denies that this lack of knowledge in any significant way threatens divine sovereignty. First, Swinburne points out that while God cannot certainly know future free acts of humans, he very accurately can predict such actions. This follows because humans are "creatures of limited knowledge in the actions and the reasons for doing them which occur to them, of habit in how they execute their actions, and of desire (i.e. inbuilt inclinations) in which actions they do . . . ."[31] Further, Swinburne notes that the limitation on divine foreknowledge is by divine choice. God does not know the future free actions of humans because he freely chooses to give humans freedom. At any moment, the deity is able to dissolve this limitation by "withdrawing from humans their free will."[32] Finally, Swinburne argues that God retains total control over the future. Since God is omnipotent and free, he is able to control whatever events unfold in the future. Indeed, at any moment, God may choose to abolish the universe completely. The deity remains sovereign into the future.

William Hasker offers a similar view of divine omniscience.

[28]Swinburne explicitly makes this point in *The Christian God* where he states: "God, if he is necessarily and eternally perfectly free, must be ignorant of his own future actions—except in so far as his perfect goodness . . . constrains him to act in certain ways." p. 134. Similar points are made in *The Coherence of Theism*, p. 266.

[29]Swinburne, *The Coherence of Theism*, p. 177, 181.

[30]Swinburne, *The Christian God*, p. 143.

[31]Swinburne, *The Coherence of Theism*, p. 181.

[32]Ibid., p. 183.

He defines omniscience as the ability to know "everything that logically can be known."[33] According to Hasker, this definition allows God fully to know the past and the present.[34] It also allows the deity to know in detail all future possibilities (a point that Swinburne does not explicitly make). Further, Hasker's definition allows God to know the probability of future events and the changing probabilities of those events as time unfolds.[35] Further still, God is able fully to know "his own purposes, and . . . how they may best be carried out."[36]

This definition, however, does not allow the deity to know future free events; for while God knows all that it logically is possible to know, it is not possible to know in advance events that will be freely enacted.[37] Hasker admits that this view of divine omniscience entails divine risk-taking.[38] But like Swinburne, Hasker believes that these limitations on divine knowledge do not curtail God's sovereignty in a major way, for "*God's capacity to control the detailed course of events is limited only by his self-restraint, not by any inability to do so.*"[39] In other words, the deity's knowledge of and power over free creatures is limited only by the divine choice to grant human freedom. Should God so choose, he is free to take away creaturely freedom.

Hasker is concerned to explain biblical prophecy which at face value implies divine knowledge of future free events. He argues, first, that many prophecies are conditional. They do not state what God knows will happen, but what he intends to do if certain circumstances should arise or if certain trends should continue. Second, many prophecies are predictions "based on

---

[33]William Hasker, "A Philosophical Perspective," p. 151.
[34]Hasker, *God, Time, and Knowledge*, p. 192.
[35]Ibid., pp. 188-189.
[36]Ibid., p. 192.
[37]Hasker, "A Philosophical Perspective," p. 151.
[38]Hasker, *God, Time, and Knowledge*, p. 197.
[39]Ibid., p. 196. Hasker's italics.

foresight drawn from existing trends and tendencies."[40] In other words, the deity is stating that highly probable events are going to occur. Third, many prophecies are straight-forward declarations of what God intends to accomplish. For example, claims Hasker, "God did not foresee the death and resurrection of his Son; he declared them as going to happen, because he fully intended to bring them about."[41] Thus, by a variety of means God may prophesy the future, without directly "seeing" it.

Richard Rice echoes many of the themes found in Swinburne and Hasker. Rice defines omniscience as knowledge of "everything logically knowable."[42] Since future contingent events are not logically knowable, God cannot know them—even though he is omniscient.[43] In this view of divine knowledge, God exhaustively knows the present[44] and the past.[45] He knows all possibilities and how to respond to any possibility that might actualize. Further, God knows the divine intentions, knowing "infallibly the content of his own future actions . . . . [and] the ultimate outcome to which he is guiding the course of history."[46] Finally—a point not made explicitly by Hasker or Swinburne—God knows those future events that "will happen as the inevitable consequence of past and present factors,"[47] events that are physically or causally necessitated by present events, events that "will happen because necessary conditions for . . . [them] . . . have been fulfilled and nothing could

---

[40]Ibid., p. 194.

[41]Ibid., p. 195. Interestingly, here, Hasker employs in a limited way what Calvin asserted for all future events, namely, that God might know them by decreeing them.

[42]Richard Rice, "Divine Foreknowledge and Free-Will Theism," Clark Pinnock et. al., *A Case for Arminianism: The Grace of God, The Will of Man* (Grand Rapids: Academie Books, Zondervan Publishing House, 1989), p. 128.

[43]Ibid., p. 129.

[44]Ibid., p. 135.

[45]Rice, *God's Foreknowledge & Man's Free Will*, p. 55.

[46]Ibid., p. 134.

[47]Ibid., p. 135.

conceivably prevent . . . [them]."⁴⁸

Like Hasker, Rice explains biblical prophecy in a variety of ways. Some prophecies "express God's intention to do something in the future irrespective of creaturely decision."⁴⁹ These are events that God intends to enact unilaterally. Other prophecies are about events whose necessary causal conditions already exist and, thus, are subject to God's present knowledge. Finally, many prophecies are conditional. They "express what God intends to do *if* certain conditions obtain."⁵⁰

Like both Swinburne and Hasker, Rice admits that his view of divine knowledge involves divine risk-taking,⁵¹ but he denies that God's providential control is unduly jeopardized. First, the deity knows "the range of options available to His creatures."⁵² And with this knowledge "God can formulate in advance an effective response to any course of action they may choose."⁵³ Further, God knows what options a creature is likely to take and, therefore, knows what responses he likely will need to make.⁵⁴ Finally, the deity determines how much freedom creatures have; he sets the limits of their available options. Therefore, God retains ultimate control.⁵⁵

From these open theist writings, the following model of divinity and of divine knowledge emerges. God is a temporal, dynamic, everlasting, personal, loving, omnipotent, and perfectly good being who knows at each moment of divine existence all that is logically knowable at that moment. He is unable to know

---

⁴⁸Rice, "Biblical Support for a New Perspective," *The Openness of God*, p. 51.

⁴⁹Ibid., p. 51.

⁵⁰Ibid.

⁵¹Rice, *God's Foreknowledge & Man's Free Will*, pp. 42-43.

⁵²Ibid., p. 65-66. The range of creaturely options is determined by the type of being and by the specific individual that a creature happens to be. See Ibid., pp. 56-57.

⁵³Ibid., p. 66.

⁵⁴Ibid., p. 57.

⁵⁵Ibid., p. 66.

propositions that are only knowable at times other than his immediate time or by persons others than himself. God also is unable to know propositions about freely enacted future events. This follows from the facts that he is temporal, backward causation and middle knowledge are impossible, and he has created genuinely free creatures. Nevertheless, there are a number of things the deity can know. He exhaustively knows all past and present events. He knows the truth of all logically necessary propositions. He knows all possibilities and how he could respond to each should it occur. God knows the present probabilities of any given future event and will know the changing probabilities of each possible future event as time unfolds. Further, the deity knows with certainty those future events whose necessary conditions already exist, those future events that currently are physically necessitated. Finally, God knows those events that he intends to bring about in the future and, consequently, he can rest assured that those events will occur.

This last point is somewhat tricky for the open theist, for part of the value of claiming that the deity cannot know future free contingencies is that it allows God's own future actions to be free. With this in mind, it seems that the open theist would not want to assert that God's current knowledge of a divine intention is logically equivalent to sure knowledge that he will perform a future act. Such an equation would imply that any action that God previously intended is not performed freely—an implication that I think freewill theists would want to avoid. Swinburne seems to be aware of this problem. He states that since God is perfectly free, God cannot "know in advance what he will do . . . ."[56] For this reason, Swinburne qualifies God's knowledge of divine future actions by stating that the deity knows those future events for which he "has overriding reason to make true . . . ."[57] In other words, the deity only knows those future divine contingent events which are required by his essential nature—especially by the

---

[56]Swinburne, *The Coherence of Theism*, p. 181.
[57]Ibid.

divine goodness.[58] Indeed, Swinburne claims that such certainly known future divine events are not free.[59] Although neither Hasker nor Rice explicitly qualify in this way their claim that God knows the future by knowing divine intentions, such a qualification works well with and may be required by their systems. Further, it may best represent Hasker's, Rice's and Swinburne's intent not to assert that God knows future divine free actions by knowing current divine intentions. Rather, their primary meaning seems to be that God currently knows the divine intentions and knows that nothing external to himself can prevent those intentions from happening. *In other words, God knows that if he should continue to want a certain event to occur in the future, nothing can stop him from bringing it about.* This is perhaps Hasker's point when he writes: "Whatever God needs to do, he has the power to do; whatever he sees is best to do happens forthwith."[60] Likewise, Swinburne comments that if God is "omnipotent and perfectly free, the future will be subject to his total control; he can do with the world as he chooses . . . ."[61] Finally, Rice comments:

. . . . God knows the range of options available to His creatures. He also is Himself responsible for those options. God determined how much freedom to allow His creatures. In so doing He limited the extent of their potential disruption of the universe. Surely God retains sufficient power to ensure the

---

[58]Swinburne states that events for which God has overriding reasons to make true "follow from his [God's] nature." *The Christian God*, p. 135.

[59]Swinburne makes this explicit when he states that God's "freedom of choice only operates for choice whether to do an action A when he does not acknowledge overriding reasons for doing A rather than refraining, or for refraining rather than doing A." *The Coherence of Theism*, p. 152. In other words, if God has overriding reasons for making a future event true and, thus, knows that it will occur, that event is not free.

[60]Hasker, *God, Time, and Knowledge*, p. 192.

[61]Swinburne, *The Coherence of Theism*, p. 181.

ultimate realization of His objectives . . . . the ultimate end of history is in God's hands.[62]

The Divine Rulership and Salvation

Flowing from these notions of the divine nature and knowledge, open theists affirm the following notions of God's rule of the universe and of human salvation. Concerning divine government, these writers maintain many of the traditional Christian claims about divine providence. They insist that God has a plan for the universe as a whole, that God sustains the being of creatures from moment to moment, and that God is active in the ongoing affairs of creation.

God's overarching purpose for creation is that humans enter into an abiding, loving, interpersonal relationship with him. Since such a relationship requires genuine freedom, God restricts the exercise of his power. The deity does not predetermine all human events nor does he foreknow freely chosen future actions. Because God does not preordain all events nor exhaustively know the future, the divine plan for the created order is only general, not meticulous. God has over-arching goals towards which he is leading the universe and he has a general plan for bringing about those purposes. But not every event that happens leads directly to some aim that God has proposed and there are many events that the deity simply does not intend. Among these are numerous good events that God may well rejoice over, but which he did not directly plan. Also among these are many evil actions that God prefers would not happen and that do not lead to some specific higher purpose. God *permits* these various good and evil events, out of respect for human personhood and freedom. But he does not specifically plan them.

Open theists also maintain, however, that God fully is capable of working good out of all events. That is, the divine wisdom is such that while many events occur that God does not directly plan nor prefer, God is able to take whatever happens and work with it,

---

[62]Rice, *God's Foreknowledge & Man's Free Will*, p. 66.

shaping events toward something positive. To the charge that such a view denigrates God's power and sovereignty, open theists reply that their view in fact is a nobler, more exalted image of divine strength and wisdom. This view says that God is wise enough, powerful enough, and secure enough to create beings with whom he can genuinely interact. God need not generate beings that simply perform every action that he dictates. Even under the conditions of genuine human freedom and rebellion, God can accomplish his overarching purposes. This is power and wisdom supreme.[63]

As noted earlier, open theists contend that even though God does not preordain the future nor know it fully, the divine rule is not seriously or ultimately threatened. First, God can predict (with considerable accuracy) many human events based on his knowledge of their basic inclinations and past behavior. Second, God can interrupt any sequence of currently occurring human activities by removing the freedom that he previously has granted them. Third, the deity knows all possibilities and can envision a divine response to each and every one of them. Finally, God can annihilate the universe or any part of it at any time. Nothing can occur that God does not permit. Whatever being and freedom the created order has is completely at the discretion of the deity. As Hasker notes: "Whatever God needs to do, he has the power to do; whatever he sees is best to do happens forthwith."[64]

Concerning salvation, open theists essentially agree with Arminianism. Humans are sinners, which means that without divine aid, individuals cannot turn to Christ or receive salvation. The Holy Spirit must provide enabling grace (prevenient grace), so that the sinner may freely choose Christ. Without such grace, no decision for Christ is possible and salvation cannot ensue. However, enabling grace is not irresistible. Upon receiving it, a

---

[63]Sanders, *The God Who Risks*, pp. 215-217. Also see, Gregory Boyd, *God of the Possible: A Biblical Introduction to the Open View of God* (Grand Rapids: Baker Books, 2000), pp. 150-153.

[64]Hasker, *God, Time, and Knowledge*, p. 192.

person still is free to reject Christ and, thus, may not receive redemption. And so, prevenient grace is *necessary* for salvation, but it is *not sufficient*. Without it salvation is not possible. With it, other conditions are still needed in order for redemption to unfold—namely, the condition of a person freely choosing Christ.[65]

Salvation remains an act of divine grace. Without the atoning work of Christ on the cross, sin could not be forgiven. In their fallen state, human righteousness is insufficient for salvation. Further, without prevenient grace, humans could not and would not be free to exercise faith in Christ. Consequently, salvation remains solely a gift from God. Without the atoning work of Christ's death and without God's influence upon the hearts of sinners, human beings could not find salvation. Again, this may be expressed by saying that God's grace (in the cross and in prevenient action on the heart) is necessary but not sufficient for salvation.

Simple Foreknowledge and Providence

A final plank in the open theist's platform is the claim that simple foreknowledge does not benefit divine providence. While such an assertion is not quite a central component of the open theist's system, it serves as an important weapon against traditional Arminianism's endorsement of divine foreknowledge. By simple foreknowledge, open theists mean a knowledge of future events that is not caused by divine foreordination. Rather, it is a knowledge wherein God knows future events not by decreeing them, but by passively being aware of them, by being affected by them. It is a knowledge similar to (although not identical to) our awareness of present events. We do not know current events by causing them, but by being causally affected by them. Presumably, the same would be true for divine "simple foreknowledge."

As noted in chapter three, one may question how such a simple or passive knowledge of the future could help God control the future. If the deity currently knows what will happen in the

---

[65]John Sanders, *The God Who Risks*, pp. 243-246.

future, there is nothing that he can do about those future events now. He cannot change them, stop them, or control them. The future simply will be as God "sees" it. Several consequences seem to flow from this state of affairs. For example, John Sanders argues that God could not have used simple foreknowledge to avoid creating sinful creatures. If God passively knew of the fall of human beings prior to the creation, he could not prevent the creation of such beings. For in foreknowing their future sin, he also foreknew their created existence; he knew of the fact that in the future he would create them. Or again, God could not use knowledge of the future damnation of some to choose not to create those persons. For again, in knowing of their future damnation, God implicitly also knows of his own future creating of them. Or yet again, God cannot even use simple foreknowledge to guide people concerning the choices they currently are making that will impact the future. For in seeing what will in fact happen to these persons in the future, there is nothing that the deity can recommend to them now to help them avoid those foreseen future events.[66] In sum, open theists maintain that simple foreknowledge renders no genuine aid to divine providential care.

Evaluating Open Theism

The open theist's model offers an intriguing alternative to traditional notions of God's nature and of the divine-world relationship. The paradigm is positive in a number of ways. First, like conventional Arminianism, open theism's endorsement of human responsibility and of libertarian freedom gels well with the Biblical affirmation of human accountability and dodges some of the more paralyzing difficulties faced by Calvinism. Specifically, it avoids the problems that Calvinistic determinism produces for

---

[66]John Sanders, *The God Who Risks*, pp. 202-205. See similar arguments in Hasker, *God, Time, and Knowledge*, pp. 59-63.

divine justice, authorship of sin and tolerance of evil. Because humans determine their own actions and, therefore, are responsible for their deeds, God is just in condemning them for their moral failures. Also, because the deity does not internally coerce humans to act, God is not the initiator of human sins. Further still, unlike Calvinism, open theism can claim that God allows evil for the sake of human libertarian freedom so that he and creatures might participate in loving, interpersonal relationships.

Open theism likewise avoids some of the proposed problems faced by traditional Arminianism. Because it denies divine atemporality, immutability and foreknowledge, this model eludes the complications associated with such claims. Specifically, open theism circumvents the difficulties that atemporality and immutability allegedly present for God's personhood and for divine-human dialogue. In turn, this model evades the dilemma that divine foreknowledge supposedly generates for human freedom. Because open theism denies divine foreknowledge of free events, no contradiction emerges between freedom and God's knowledge. (In later chapters, we will consider the warrant of some of these charges against traditional Arminianism). In spite of its advantages, open theism faces a number of challenges. We now turn to some of these.

Sovereignty, Works-Righteousness and Freedom

Because of their similarity, open theism confronts many of the complications that are met by Arminianism. In particular, open theism encounters the charges that it tacitly denies divine sovereignty, that it endorses works-righteousness, and that its view of libertarian freedom is nonsensical. We already have addressed these difficulties in our discussion of Arminianism and so little more needs to be said here. In passing we may note that two key issues still need clarification for open theism (and traditional Arminianism). These are (1) whether creatures can affect God (which influences both the notion of divine sovereignty and divine grace) and (2) whether the Bible teaches that God is the cause of all events (which especially pertains to divine sovereignty). As noted in our discussion of Arminianism, we will address these questions in chapters five and six.

Freedom and Interpersonal Relations

Much of the force behind open theism—and that which most clearly distinguishes it from traditional Arminianism—is its dual declarations (1) that foreknowledge is incompatible with freedom, and (2) that a timeless/static being cannot engage in interpersonal relations. Because of these beliefs, the open theist denies that God has foreknowledge and rejects the traditional view of God as timeless. However, if these claims can be undermined, then much of the rationale for endorsing open theism can be diffused, and the case for traditional Arminianism can be strengthened. We will consider these issues also in chapter six.

Divine Foreknowledge and the Bible

A major challenge to the open theist's position concerns its denial of divine foreknowledge. Such a disavowal can be criticized from a number of angles. First, some say that the denial of foreknowledge is a flat rejection of Bible-teaching.[67] Numerous scriptures appear to affirm divine knowledge of future events, including various prophetic passages. For example, Acts 2:23 says that Jesus was handed over to be crucified by "God's set purpose and foreknowledge . . . (NIV)." Romans 8:29 declares that "those God foreknew he also predestined . . . (NIV)." In Luke 22:34, Jesus predicts that Peter will deny him three times before the rooster crows, indicating knowledge of specific future events. In Matthew 1:22, 2:6, 2:18, 3:3, 4:14, various aspects of Jesus' birth and early life are perceived to be fulfillment of Old Testament prophecy. In short, the Bible seems to affirm divine foreknow-

---

[67]Edwards, p. 239. Also see Bruce Ware, *God's Lesser Glory: The Diminished God of Open Theism* (Wheaton, Illinois: Crossway Books, 2000), pp. 99-141.

ledge.

Open theists reply to such a claim by asserting that it is not abundantly clear that the Bible affirms an absolute and exhaustive divine foreknowledge. While some passages indicate a thorough and precise knowledge of diverse future events, others suggest a more general and vague divine awareness of the details of the future.[68] And there are a few occasions where the text implies that God does not know about a future event until it actualizes.[69] All of this insinuates that parts of the future may be known by God, but other portions are open and unknown or sketchy.[70] Of those divine predictions that are precise, open theists contend that God may be articulating his knowledge of future events that are presently causally necessary,[71] or that are highly probable, or that the deity simply intends to bring about regardless of future creaturely actions.[72] Concerning more vague predictions, these may be general goals that God intends to bring about, the specifics of which are not yet worked out.[73] Or they may be general states of affairs that God anticipates will unfold, the details about which he is not certain.

As we noted earlier in this chapter, open theists also point out that many biblical prophecies appear to be conditional; they are qualified by future human actions. Examples of such conditional prophecies are God's declaration that he will destroy the people of

---

[68]Sanders particularly makes this claim concerning Jesus' fulfillment of Old Testament prophecies about the Messiah. He writes: "Prophecies undergo multiple fulfillments and are not stated with a high degree of specificity . . . . There is nothing specifically said in the Old Testament that would have led one to predict a dying and raised Messiah." Sanders, *The God Who Risks*, pp. 133.

[69]After Abraham's trial wherein he is asked by God to sacrifice Isaac, the Lord declares that now he knows of Abraham's genuine faith. Genesis 22:12. See Sanders' comments, *The God Who Risks*, p. 52.

[70]Boyd, pp. 32-33.

[71]Rice, *God's Foreknowledge and Man's Free Will*, p. 77.

[72]Hasker, *God, Time, and Knowledge*, pp. 194-195.

[73]Sanders, *The God Who Risks*, pp. 50-51.

Nineveh (Jonah 3:4,10) and God's announcement that king Hezekiah soon will die (2 Kings 20: 1-6). In each case, a prophecy is made and rescinded based on a change in the attitudes/actions of those who previously had been condemned.[74] Indeed, Hasker notes that Jeremiah 18:7-10 may imply that all prophecies tacitly are conditional.[75] It reads:

> If at any time I declare concerning a nation or a kingdom, that I will pluck up and break down and destroy it, and if that nation, concerning which I have spoken, turns from its evil, I will repent of the evil that I intended to do to it. And if at any time I declare concerning a nation or a kingdom that I will build and plant it, and if it does evil in my sight, not listening to my voice, then I will repent of the good which I had intended to do to it (RSV).

Open theists admit that their view of divine knowledge makes it possible for God falsely to predict an event. But this is not a divine mistake, so long as one understands that in making such predictions God is not declaring that the event infallibly will occur, but only pronouncing that the happenstance likely will occur, and/or that God currently intends for it to transpire.[76] In sum, open theists maintain that the biblical case for exhaustive divine foreknowledge is not as strong as their opponents believe it to be.

Obviously, opponents of open theism are not without rejoinder in these matters. Bruce Ware contends that while some scriptural passages *suggest* divine ignorance of future events, others clearly imply a precise knowledge of the future. Examples include God's predicting of

> Israel's 400 years in Egypt; Judah's seventy-year captivity; the destruction of Jeroboam's altar (predicted 300 years in advance), specifically indicating Josiah by name as the king to

---

[74]Ibid., pp. 70-71.
[75]Hasker, *God, Time, and Knowledge*, p. 194.
[76]Sanders, *The God Who Risks*, pp. 134-135.

carry out this destruction (1 Kings 13:1-3); and Jesus' death by crucifixion, with the casting of lots for his clothing (Psalm 22:18), his bones not being broken (Psalm 34:20), and his being buried in the tomb of a rich man though he should have been with the two thieves (Isa. 53:9) . . . .[77]

Other examples consist of God naming Cyrus to be the king who would return the Jewish exiles to Judah from Persia—many years before it happened (Isaiah 44:24-28); Jesus' prediction that Peter would deny him three times (Luke 22:34);[78] prognostications concerning Christ's "birth in Bethlehem, the slaughter of the infant boys, the flight to Egypt . . ."[79] etc.

Indeed, some scriptural texts imply that God's knowledge of the future is exhaustive. For example, says Ware, certain verses in Isaiah assert that God's knowledge of and sovereignty over the future is that which distinguishes Yahweh from false gods. Isaiah 41:21-23 reads:

Set forth your case, says the Lord; bring your proofs, says the King of Jacob. Let them bring them, and tell us what is to happen. Tell us the former things, what they are, that we may consider them, that we may know their outcome; or declare to us the things to come. Tell us what is to come hereafter, that we may know that you are gods (RSV).

Ware notes that, in these verses, there is no hint of partial knowledge of the future; rather, exhaustive divine foreknowledge seems to be implied. Further, accurate prediction is used as a standard by which to demonstrate the Lord's deity and the lack of divinity of idols.[80] A similar criterion is evoked in Deuteronomy 18:20-22, which declares:

---

[77]Ware, p. 137.
[78]Ibid., p. 81.
[79]Ibid., p. 139.
[80]Ibid., p. 103.

"But the prophet who presumes to speak a word in my name which I have not commanded him to speak, or who speaks in the name of other gods, that same prophet shall die." And if you say in your heart, "How may we know the word which the Lord has not spoken?"— when a prophet speaks in the name of the Lord, if the word does not come to pass or come true, that is a word which the Lord has not spoken . . . (RSV).

In sum, diverse scriptural passages seem to affirm precise, perhaps even exhaustive, divine foreknowledge, and a few evoke foreknowledge as a test for determining the divine authority of prophetic utterances.

Concerning Biblical passages that seem to imply divine ignorance of the future (such as Genesis 22:12), Ware contends that a straightforward reading of such texts is not the best hermeneutic. This is analogous to passages that imply that God has a body or that God is ignorant of past or present facts. For example, Genesis 3:8 speaks of God "walking" in the Garden of Eden, as if the deity had legs; and Genesis 3:9 depicts God calling out, asking Adam "Where are you?," as if the Lord did not know where Adam presently was. In each case, argues Ware, the open theist would reject the straightforward interpretations of these texts, precisely because other scriptures (not to mention the open theist's theological system) clearly indicate that God has no body and that the deity's knowledge of present events is perfect. In like manner, Ware contends that we have reason to reject the surface meaning of passages that seem to imply divine ignorance of the future, in light of the fuller testimony of scripture.[81]

Not surprisingly, open theists are not convinced by argumentation such as Ware's. First, they are not persuaded that the scriptural testimony for exhaustive foreknowledge is unassailable. Much of their recent writing has been an attempt to make this case.[82] Further, open theists believe that numerous theological

---

[81]Ibid., pp. 74-76.
[82]See Sanders, *The God Who Risks*, and Boyd.

considerations work against the case for exhaustive divine foreknowledge and, subsequently, this gives reason for questioning the straightforward meaning of those texts that seem to endorse comprehensive divine foreknowledge.

We seem, then, to come to an impasse. Evoking essentially the same hermeneutical principle, open theists and writers like Ware come to opposing conclusions–one side insisting that passages that seem to teach exhaustive foreknowledge must be reinterpreted, the other side contending that texts that imply divine ignorance of future events must be reevaluated. Who is right? Flipping a coin probably will not help. There likely is an element of truth in each position. It may be that differing portions of scripture endorse/assume somewhat different models of the divine attributes and of divine interaction with creatures, so that a precise systematization of these diverse models may not be possible–at least not without seriously straining important rules of interpretation. Living with such ambiguities may be one of the trials of faith that the believer must endure. In turn, proof-texting likely will not solve the impasse.

It does seem to me that at least some scriptural passages assume a thorough divine knowledge of the future, but this need not require that all scriptures assume this, or that there are no scriptures that implicitly perceive the divine knowledge in a different fashion. In the end, hermeneutical spade-work may well not solve the dilemma. Rather, appeal to broad theological and even philosophical considerations may be the only means through the deadlock, particularly if one hopes to build a coherent model of divine providence. For example, if it can be shown that divine foreknowledge truly truncates human freedom and responsibility, and that this goes against central scriptural teaching, then considerable force is given to the open theist's case against such foreknowledge–especially if it can be shown that the scriptural testimony concerning foreknowledge is ambiguous or diverse. On the other hand, if the claim that foreknowledge is compatible with human freedom and responsibility can be substantiated, then the case for divine foreknowledge can be strengthened, especially in light of the fact that at least some scriptural passages prima facie endorse such knowledge. In chapter six, we will consider the case for the compatibility of foreknowledge and free will. In the meantime, let us close this section by concluding that the Bible's teaching on divine foreknowledge is not abundantly precise. Many passages seem to support thorough divine foreknowledge; others are less clear. Subsequently, through exegesis alone, an iron-clad case cannot be made either for or against the traditional doctrine of divine foreknowledge. Scripture writers may not have had a clear or precise conceptualization of foreknowledge when they wrote, and this ambiguity seems to have carried over into their writings.

Divine Foreknowledge and Providential Control

Another attack on open theism's denial of foreknowledge is that such a view disallows a comprehensive divine providential control. As we saw in chapter three, Cottrell champions divine foreknowledge because he feels that it allows God to construct a meticulous plan for the future and to exercise exhaustive providential control over future creaturely events. According to Cottrell, divine foreknowledge enables God to choose ahead of time which future events he will permit and not permit. Further, foreknowledge empowers the deity to anticipate his own responses to all future events. Therefore, foreknowledge allows God to construct a thorough plan for the future and permissively to control all future events.[83]

Open theists offer a two-fold response to these assertions. First, they admit that their own position prohibits a meticulous divine plan for the future. However, they insist that this is acceptable. For them, God does not fully anticipate or plan every future event, nor does he decide ahead of time which specific

---

[83]Jack Cottrell, *What the Bible Says About God the Ruler* (Joplin, Missouri: College Press Publishing Company, 1984), pp. 214-217.

events he is going to permit. Rather, the deity's plan is general, not exhaustive. This is not to say that God is not in control. As the present unfolds, the deity exercises complete control over what he will and will not permit, or what he will or will not cause. God simply does not decide *in advance* how every event is to develop. Nevertheless, claim open theists, God is wise and secure enough to ensure that eventually his *ultimate goals* will be met, even though many occurrences are not a part of and even run contrary to his overarching aims.[84] In short, open theists endorse general providence, not meticulous providence.

Second, open theists maintain that, contrary to claims like Cottrell's, simple foreknowledge *does not* enable God in advance to exercise complete control over future creaturely events. By the time God knows that a given event will occur, it is outside of the scope of the divine power to allow or disallow that event. It simply will happen as God "foresees" it. Subsequently, contrary to Cottrell's claim, divine simple foreknowledge does not enable God to choose which future events he will permit or not permit. We will consider these issues more fully in chapters six and seven. For now, we may comment that the open theist perspective does seem to negate the possibility of an exhaustive divine plan for the future; but this is a point that open theists readily concede. Further, it remains to be seen whether the Arminian appeal to simple divine foreknowledge fares any better.

Divine Risk and Trustworthiness

A final, perhaps most disturbing, problem remains for the open theist's view of divine knowledge. In spite of their claims to the contrary, one may question whether the God of open theism can know of (1) future physical necessities, (2) future physical probabilities, or even (3) future occurrences that are required by the divine nature. In turn, such limitations imply far greater risk than typically is admitted by open theists and, ultimately, challenge

---

[84]Sanders, *The God Who Risks*, pp. 215-217. Boyd, pp. 153-156.

the very trustworthiness of God. The extended case for these charges is beyond the scope of this book.[85] However, the basic argument proceeds as follows.

If we keep in mind the open theist's (especially Swinburne's) assertion that God cannot know of his own future free acts, then it seems to follow that the deity cannot know of any currently physically necessitated future events. This is the case because the entire physical universe depends on God for its continued existence, including the physical patterns that make some future events currently physically necessary. Presuming that in the future God will be free *to cease sustaining* part of or all of the physical processes of the universe, then it follows that no future physical event truly is currently physically *necessary*. Since (per the open theists) God does not know what he freely will do in the future—that is, since the deity does not know what processes he freely will sustain in the future—God cannot know what future events will be physically necessary.

In turn, because knowledge of probabilities is based on the assumption that the physical patterns of the universe will continue to behave in the future as they have in the past, and since such patterns depend upon God's ongoing and free sustaining of those regularities and, further, since God does not know with certainty what he freely will do in the future, then the deity (of open theism) cannot know the probability of any given future event. In other words, all probabilities are subject to the future free acts of God sustaining the universe, and because God does not know with certainty these divine events, he cannot know physical probabilities.

At this point, open theists might protest that in their system while God may not know with certainty what events he freely will choose to perform in the future, the deity at least can know that if he should continue to want to perform any given divine act in the future, he will be able to do so. In turn, this implies that God can

---

[85]For a more comprehensive version of this argument see Robinson, 251-275.

know that if he should want to continue sustaining the natural physical patterns of the universe—those patterns that make some future events physically necessary and others probable—the deity will be able to do so. God can do this because he is and always will be sovereign. Whatever he will continue to want to do, he will be able to do so. This is the point that Hasker seems to be making when he asserts that "[w]hatever God needs to do, he has the power to do; whatever he sees is best to do happens forthwith."[86]

Such a rejoinder to my argument faces two significant difficulties. First, even if correct, this response offers to God little concrete information concerning actual future (necessary or probable) events. Essentially all it tells us is that God knows the truth of the following hypothetical statement: if God sustains the regularities of nature, then certain events will be necessary and others will be (more or less) probable. But what this hypothetical claim does not tell us is whether or not God will maintain the uniformities of nature and subsequently whether certain events in fact will be necessary and others probable. Because God, according to open theism, does not know whether he will maintain such uniformities, then the deity cannot know what future events are necessary or probable.

The second difficulty with this (potential) open theist response is that it is not abundantly clear that the God of open theism can know of his own future sovereignty! If he cannot, such a deity could not even know the truth of the conditional claim that if he should continue to want to perform some action in the future, he will be able to do so. But why should anyone think that the God of open theism cannot know of his own future sovereignty?

To answer this question we may begin by considering *how* God might know of his own future sovereignty. At first, this seems like a silly concern. The open theist simply may assert that God essentially, necessarily is such a being. That is, sovereignty is an essential quality of divinity; it is a necessary attribute of God. Swinburne and Rice each claims that God is a necessary being, *that*

---

[86]Hasker, *God, Time, and Knowledge*, p. 192.

the deity necessarily exists and necessarily has the attributes that he has. And so, since God necessarily exists, he always will exist, and since he necessarily has the attributes that he has, he always will have those attributes, including sovereignty.

But a question now emerges: How might God know that he is a *necessary being*, that he always will exist and always will have the qualities that he has? The answer is not immediately apparent for open theism. It does not seem that the God of open theism *experientially* could know this. If God were timeless, he experientially could know that he always exists and always has the attributes that he has. That is, if there were only a single eternal moment and the deity existed and had certain attributes in that moment, and if God were aware of his existence and attributes in that moment, then God could know that he "always" exists and "always" has those attributes—including sovereignty. Or again, if God were temporal and had foreknowledge, he could foreknow his endless future existence and unchanging future nature and, subsequently, could know that he always will exist and always will have the nature that he has. But open theists deny both that God is atemporal and that God has experiential foreknowledge. Consequently, it seems that such a deity could not know of his own necessary nature and existence in these ways.

Further, there seems to be no way for a temporal God *without* foreknowledge experientially to know that he always will exist or always will have the attributes he now has. Such information could not be induced from past and present experience. One cannot verify a universal statement based on inductive reasoning, based on temporally limited experience. Even if the deity always has existed and always has had the attributes he currently possesses, it does not confirm that in the future God will continue existing or will continue having these attributes. In sum, there is no clear way for the God of open theism experientially to know that he will always exist or always will have the attributes he now has.

But perhaps God could know this in another, non-experiential, way. Perhaps he could know of his necessary existence through analytical reasoning, through deduction. Maybe God is an analytically necessary being and, subsequently, through analyzing the concept "God," the deity could know of his own endless existence and nature.[87] By an analytically necessary being I mean one whose nonexistence is analytically impossible and for whom it is analytically incoherent to suppose that being not having the properties it has. An analogy may be helpful. It is logically incoherent to suppose that a triangle fail to have three angles. By definition a triangle has three angles. In like manner, one could claim that it is logically impossible for God to fail to exist or fail to have the attributes that he has. By definition God has such characteristics and, thus, must exist. Since presumably God knows all logical necessities, then he could know of his own analytically necessary existence and nature and, consequently, could know that he always will exist with the attributes he now has.

But is God an analytically necessary being? Interestingly enough, many theists say no, including open theist Richard Swinburne. He writes:

> . . . a world without a particular substance or a particular kind of substance seems always to be a coherent supposition and to involve no contradiction; no set of propositions which describe such a world seem to entail a self-contradiction. The supposition of the existence of a Godless universe (either one without any divine being or one without the particular one that I suppose this is) seems evidently coherent, and so should be taken to be so in the absence of positive counter-argument. All ontological arguments known to me that purport to show the logical necessity of God's existence seem to me unsound.[88]

According to Swinburne, God is not analytically necessary but ontologically necessary. That is, God's existence and nature are

---

[87]This is the central claim of Anselm's ontological argument—namely, that in knowing the concept of "God" alone, one also understands that God must exist (with certain perfections).

[88]Swinburne, *The Christian God*, pp. 144-145.

simply ultimate brute facts of reality. God exists with the nature that he has with no cause, indeed with no explanation. God simply everlastingly is. If Swinburne is correct, however, if no being—including God—is analytically necessary, then the deity cannot learn of his necessary future existence and nature through deductive/analytical reasoning. It always is logically possible for any being not to be or not to have certain attributes.[89] And so again, the way is blocked for the God of open theism to know of his own necessary existence and necessary attributes, including the attribute of sovereignty.[90]

Troublesome ramifications for open theism flow from these conclusions. First, God could not know of his own future sovereignty and, so, the deity could not know that if he should want to perform some task in the future, he will be able to do so. He could not know that in the near or distant future he will be able to destroy the universe, work a miracle, or eradicate creaturely freedom. God could not know that good will win, that he will save the world, that evil will not overrun the created order. Second, even more radically, God could not know of other key future divine attributes; particularly he could not know of his own future goodness, faithfulness, and mercy. He could not know that he will not become evil one day! Third, and perhaps most disturbing of all, the deity could not know of his own future existence! He could not certainly know that he will be around in the future to heal the sick, raise the dead, save the world. This is troublesome indeed!

Numerous writers have voiced concern over the implications for divine sovereignty of denying foreknowledge to God. But few, if any, have explicated the difficulties to the degree suggested here.

---

[89]The issues are a bit more complex than this, but the preceding argument is sufficient to make the point. For more details see Robinson, especially 264-268.

[90]One could claim that God simply innately knows of his own future existence and nature. But such a claim is not particularly explanatory. (One could equally say that God uses a magical crystal ball to know such things. But this would satisfy few).

For example, Jonathan Edwards complains that if God does not know the future choices of morally free creatures, then the deity cannot know the future chains of events that will flow from those choices–series of events that may well string out into virtual infinity. In turn, claims Edwards, such a scenario implies that immediately after the creation of humans, God would have been ignorant of whether or not his creatures were going to fall into sin, whether the cross of Christ were going to be necessary, whether any humans would eventually exercise faith in Christ and thus be saved, etc.[91] Edwards' charges appear to be genuine impediments faced by open theism (and, as we will see, by traditional Arminianism). Nevertheless, these concerns do not quite plumb the depth of the problem as I see it. In fact, open theists often grant Edwards' reasoning to this point, agreeing that prior to the first human sin, God did not know that humans would fall into sin, that the cross would be necessary, or that any would turn in faith to Christ. John Sanders has gone so far as to claim that the deity likely was surprised by the fall of humans because such an event was improbable in light of all that God had done for them.[92] Still, as problematic as these concessions may be for some, I think the difficulties go deeper. For neither Edwards nor open theists have discussed this dilemma in terms of divine ignorance about God's own being. Each agrees that divine ignorance of future human choices diminishes God's knowledge of *how* he will control future creaturely events, but neither suggests that ignorance of the future threatens God's knowledge of his own future sovereignty, character, or existence. Each assumes that God will be and can know that he will be sovereign and good in the future. But if the reasoning offered above is sound, such an assumption is unwarranted. Again, this is quite troublesome!

Indeed, let us try to imagine what all of this could mean for the divine mental life. Since God could not know of his own future existence, the possibility of the dread of non-existence awakens

---

[91]Edwards, pp. 240, 255.
[92]Sanders, *The God Who Risks*, pp. 46-49.

within the divine mind. Since God could not know of his future moral perfection, room for fear of moral failure surfaces. Since God could not know of his future omnipotence, the potential for disquiet over failed plans and broken promises dawns. In sum, many of the deepest human anxieties potentially well-up within the divine psyche. Notice that I am not saying that God will fail, or that such fears will come to pass, or even that God is not a necessary being—one whose existence and nature are not necessary. All I am claiming is that the God of open theism could not know any of this. God could not know that he forever will exist with those good and great attributes he now has. In turn, if God could not know this, neither could we. Such a state of affairs is theologically problematic.

As we have seen, open theists acknowledge that their model of God involves divine risk-taking, but they quickly assert that the risk is minimal. Allegedly, God remains utterly in control of the future. At any moment, God can abolish the universe, ending any threat of creatures foiling the divine plan. At any moment, God can work a miracle, breaking into creaturely history and forcing his will upon natural processes. At any moment, God can curtail creaturely freedom, forcing creatures to perform as he deems appropriate. But if my reasoning is sound, open theists grossly have under-estimated the risk. For God cannot *know* of his future sovereignty (or of any other future divine attributes). For many this is not an acceptable view of God. It involves the deity in far too great of risk-taking.

Preliminary Conclusion

Open theism is a fascinating alternative to traditional theism. It avoids many of the problems discernable in both Calvinism and Arminianism. Nevertheless, it suffers from some of the problems encountered by Arminianism and picks up additional difficulties along the way. Specifically, with traditional Arminianism, open theism confronts the following concerns: (1) Can God in any way depend on creatures?, (2) Does the Bible teach that God is the direct cause of all things?, and (3) Does the Bible allow for belief in prevenient grace?   Questions (1) and (2) emerge from Calvinistic concerns over divine sovereignty. Questions (1) and (3) derive from issues arising from the notion of divine grace. Open theism also faces challenges not encountered by traditional Arminianism. These include the charges (4) that its rejection of complete divine foreknowledge is contrary to scripture teachings and (5) that its view of deity tacitly abnegates God's capacity to know of his own future existence, sovereignty and trustworthiness.

I will presume that the case made in this chapter shows that the open theistic system truncates the divine ability to know of his own future existence and nature, and that this is theologically unacceptable. Further, I will assume that while the open theist makes an impressive case for an augmented view of divine foreknowledge, the traditional notion of such knowledge also has much to commend it, and ought not to be abandoned unless clearly shown to be scripturally or logically unsound. Indeed, I maintain that at very least affirmation of divine foreknowledge avoids denying to God knowledge of his own future existence and nature and this, in itself, offers considerable practical advantages over open theism. I will address some of these practical benefits in chapter seven.

In chapter five, we will consider the Biblical case for and against our three models of divine providence. We especially will focus on whether the Bible teaches complete divine causal influence on the world and on whether the scriptures allow for prevenient grace. In chapter six, among other issues, we will address whether theism requires that God not be influenced by the created order. We now turn to these quandaries.

Chapter 5

Navigating the Storm I:
Steering Toward the
Biblical Lighthouse

As we have seen, each of our models of the divine-world relationship faces challenges. Because it endorses theological determinism, Calvinism cannot easily explain why God tolerates evil, nor how the deity justly condemns humans, nor why God is not culpable for sin. Indeed, in chapter two, I expressed my conviction that Calvinism does not and cannot deal adequately with these problems. Arminianism, on the other hand, faces the largely Calvinistic allegations that it negates divine sovereignty and endorses works-righteousness. Closely related to these concerns is the question of whether a genuinely sovereign and gracious God can be affected by creatures. Further, Arminianism must address whether freedom and divine foreknowledge are compatible and whether foreknowledge benefits divine providence–two challenges advanced mostly by open Theists. *Both* Calvinism and Arminianism encounter the further conundrums associated with the static model of God. How can a changeless being be personal or engage in interpersonal relations and how can the events of all time be simultaneous with one another? Open theism, in turn, braves some of the obstacles confronting traditional Arminianism—the charges that it denies God's sovereignty and denies salvation by grace alone. Beyond these, open theism faces challenges unique to itself. It finds it difficult to explain how the deity might know of his own necessary existence, sovereignty, and nature. Finally, each of these theological systems confronts scriptural anomalies, Biblical passages that do not gel well with its peculiar theological outlook. In broad terms, Calvinism must address whether its views on theological determinism conform to the Bible's affirmation of human responsibility. Arminianism needs to consider whether the Bible teaches divine pancausality and whether a scriptural case can be made for prevenient grace.

Some of these challenges are stronger than others. In the next three chapters, we will assess the warrant of these various problems and, in turn, will attempt to construct a logically coherent and theologically satisfying model of divine providence. In evaluating these theological paradigms, we will employ the three criteria mentioned in chapter one—namely, faithfulness to the Bible, logical coherence, and compatibility with life-experience. We will focus on the first of these standards in this chapter, on the second criterion in chapter six, and on the last principle in chapter seven. My overarching thesis is that a modified version of traditional Arminianism provides theologically and philosophically the most satisfying paradigm for the divine-world relationship.

We begin our assessment by looking at the Biblical materials. Two critical hermeneutical issues have arisen from our study: (1) What does the Bible teach about God's causal influence on the world?, and (2) Does the Bible allow for prevenient grace? Let us first examine the Biblical teaching concerning divine causality.

Divine Causality

Each of our theological models has some scriptural support. Because Arminianism and open theism share much in common, we begin with verses that mutually support these systems.

Arminian/Open Theistic Passages

Central to Arminianism and open theism are the claims that humans freely perform sinful acts, that God holds persons responsible for such deeds, and that God does not cause nor want humans to sin. At first glance, a number of scriptures confirm this position. Genesis 3:6ff informs us that when Eve saw that the fruit of the forbidden tree was good, pleasing and desirable, *she took* some and ate it; and her husband did likewise. There is no indication in the text that God willed that they do this or caused them so to act. Indeed, quite to the contrary, we are told that God explicitly commanded them not to do this (Gen. 2:16-17), and that upon their performing the deed the deity held them responsible, exacting punishment on them (Gen. 3:14-19). This pattern reverberates throughout the Old and New Testaments: (1) Humans perform an act that (2) God has commanded or desires that they not do; (3) God holds them responsible for the action and (4) there is not the slightest hint that the deity (secretly) willed or caused them to perform the action. Consider the following passages: Genesis 4:4-16, 6:5-13; 18:20-21, 19:1-26; Exodus 1:8-14, 3:7-10, 16:1-30, 17:1-3, 32:1-8; Leviticus 10:1-2; Numbers 14:1-45; Joshua 7:1-26; Judges 2:11-19; 2 Samuel 12:7-10; Isaiah 1:1-31, 2:6-4:1; Jeremiah 2:1-3:5, 4:5-31, 5:1-13; Ezekiel 3:17-21, 16:1-63; Hosea 4:1-19; Amos 5:1-27; Matthew 7:15-29, 23: 1-39, 25:31-46; Luke 12:13-21; Acts 5:1-11, 8:9-25; 1 Corinthians 5:1-13. These texts in no way exhaust the list. Indeed, it is safe to assert that this is the predominant pattern of scripture. Normally, where human sin is discussed, divine condemnation is explicitly or implicitly affirmed, and there is no mention of God's secretly willing that the perpetrators sin.

Similar to these verses are those that indicate that God does not want humans to sin. Throughout the Bible, God commands that humans not perform certain actions and issues warnings to those that do. This phenomena is so common that a list of such passages need not be generated. And yet, the Calvinist system seems to imply that God is insincere in his demand that people not sin, for in fact God wills that some persons (indeed many persons) sin. God decrees and determines that they do sin. As William Hasker points out, such a perspective produces a logically incoherent view of God's relationship with evil. It intimates that God desires that which he hates![1] In light of this tension, the Arminian and open theist interpretation of such passages seems much more natural and leads to no such contradiction. When God commands persons not to perform some action, the deity truly does not want them to do it. Certainly, God may permissively allow them to perform such deeds, but this is not because God secretly wants such actions per se to occur but because he wants creatures to be free to choose or to reject him.

Another important element of the Arminian and open models which finds support in scripture is the affirmation that God is unwilling that sinners should perish and wants all to be saved. 1 Timothy 2:4 declares that God "wants all men to be saved and to come to a knowledge of the truth (NIV)." 2 Peter 3:9 states: "The Lord is not slow in keeping his promise as some understand slowness. He is patient with you, not wanting anyone to perish, but everyone to come to repentance (NIV)." Ezekiel 33:11 says: "Say to them, 'As surely as I live, declares the Sovereign Lord, I take no pleasure in the death of the wicked, but rather that they turn from their ways and live . . . (NIV) .'" In Matthew 23:37, Jesus declares that he has longed to gather the children of Jerusalem together "as a hen gathers her chicks under her wings (NIV)," but the *people* were not willing. The first three passages insinuate that God does not desire to destroy any of the wicked but wants all to turn in repentance. The last passage indicates, at least in the case of the people of Jerusalem, that it was the unwillingness of the people and not the will of Jesus that kept them from being comforted and cared for by Christ. The Calvinistic interpretation of these passages often is strained, at best. For example, Augustine interprets 1 Timothy 2:4 to mean that God desires men from every

---

[1]William Hasker, "A Philosophical Perspective," *The Openness of God: A Biblical Challenge to the Traditional Understanding of God* (Downers Grove: InterVarsity Press, 1994), p. 143.

tribe/nationality to be saved, not that God wants all humans saved.[2] Or another example: Luther insists that Ezekiel 33:11 is stated from the perspective of "God preached" and not from the perspective of "God hidden." In other words, while the God revealed in the gospel is portrayed as offering salvation to all so that the elect will be encouraged to come, in fact God hidden does not desire that all sinners avoid destruction.[3] For many interpreters, myself included, these expositions are examples of theologians allowing their theological systems to overcome the rather clear meaning of the scriptural texts.

In addition to these passages, there are a number of Biblical verses that seem to endorse the Arminian/open theistic affirmation of the universal atonement of Christ's death. 1 Timothy 2:5-6 speaks of "the man Christ Jesus, who gave himself a ransom for all men . . . (NIV) ." John 3:16-17 declare that God so loved the *world* (not some or part of the world) that he gave his Son, "for God did not send his Son into the world to condemn the world, but to save the world through him (NIV)." Hebrews 2:9 states: "But we see Jesus . . . now crowned with glory and honor because he suffered death, so that by the grace of God he might taste death for everyone (NIV)." In Isaiah 53:6, which speaks of the suffering servant of the Lord and which traditionally was interpreted by the early Church to refer to the Christ, the author says: "All we like sheep have gone astray; we have turned every one to his own way; and the Lord has laid on him the iniquity of us all (RSV)." Certainly, at first glace, these verses endorse a universal atonement of Christ's death. That is, they suggest that Christ's death in principle has atoned for all human sin—even though the Arminian

---

[2]Augustine, *Enchiridion*, trans. J. F. Shaw, *On the Holy Trinity, Doctrinal Treatises, Moral Treatises*, Nicene and Post-Nicene Fathers, vol. 3, ed. Philip Schaff (Peabody, Massachusetts: Hendrickson Publishing, Inc., 1995), 27.

[3]Martin Luther, *The Bondage of the Will*, trans. J. I. Packer and O. R. Johnston (Grand Rapids, Michigan: Revell, Baker Bookhouse Co., 1957), pp. 169-171.

would wish to deny the universal reception of these benefits by all humans.

Of course, none of these passages *demonstrates* the truth of the Arminian and open theism interpretations. Each is subject to a different interpretation from a Calvinistic (or other) perspective. However, one must admit that initially these (and other) passages seem to support Arminianism and open theism. Specifically, they seem to affirm the idea that God does not directly cause all that happens and that some things occur that God does not directly will. Further, they seem to maintain that human free will plays an important role in the human-divine interface and in saving faith. Let us turn to verses that appear to affirm the Calvinistic model of divine causality.

Calvinistic Passages

A key claim of Calvinism is that God's plan for and rule over the universe is exhaustive, meticulous and utterly efficacious. God's will pertains to all events and whatever God wills certainly happens. Subsequently, all that happens is by divine design and decree. A number of Biblical passages, when combined, seem to point toward such a conclusion. First we note texts that attribute various natural events to the workings and rule of God. Psalm 135:5-7 states:

> For I know that the Lord is great, and that our Lord is above all gods. Whatever the Lord pleases he does, in heaven and on earth, in the seas and all deeps. He it is who makes the clouds rise at the end of the earth, who makes lightnings for the rain and brings forth the wind from his storehouses (RSV).

Matthew 5:45 notes: "Your Father who is in heaven . . . makes his sun rise on the evil and on the good, and sends rain on the just and the unjust (RSV)." Psalm 104:21-29 and I Kings 17:4 announce that various animals carry out God's will. And Matthew 10:29 declares that no sparrow falls to the ground without the Father's will. Even seemingly chance events appear to be under divine control; and so, Proverbs 16:33 insists that "the lot is cast into the lap, but the decision is wholly from the Lord (RSV)."

Perhaps more profoundly, multiple passages accredit various human events to the work and will of God. Isaiah 37:26 speaks of how God planned the actions and victories of the king and nation of Assyria; Psalm 139:16 suggests that God has a day by day plan for the lives of individuals; 1 Samuel 2:6-7 says that "the Lord makes poor and makes rich; he brings low and also exalts (RSV);" Acts 2:33 indicates that Jesus was delivered into the hands of the wicked to be crucified according to God's plan. Several scriptures profess that God directs the very wills and choices of humans. Proverbs 21:1 declares that "the king's heart is in the hand of the Lord; he directs it like a watercourse wherever he pleases (NIV)." Jeremiah 10:23 says: "I know, O Lord, that a man's ways is not in himself, nor is it in a man who walks to direct his steps (RSV)." This suggests that human actions are not in fact their own, but are secretly directed by God. Specific instances where God directs the wills, decisions, and attitudes of persons include the following. 1 Chronicles 5:25-26 informs us that because the heads of the tribe of Manasseh were unfaithful to God, the Lord "stirred up the spirit of Pul king of Assyria . . . (NIV)" and that king took Manasseh and other tribes into exile. 2 Chronicles 21:16 states that "the Lord aroused against Jehoram the hostility of the Philistines and of the Arabs who lived near the Cushites. They attacked Judah, invaded it and carried off all the goods found in the king's palace . . .(NIV) ." Isaiah 13:17 declares God's intention to "stir up" the Medes against the Babylonians as punishment for the latter's wickedness. In Deuteronomy 2:25 God promises the Hebrews: "This very day I will begin to put the terror and fear of you on all the nations under heaven (NIV)."

Even evil human actions—choices that God condemns—are sometimes attributed to divine action. Deuteronomy 2:30 explains that the reason king Sihon refused to let the people of Israel pass through his kingdom is because "the Lord . . . had made his spirit stubborn and his heart obstinate in order to give him into your hands as he has now done (NIV)." Isaiah 63:17 apparently assumes that God plays some role in persons turning *from* him, for it asks: "Why, O Lord, do you make us wander from your ways and harden our hearts so we do not revere you (NIV)?" Concerning the Egyptians, Psalm 105:25 insists that the Lord turned their hearts "to hate his people, to conspire against his servants (NIV)." As punishment against David for his sin with Bathsheba, the Lord announces in 2 Samuel 12:11 that "out of your own household I am going to bring calamity upon you. Before your very eyes I will take your wives and give them to one who is close to you, and he will lie with your wives in broad daylight (NIV)." This proclamation is fulfilled in 2 Samuel 16:21-22, when David's son Absalom does precisely what God said would happen. In these passages, God seems to be credited with causing Absalom to commit adultery! In Jeremiah 19:9, the Lord declares concerning the people of Jerusalem: "I will make them eat the flesh of their sons and daughters, and they will eat one another's flesh during the stress of the siege imposed on them by the enemies who seek their lives (NIV)." Here the horrific act of cannibalism enacted by a people under siege is attributed to the divine directive will.

In turn, a number of Biblical passages support the idea that God sometimes prevents people from turning to him. As noted above, Deuteronomy 2:30 claims that God made king Sihon's heart stubborn so that the people of Israel might rise up against the king's nation. 2 Thessalonians 2:11 predicts a time when God will send a "powerful delusion" so that certain people in the end times will believe the Satanic lie. In Romans, the apostle Paul claims that God "hardens whom he wants to harden (9:18, NIV), and that "Israel has experienced a hardening in part until the full number of the Gentiles has come in (11:25, NIV)." Of course, the classic text for divine hardening is that of God's hardening of Pharaoh's heart in Exodus. In Exodus 4:21, the Lord announces to Moses his intention to harden Pharaoh's heart "so that he will not let the people go (NIV)," so that, in turn, God will be able to bring the people of Israel out of bondage with a mighty hand. Several times throughout the narrative the reader is informed that God hardened Pharaoh's heart, to the effect that the earthly king would not let the Hebrews go and God worked yet another mighty plague upon the

Egyptians (Exodus 10:20, 27; 11:10; 14:8).

In addition to passages that seem to teach that God sometimes prevents persons from turning to him or doing what is right, there are those that seem to say that only persons whom the deity chooses and draws to himself can be saved. In John 6:44 Jesus proclaims: "No one can come to me unless the Father who sent me draws him . . . (NIV, compare with John 6:65)." In a similar vein, Acts 13:48 declares of certain Gentile believers that "all who were appointed for eternal life believed (NIV)." Ephesians 1:4-5 speaks of how in Christ, God chose us "before the creation of the world to be holy and blameless in his sight. In love, he predestined us to be adopted as his sons through Jesus Christ, in accordance with his pleasure and will . . . (NIV)." In John 15:16, Jesus informs his disciples: "you did not choose me, but I chose you and appointed you to go and bear fruit—fruit that will last (NIV)." And in John 6:37, Jesus intimates that all whom the Father chooses turn to him and find salvation. Jesus states: "All that the Father gives me will come to me, and whoever comes to me I will never drive away (NIV)."

Finally, there are some verses that seem to declare that God's plan and rule concerns all that happens in the universe. Isaiah 46:9-10 proclaims: "I am God, and there is no other; I am God, and there is none like me. I make known the end from the beginning, from ancient times, what is still to come. I say: My purpose will stand and I will do all that I please (NIV)." Ephesians 1:11 indicates that God "works out everything in conformity with the purpose of his will . . . (NIV)." Further, some verses insinuate that God's plans cannot be impeded. In Isaiah 14:24, 27, the Lord is reported as saying: "As I have planned, so shall it be, and as I have purposed, so shall it stand . . . . For the Lord of hosts has purposed, and who will annul it (RSV)?" The obvious answer is that no one can oppose God's designs.

When all of these verses are combined, an impressive case can be made for the Calvinist belief that God's plan and rule not only concerns everything that happens in the created order but also that God determines all that happens. However, as was the case with

Biblical passages that support Arminianism and open theism, the texts promoting Calvinism are not indisputable.

Strategies for Evaluating the Biblical Data

Verses can be cited both in support of Calvinism and in support of Arminianism/open theism. What are we to make of the diversity found in the Biblical record? Can this tension be resolved? Two key strategies are available. The first option is to subsume one set of scriptures under the other. This occurs in one of two ways: (1) either by submitting Arminian/open theistic verses to Calvinistic interpretation or (2) by surrendering Calvinistic texts to Arminian/open theist interpretations. The assumption behind each of these solutions is that a broad logical harmony exists (indeed, must exist) in the teachings of the scriptural corpus. An example of the first of these approaches is when Calvinists deny libertarian freedom to humans, thus, resolving the contradiction between claiming that humans make choices and that God completely determines their choices. The reverse of this strategy is when Arminians, for example, insist that God's hardening of Pharaoh's heart in fact refers to a divine attempt to win over Pharaoh's heart to God's purposes, an attempt that only was met by a growing and deliberate stubbornness on the part of the Egyptian king.

There are advantages to subsuming one set of passages under another. First, it assumes the overall logical consistency of scripture. Second, in some cases, it may allow for a better exegesis of a text. Sometimes traditional Calvinistic and/or Arminian interpretations of their "favorite" verses involve ignoring important features of the passages in question. And so, approaching a passage from a different frame of reference brings out nuances otherwise overlooked. The disadvantage of this approach is that it can result in eisegesis, in forcing the text to say things not intended by its author/s.

A second broad strategy for dealing with the tension found in scripture simply is to embrace it, to admit that in some sense there is disharmony among various passages. The benefit of such a tactic is that at times it may be more honest with the texts; it may reflect accurately the way things are. The disadvantages will become apparent in a moment. There are three different ways this second strategy might be expressed. First, one may claim that there are irreconcilable logical contradictions in the Bible and that it simply is not rational to affirm many of its conflicting teachings. When stated so bluntly, such a position is hardly acceptable to most theologians. Hopefully, there is a gentler and more positive strategy for dealing with scriptural disagreements.

A second option is to appeal to mystery. In this case, one concedes that key scriptural teachings are not rationally reconcilable (at least not readily so), but one insists that somehow each set of doctrine is true anyway. Accordingly, while an individual cannot fully understand how each set of teachings can be true, that person nevertheless submits to the authority of the text.[4] There is some warrant to the appeal to mystery. Certainly (perhaps many) aspects of the Christian faith ultimately are beyond human comprehension—the Trinity and Incarnation to name two. At key places, the believer simply may need to exercise faith in the face of the human inability to comprehend. Still the appeal to mystery must be a card cautiously and infrequently played. This is the case for several reasons: (1) it truncates rational dialogue concerning Christianity both inside and outside of the Church; (2) it opens the door for contradictory views throughout the Christian system of beliefs; anytime something does not make sense, one might be tempted to call it a mystery; (3) it can become an excuse for lazy scholarship and/or closed-mindedness. While appeal to mystery may be appropriate at times, wisdom calls for its sporadic use only.

A third option for those who admit a genuine logical tension in the scriptures is to invoke some notion of progressive revelation. Here one recognizes development in the scriptural testimony concerning God and development in the interpretation of that

---

[4]This appears to be the perspective of C. G. Berkouwer, *Studies in Dogmatics: The Providence of God* (Grand Rapids: Wm. B. Eerdmans Publishing Company, 1952), pp. 125-160.

material. These progressions can be accounted for both in terms of the divine revelation per se and in terms of the development of cultural distinctions among the people of the Bible. In short, what is revealed about God in the Bible develops through history both because of the variant details of God's own self-disclosure and because of the changing cultural perspectives (including language, idioms, and general conceptual frames of reference) of those to whom God was revealed. That scriptural perspectives vary over time can hardly be challenged. Some of the more significant shifts from Old to New Testaments include changing attitudes toward the role of the law in salvation, the work and nature of the Messiah, the extent of God's love for and saving activity toward Gentiles, the nature of life after death, etc. By appealing to progressive revelation, one can explain some of the tension in scripture as the result of a shifting and growing understanding of the nature of God and of his activity in the world. We will discuss the difficulties with this approach below.

Which of these strategies and substrategies for dealing with the tensions in scripture should one endorse? Two options seem most palatable to me: (1) subsume "Calvinistic" passages into an Arminian framework or (2) appeal to progressive revelation. My rationale for the first alternative is that I do not think the Calvinistic model can overcome the logical difficulties inherent in its system. Many of the criticisms offered against it in chapter two are sound. The model cannot rationally explicate the notions of human responsibility and divine justice, nor can it deny divine authorship of sin—each of which, in my judgment, is a cardinal affirmation of the Biblical testimony. On the other hand, as we will argue in more detail in chapter six, many of the difficulties faced by Arminianism (that were mentioned in chapter three) can be ameliorated. And so, if a harmony of scripture can be discerned from the Arminian perspective, it should be elaborated. Further, in a number of cases, an Arminian interpretation of a given passage is as cogent or even more cogent than the traditional Calvinistic spin.

My rationale for appealing to progressive revelation is that admittedly there are some Biblical passages for which an "Arminian" interpretation is strained and questionable. In such cases, it may make sense to assume that the text is limited by its own historical and culture context and/or by the degree of divine self-disclosure that it entails.

An Arminian Interpretation

Let us first consider the case for an Arminian interpretation of passages traditionally claimed by Calvinists. Jack Cottrell offers such an exposition. Cottrell notes that while the Bible affirms divine control of natural and human events, in most cases it does not specify *how* God exercises such control and this leaves room for speculation concerning the precise meaning of the texts in question. Such verses may indicate direct causal control or they may refer to divine permissive control. Further, Cottrell distinguishes between two broad sets of passages that deal with divine providence–those concerned with general providence and those relating to special providence. General providence is God's rule of the routine ebb and flow of events in the physical world. Special providence is the divine governance of specific creaturely events with an eye toward achieving particular purposes. While the Bible does not explicitly demarcate these distinctions, Cottrell believes that such a differentiation is implicit in the scriptures.

Among the passages that point toward a divine general providence are those that speak of God's control over and/or creation of various natural events such as the workings of celestial bodies (Psalm 104:19; Job 38:31-33), the feeding and care of wild animals (Psalm 104:10-28; Job 39:1-27; 38:39-41; Matthew 6:26), the changing of the seasons and of various weather patterns (Psalm 135:6-7; Job 36:27-28; Matthew 5:45), etc.[5] Cottrell renounces the theory of concurrence, the notion that somehow both God and created entities simultaneously cause the same events. If rightly

---

[5]Jack Cottrell, *What the Bible Says about God the Ruler* (Joplin, Missouri: College Press Publishing Company, 1984), pp. 93-96.

conceptualized, the theory of concurrence may have merit, claims
Cottrell. But typically Calvinistic interpretations of this doctrine
make it indistinguishable from the pantheistic notion that God is
the sole cause of all actions. Cottrell writes:

> the doctrine of concurrence must be questioned because
> however much emphasis it puts on the reality of natural laws,
> these secondary causes are engulfed by and negated by the
> Primary Cause . . . . If no creature can act until God acts upon
> it, if "nothing created can originate action" [as Charles Hodge
> claimed], if every natural process is determined each moment
> by the divine will, then how is this view really different from
> the . . . view . . . that God is the sole cause of natural events?
> As the doctrine of concurrence is explained [by theological
> determinists], there would seem to be no need of second causes
> at all *in the sense of causes.* It would seem more appropriate
> to speak of instruments or means, since an instrument is simply
> a tool in the hand of a user and need not contribute anything of
> its own.[6]

With this denial in mind, Cottrell proposes the following
understanding of passages that deal with general providence. First,
they teach that God is the *ultimate* cause of cosmic events in the
sense that he created the universe; second, God is the *immediate*
cause of creaturely occurrences in the sense that he *sustains* the
created order and *permissively grants* any event that unfolds. In
other words, creation operates according to divinely ordained
natural laws, but these laws only function because God preserves
the created order in its being and because the deity permissively
allows such events and laws to happen.[7] God does not directly
cause such happenings and, so, a genuine although limited
autonomy persists in creation. Cottrell's interpretation of general
providence appertains to much of human activity as well. He
writes:

---

[6]Ibid., p. 105. Brackets are mine.
[7]Ibid., pp. 106-109.

[T]he principle of *relative independence* applies to God's moral creatures in their exercise of free will just as much as, if not more than, it applies to the operation of physical laws in the realm of nature. In many if not most cases God permits human beings to make their own choices and chart their own courses without any special intervention.[8]

Turning to special providence, Cottrell identifies a number of Biblical passages that denote divine control of specific events, often with a view to accomplishing precise goals. Examples within the realm of human actions include the hardening of Pharaoh's heart (Exodus 10:20, 27), the placing of dread into the hearts of Israel's enemies (Exodus 23:27), and the use of the Assyrian king and armies against Israel (1 Chronicles. 5:26). Cottrell argues that Arminians are free to interpret such events as cases of either *direct or indirect* divine control. For example, in the case of the hardening of Pharaoh's heart, *direct control* would entail the deity acting immediately upon the *will* of the king, causing it to be stubborn. *Indirect control* would involve God bringing to bear influences exterior to the king's will itself. These influences could be either inner or outer. Outer influences might involve the words of other persons, the general beliefs of the Pharaoh's society, the king's family tradition and upbringing, etc. Such outer influences would *entice* or *incline* the Pharaoh toward a definite action without directly causing his will to act. Inner influences, on the other hand, would involve God placing a specific thought into the king's mind or causing some memory to surface. These thoughts/memories would work upon the king's psyche, helping persuade him to act in a given way, but they would not directly cause the Pharaoh's will to act. According to Cottrell, whether divine control were direct or indirect it would remain accurate to assert that God brought about the event.[9]
Cottrell tempers his interpretation of special divine provi-

---

[8]Ibid., p. 113.
[9]Ibid., pp. 195-204.

dence. Concerning direct providential control, he insists first that God does not directly move the human will to accept or reject *salvation*, for this would contradict the deity's express desire that persons come to salvation freely. And so, if it occurs at all, direct control applies to God's action upon human hearts with a view toward producing decisions that do not directly impact salvation or damnation. Second, even if direct divine control of the human will does occur occasionally, "we do not have any warrant for generalizing from these cases and assuming that this is the way God works with every decision of every will."[10]   Indeed, Cottrell is inclined to believe that direct divine control is seldom used and that indirect control is the primary technique employed in special providence. Concerning indirect providential control, Cottrell contends that it too must be consistent with God's broad purpose to save those "who freely choose to serve him."[11]   Further, one must stress that indirect control leaves up to the individual will *all decisions*, not only those directly impacting salvation. And so, through indirect providential control God only *influences* human choices; humans themselves (their wills) make the actual decisions.[12]

Cottrell's proposal offers a broad matrix through which a number of biblical passages might be explained. For example, many (perhaps most) of the verses that speak of the divine causal influence over natural events, such as rain (Matthew 5:45), clouds, sea, lightning, and wind (Psalm 135:5-7) can be understood as declarations of God's general providence, of the deity being the ultimate, sustaining and permissive cause of such phenomena–but not necessarily of God being the direct cause. Likewise, some passages about human events may fall under this rubric, such as 1 Samuel 2:6-7 where we are informed that God makes poor and rich, and brings humans low or exalts. Here the events described seem to concern general socio-economic patterns. The divine causal influence simply may be permissive and sustaining, rather

---

[10]Ibid., pp. 196-197.
[11]Ibid., p. 204.
[12]Ibid., 207-208.

than direct.

In turn, numerous texts dealing with divine control over human affairs may be interpreted as examples of indirect providential control, where God brings various internal and external influences upon persons in an effort to evoke specific actions from them. This may be the case with God's stirring of king Pul against Manasseh (1 Chronicles 5:25-26), the divine provoking of the Philistines and Arabs against Judah (2 Chronicles 21:16), and the general fear that emerged among the enemies of Israel in Canaan (Deuteronomy 2:25). Even less than ideal human actions partially may result from indirect divine influence. Examples might include king Sihon's refusal to let the people of Israel pass through his territory (Deuteronomy 2:30), the Egyptian population's hatred of the Hebrew slaves (Psalm 105:25), or the Pharaoh's stubborn refusal to let Israel go free.[13] Here, in light of specific providential goals, God may have reinforced (through indirect influences) the evil that certain persons were already inclined to perform. The evil actions themselves were the result of the free will decisions of the people in question, but God did indirectly (without utter efficacy) influence them toward these decisions. Presumably God did this for the sake of achieving some specific and righteous goal.

But what of God's influence upon people toward salvation? Is God's call/election irresistible? Cottrell maintains that God's influence on persons toward salvation is best understood as indirect control and, so, the divine election or call need not be understood as irresistible. Scriptures that are often interpreted as teaching divine determinism unto salvation should be understood accordingly. For example, Cottrell argues that the principal indirect means by which God draws persons to salvation is through the hearing of the gospel. Many biblical verses that are often understood as teaching divine determinism can better be comprehended as claiming that God exercises indirect influence upon the human heart through the persuasiveness of the gospel. For instance, where Acts 18:27 speaks of persons who "believed

---

[13]Cottrell specifically cites the example of Pharaoh. Ibid., p. 203.

through grace," the reference to grace is not to some hidden and overwhelming divine causal influence. Rather, it "probably refers to the preaching of 'the word of His [God's] grace' (Acts 14:3; 20:24)."[14] In turn, Matthew 15:13 declares that "every plant the Father did not plant will be pulled up by its roots (NIV)." But this easily can be understood in light of the fact that God "plants" via the preaching of the Word (Luke 8:11-15). In short, this verse points toward the necessity for salvation of hearing and responding to the gospel, not to the necessity of being preselected and given faith by God. Again, in John 6:44 Jesus says: "No one comes to me unless the Father who sent me draws him (NIV)." But this must be considered in the context of Jesus' further and similar statement that "But I, when I am lifted up from the earth, will draw all men to myself (John 12:32, NIV)." When put together, these verses indicate that "the gospel of the grace of God in the cross of Christ is the drawing power that brings people to Jesus (Romans 1:16). No one can come unless he is drawn, that is true; but the word of grace is the principal means of that drawing."[15] And so, numerous biblical passages that suggest divine causal influence toward salvation can be interpreted as expressing indirect divine control, which leaves room for human freedom.

In a similar manner, verses that speak of divine hardening of hearts should not be understood to refer to God's deterministic denial of persons to salvation (and thus of God's deterministic consignment of people to reprobation). Rather, in most if not all instances such texts speak of an indirect divine influence (which leaves the will free) toward actions that do not directly affect salvation or damnation. Presumably, then, God's hardening of Pharaoh's heart was an influence (1) that did not force Pharaoh to act as he did and (2) did not directly result in the eternal damnation of Pharaoh. The same might be said of other cases of divine hardening. Cottrell insists that a distinction must be drawn between God's causally influencing persons toward some divinely

---

[14]Ibid. Brackets are mine.
[15]Ibid.

intended *service* and God's calling/electing/causally influencing persons toward salvation. Recognition of this distinction is critical for understanding passages such as Roman 9-11. These chapters should not be perceived as a discussion of the divine choice of individuals *for salvation or damnation*, but of God's election of certain individuals and nations to roles of *service* in his overarching providential plan.

According to Cottrell, the apostle Paul makes four central points in Romans 9-11. First, God can choose or reject anyone he wants for the purpose of bringing about a divinely intended goal, including the aim of having individuals help bring salvation to the world through Christ. And so, God is free to choose Gentiles in the place of (or in addition to) Israel as the key instruments by which the gospel of Christ is now shared with the world. This is analogous to God's choosing Isaac over Ishmael, Jacob over Esau, and even Moses over Pharaoh. In each case, the choice is not of an individual for personal salvation (or damnation) but of a person as an instrument to help bring about the eventual advent of God's saving work in Jesus Christ. A second point in these chapters is that although God chose Israel for service, their role largely has been fulfilled with the coming of Christ. Indeed, God had tolerated the unbelief of many Jews up to this point precisely because he had chosen them as preparatory agents for the coming of Christ. But now a new set of servants has been selected whose purpose (in part) is to offer salvation in Christ. These servants are "the church as composed of believing Jews and Gentiles (9:23ff)."[16] Paul's third principal claim is that the whole nation of Israel has not been rejected—neither as servants of God nor as persons saved. Only those who refuse to believe in Christ have been rejected, but there is and always has been a remnant of faithful believers in Israel. Finally, Paul asserts that the reason any person, a member of Israel included, is rejected for salvation is due to his/her unbelief in Christ. This rejection is not the result of some arbitrary choice on

---

[16]Ibid., 206.

God's part.[17] And so, according to Cottrell, Romans 9-11 does not teach the arbitrary divine selection of individuals either to salvation or damnation but the divine sovereignty to choose diverse persons *for service* especially in the history of salvation. Whether one is saved or not remains a matter of responding in faith to God through Jesus Christ.

Cottrell's general interpretation of scripture is echoed in the writings of other Arminian and open theistic authors. John Sanders insists that the overall flow of scripture suggests an authentic divine-human interchange where God grants humans genuine freedom and where humans both can and do disappoint the deity's intentions. In light of this, passages that seem to affirm divine pancausality must be interpreted carefully. In many cases, such verses can be understood as descriptions of God's actions in specific instances, and not of the deity's universal activities. For example, Isaiah 45:7 states: "I form light and create darkness, I make weal and create woe; I . . . the Lord . . . do all these things (RSV)." According to Sanders, this "refers to the specific experiences of Israel in exile and not to divine pancausality." It "alludes to the promise of the return from exile, not to every single event that happens in life."[18] Gregory Boyd makes a similar comment concerning Isaiah 46:11, which says "I have spoken, and I will bring it to pass; I have proposed, and I will do it (RSV)." According to Boyd this verse indicates that God "declares that the future is settled to the extent that he is going to determine it, but nothing in the text requires that we believe that *everything* that will ever come to pass will do so according to his will . . . ."[19]

Sanders further contends that Calvinist interpreters sometimes stretch Biblical metaphors beyond the meaning supplied by the

---

[17]Ibid., 206-207.

[18]John Sanders, *The God Who Risks: A Theology of Providence* (Downers Grove, IL: InterVarsity Press, 1998), p. 82.

[19]Gregory Boyd, *God of the Possible: A Biblical Introduction to the Open View of God* (Grand Rapids, Michigan: Baker Books, 2000), p. 30.

text. For example, in scripture the God-human relationship sometimes is compared to that of the relationship between a potter and clay. Such is the case in Isaiah 29:15-16, Jeremiah 18:7-10, and Romans 9:19-24. From this the conclusion often is gleaned that God determines every aspect of human life. But such an exegesis fails to detect that the analogy is only partial, that God is only partly like a potter and humans are only somewhat like clay. Indeed, humans are quite disanalogous to clay in that they willfully "resist the will of the potter."[20] For this very reason these passages blame the clay for its recalcitrance.

Arminian interpretations of various "Calvinistic passages" could be multiplied, but those cited here suffice to show that such a rendering is possible and in many cases more plausible than standard Calvinist interpretations. Again, the advantage of this approach is that it harmonizes the scriptures in a way that preserves human freedom/responsibility and divine justice. Further, at times it offers more natural interpretations of the Biblical passages. However, another method for resolving the tensions in scriptures is available–namely appeal to progressive revelation. We turn now to consider this approach.

Appeal to Progressive Revelation

While an Arminian interpretation of various "Calvinistic" passages offers considerable advantages, it may be problematic in places. At times such an exposition seems to strain the natural meaning of certain texts. No doubt, Cottrell is correct that usually scriptures depicting divine causal influence do not specify *how* the deity exercises such control. It is less clear, however, that Cottrell is right in asserting that this allows one to postulate that God's causal activities primarily are permissive and indirect rather than direct. A number of Biblical exegetes, with no particular Calvinistic axe to grind, observe a tendency in Biblical writings to affirm

---

[20]Sanders, p. 86.

a kind of divine pancausality. While the precise mechanism by which God causes events seldom is detailed, often direct causal influence naturally is inferred.

Joseph Fitzmyer speaks of the Bible's tendency to use protological language in describing God's causal influence on creation. "In such thinking, God is considered responsible for all that happens to his people and his creation, good or evil."[21] Fitzmyer detects this perspective in the apostle Paul's writing and believes it to be a carry-over from Old Testament thinking.[22] Fitzmyer's claim fits well with the wide variety of Biblical passages cited above (in our discussion of "Calvinistic" passages) where a full range of creaturely activities is attributed to God—occurrences like rain, wind, warfare, the hardening of human hearts, etc. Further, his thesis is bolstered by the use of the term *bara'*, "create," in the Old Testament. Throughout the Old Testament the word used to speak of God's generation of the entire universe (Genesis 1:1ff) also is employed to speak of the deity's producing of events within the natural order. God is said to *create* things such as individual humans (Ezekiel 21:30), generations of people (Psalm 102:18), individual animals (Psalm 104:30), the wind (Amos 4:13), the nation of Israel (Isaiah 43:1, 7, 15), redemption (Isaiah 41:20), praise on the lips of worshipers (Isaiah 57:19), darkness and disaster (Isaiah 45:7), and the smith and the destroyer (Isaiah 57:19).[23] In turn, often scripture writers discern divine retribution in "any unexpected and terrifying disaster,"[24] so

---

[21]Joseph A Fitzmyer, *The Anchor Bible*, vol. 33, *Romans: A New Translation with Introduction and Commentary* (New York: Doubleday, 1993), p. 108.

[22]Ibid., pp. 108, 568.

[23]John H. Stek, "What Says the Scripture?" *Portraits of Creation: Biblical and Scientific Perspectives on the World's Formation*, ed. Howard J. Van Till (Grand Rapids: William B. Eerdmans Publishing Company, 1990), p. 212.

[24]Walther Eichrodt, *Theology of the Old Testament*, vol. 1, trans. J. A. Baker, Old Testament Library (Philadelphia: The Westminster Press, 1961), p. 259. Examples of divine wrath include: Exodus 9:14; 1 Samuel

that sickness, injury and misfortune often are attributed to divine wrath. In light of all this, it is not surprising that a number of interpreters (many of whom are not particularly sympathetic to theological determinism) reject an Arminian construal of various "Calvinistic" passages because such an interpretation does not deal with some texts adequately. For these expositors, the Biblical sources often implicitly endorse pancausality.

But this does not necessarily vindicate the Calvinist perspective. Let us suppose that Biblical authors tended to think in pancausal categories. It need not follow that they *intended* to affirm theological determinism, because as we have seen many passages—in both the Old and New Testaments—also point toward the authenticity of human freedom and responsibility. And so, rather than assume that the scriptures affirm determinism, we might conclude that the Biblical writers affirmed both divine pancausality and human freedom/responsibility *without fully recognizing the incompatibility of the two*. Perhaps they missed this because it never occurred to them to look for it and/or because they simply did not have the intellectual tools needed to engage in such subtle abstractions. In turn, we may speculate that their endorsement of pancausality resulted less from an affirmation of the full deterministic ramifications of such a notion (as later spelled out by Augustine, Calvin, and others) and more from an *intuitive* desire to maintain (as Cottrell suggests) that God is the ultimate, sustaining and permissive cause of all things. In this case, one could give an "Arminian" interpretation to various passages without insisting that this is directly what the Biblical writers *intended* to teach. In truth, the Biblical writers may have not endorsed either theological determinism or libertarian freedom, at least not as ironed out by later theologians. Still the Arminian perspective may best fit the viewpoint of these authors precisely because it affirms what they implicitly maintain–namely human responsibility and ultimate divine control. In short, a certain progression or clarification of thought is found in Christian history,

---

6:4; 2 Samuel 24:21, 25; Numbers 14:37; 25:8.

a progression not fully developed in the Biblical literature but implicit in the various assumptions found there. This progression may be the result of the varying degree of divine self-disclosure and/or of the variations/limitations of the Biblical writers' cultural and linguistic frames-of-reference.

Analogous cases are located in other areas of scriptural teaching. For example, it is widely recognized that Biblical literature reflects a tri-level understanding of the cosmos–one wherein a flat earth is thought to be surrounded by a domed sky above and by some sort of underworld beneath.[25] Contemporary interpreters seldom feel obligated to accept this physical cosmology, even though they fully subscribe to certain spiritual truths that are often associated with it–for example, that there is an abode of God beyond this world, or that this world is a primary place of divine interest, or that God is the creator of all including that which is spatially above the surface of our planet, etc. Yes, the ancient writers tended to think of the universe as tri-level. But modern Christians need not feel obligated to endorse the same. In a similar manner, even if ancient writers tended uncritically to affirm divine pancausality, it may not necessitate contemporary critical thinkers to believe the same, particularly in light of the tension that exists between this view and the Bible's affirmation of human freedom/responsibility. What empirical observation will not allow one to affirm about physical cosmology, deductive and moral reflection may not allow one to accept about divine determinism in the world. This is the case, even though the Biblical writers tacitly tended to think of the physical universe as tri-level and of divine interaction with creation pancausally.

Or consider another analogous situation. As pointed out above, the Old Testament often ascribes to God the creating (*bara'*) of a large number of events in the natural realm–children, generations, smiths, animals, etc. Theological reflection (even among Calvinists) quickly interprets these claims to mean *not* that

---

[25]Such a view seems to be implicit in the Genesis narrative of creation (Gen. 1:1-8), as well as in passages like Philippians 2:10.

the deity generates these things *ex nihilo*, but that God brings them about in, through and with causal networks in the created world. This is not explicitly taught in the various texts, but it is reasonably extrapolated from our own awareness of causal connection in the world and from the claims of scripture itself. As John Stek points out even though the Bible attributes to God the *creation* of new generations, the scripture writers did not think that such events were "unrelated to the sexual union of male and female."[26] Now, if contemporary (Calvinistic and otherwise) interpreters may be granted this level of abstraction concerning the dual (divine and human) causal mechanics of procreative acts, then it is difficult to see why Arminian exegetes cannot push the degree of abstraction a step further and assert that the scripture writers were attempting to affirm God's ultimate, preserving, and permissive causal working in such events and were not denying libertarian freedom or endorsing divine determinism. At any rate, it is plausible to maintain that even though Biblical literature reflects pancausal thinking, it need not follow that the sacred authors intended to teach divine determinism or to deny human libertarian freedom.

Not everyone will be comfortable with this appeal to progressive revelation or progressive interpretation of scriptures. If not, the more direct Arminian interpretation of "Calvinistic" passages may be preferred. The end result is much the same for each approach. In each case, one declares that in the divine providential activity God is the ultimate, sustaining and permissive cause of all that happens but not usually the direct cause. God is the ultimate cause in the sense of being the source of the initial creation. God is the continuing cause in the sense that God sustain things in their existence and permits any occurrence that happens. The chief difference between these two strategies is that unlike the direct Arminian interpretation of Calvinistic passages, the appeal to progressive revelation need not claim that the Biblical writers precisely taught or even intended to teach these doctrinal nuances. Rather, the latter approach simply proposes that such teachings are

---

[26]Stek, p. 215.

the logical consequences of the Bible's affirmation of both divine pancausation and of human freedom and responsibility. I conclude that an Arminian interpretation of divine control best accommodates the varied teachings of scripture, particularly the Bible's affirmation of both God's causal interaction with the world *and* human moral responsibility. But what of the Arminian view of divine grace? Is there Biblical support for such a perspective? We turn to this issue in the next section.

Prevenient Grace[27]

As pointed out in chapter three, the doctrine of prevenient grace, as envisioned by Arminius and Wesley, presupposes the basic Augustinian/Calvinistic doctrine of human depravity. These writers assume that human beings are enslaved by sin and, consequently, are unable to turn to Christ by their own natural power. Rather, humans must receive inner divine spiritual aid in order to desire and to turn to Christ in faith. Indeed, Arminius and Wesley believed that this human sinful nature was somehow transferred to or conferred upon humans through the original sin of Adam and Eve. The close tie between the traditional Arminian doctrine of prevenient grace and the doctrine of human depravity leaves the contemporary Arminian with two fundamental options in defending the core elements of the Arminian model of providence. One option is to accept, with Arminius and Wesley, the notion that humans utterly are corrupted by sin and unable positively to respond to Christ without some direct divine spiritual aid. A second option is to reevaluate the alleged impact of the sinful nature upon humans, questioning whether such a nature makes it impossible for humans to respond in faith to Christ. We

---

[27]Considerable portions of this section are used by permission and appear in my article "Is Faith in Christ a Sinful Act?" *The Asbury Theological Journal* 57-58 (Fall 2002, Spring 2003).

will consider each alternative in turn. First, let us consider a defense of prevenient grace as originally articulated by Arminius and Wesley.

A Traditional Arminian Defense of Prevenient Grace

As we have just noted, the traditional Calvinist and Arminian models agree that humans are depraved to such a degree that they are unable to desire or actually to turn to Christ in faith. For each theory, a special act of divine inner influence must enable the sinner to exercise faith. Where these models diverge is in the matter of the human's ability to resist such inner divine empowering. Augustine and Calvin insisted that God's gracious influence is irresistible, that faith in Christ is directly given to the individual by God, and that salvation certainly follows from that divinely given faith. Sorrowfully, faith is not given to all persons, but only to a few—to those predestined to salvation by God. Contrary to these tenets, Arminius and Wesley contended that God's grace can be (and often is) resisted by humans. Those who accept this gracious aid are able to exercise faith and are saved. Those who reject this influence do not believe and, subsequently, reject salvation. Further (and here the notion of prevenient grace especially emerges), Arminius and Wesley maintain that the divine inner spiritual influence is made available to all persons, not just to a select few. The result is that all persons are given a genuine opportunity to respond positively to Christ (or at least, each person genuinely could respond if given the opportunity). In other words, God universally offers a spiritual influence that neutralizes the disabling effect of the sinful nature to a degree sufficient for each sinner potentially to desire and to exercise faith in Christ. In her freedom, with the aid of God's gracious spiritual empowerment, the individual is free either to accept or to reject Christ.

Calvinists often charge that such a doctrine of prevenient grace simply is not affirmed in the Bible. The Arminian must admit that the scriptures do not explicitly teach "the doctrine of prevenient grace." In its developed form, this teaching is the result of systematic theological reflection upon diverse claims found in the Bible. It is interesting to point out, however, that a similar charge might be leveled at Calvinism. The Bible does not *explicitly* teach that God's call to salvation is irresistible, nor that humans are totally depraved. While certain Biblical passages may hint at these assertions, none explicitly affirms them in the detail outlined by later theologians. These doctrines also are the result of later systematic theological reflection. In light of this, the Arminian might argue that while the doctrine of prevenient grace is not explicitly affirmed in scripture, it is implied at key points. And here a positive case materializes for the doctrine of prevenient grace as formulated by Arminius and Wesley.

Several scriptural considerations lend support to affirming this traditional Arminian doctrine. First, the Bible indicates that God is gracious, merciful, and loving and that he desires that all persons come to salvation. But if this is the case, it hardly makes sense to claim that God, in fact, refuses to grant to humans the grace necessary for them to choose salvation. Consider the following passages, listed by Vernon Grounds:[28]

> Behold the Lamb of God, who takes away the sin of the world. (John 1:29)

> For God so loved the world that he gave his only Son, that whoever believes in him should not perish but have eternal life. (John 3:16)

> For God has consigned all men to disobedience, that he may have mercy upon all. (Romans 11:32)

> For there is one God, and there is one mediator between God and men, the man Christ Jesus, who gave himself as a ransom for all, the testimony to which was borne at the proper time. (1

---

[28]See Vernon Grounds, "God's Universal Salvific Grace," *Grace Unlimited*, ed. Clark Pinnock (Eugene, Oregon: WIPF and Stock Publishers, 1999), pp. 21-30.

Timothy 2: 5-6)

> But we see Jesus, who for a little while was made lower than the angels, crowned with glory and honor because of the suffering of death, so that by the grace of God he might taste death for every one. (Hebrews 2:9)

> The Lord is not slow about his promise as some count slowness, but is forbearing toward you, not wishing that any should perish, but that all should reach repentance. (2 Peter 3:9)[29]

Obviously, these verses do not directly teach prevenient grace. But they do proclaim that God is gracious, that his grace has been extended to the whole world (all persons) through Christ, and that he is unwilling that any should perish. Surely these texts at least suggest a pervasive grace that works toward achieving God's desire to bring all sinners to him.

A second biblical support for the doctrine of prevenient grace is that throughout scripture God admonishes persons to exercise faith in him and in Christ (2 Chronicles 20:20, Isaiah 43:10, John 6:29, 14:1, Acts 16:31, etc.), and encourages them to repent of sin (1 Kings 8:47, Matthew 3:2, Mark 1:15, Luke 13:3, 5, Acts 3:19, 2:38, etc.). In turn, often failure to exercise faith and to repent of sin is directly condemned by God (John 3:18). Here, it makes little sense to suppose that God calls persons to repentance and asks them to believe, then condemns them for failing to do so, all the while knowing that they cannot repent or believe without his aid and in turn refusing to grant them such assistance.[30]

A third justification for the doctrine of prevenient grace is that some scriptures insinuate that God's enlightening and convicting power is active in all persons, and is drawing all to Christ. John

---

[29]Each rendering of these passages is from the Revised Standard Version (RSV).

[30]For a similar argument see Henry Thiessen, *Lectures in Systematic Theology* (Grand Rapids: Wm. B. Eerdmans Publishing Company, 1949), pp. 155-156.

1:9 speaks of the Logos which "gives light to every man (NIV),"
suggesting that some measure of knowledge of God is available to
all humans through the enlightening power of Christ. Romans
2:14-15 asserts that through conscience Gentiles often show that
the requirements of God's law are "written on their hearts . . .
(NIV)." Sometimes this awareness condemns their actions;
sometimes it defends them. Presumably the source of this knowledge is God, and through it persons are aware that some of their
actions are good and others evil. John 16:7-11 speaks of the role
of the Holy Spirit in convicting "the world of guilt in regard to sin
and righteousness and judgment (NIV)," intimating that God's
inner spiritual testimony is made to all persons. In turn, in John
12:32, Jesus proclaims that when he is lifted up (on the cross) he
will "draw all men to (NIV)" himself, possibly implying that the
human heart will be drawn/dragged to Christ by the powerful
picture of grace that Calvary manifests. None of these passages
explicitly speaks of a divine prevenient grace which overcomes the
effects of the sinful nature, but each leaves room for just such an
idea. Here we see advocated a universal divine influence upon the
hearts of all persons, both convicting of sin and making persons
aware of or even drawing them toward the divine righteousness.

In light of these biblical considerations, there is some warrant
for affirming the doctrine of prevenient grace as originally
formulated by Arminius and Wesley. While the doctrine is not
explicitly taught, it fits well with the general tone of these scriptural principles. This particularly is true if one assumes that in
their corrupt state humans cannot exercise faith in Christ without
inner divine influence. For if this is the case, and if God is sincere
in his willingness to save all and earnest in his call to all persons
to repent and believe, then there must be some mechanism by
which the deity frees humans sufficiently to enable them to
respond positively to his call.

But the Arminian defense of divine grace need not stop here.
For it also is possible for one to question whether the Bible teaches
that the sinful nature makes it impossible for humans to respond in
faith to Christ. To this second defense we now turn.

Alternative Arminian Defenses of Prevenient Grace

As we have seen, the traditional Arminian doctrine of prevenient grace assumes that humans are depraved to such a degree that they cannot want or exercise faith in Christ without special divine aid, without an inner spiritual aid that neutralizes the power of the corrupt nature. But if this assumption could be challenged, the need for the doctrine of prevenient grace (understood as a divine empowering of sinners so that they might desire and exercise faith in Christ) largely could be eliminated. This assumption concerning human inability can be challenged in either of two ways. First, one can question whether the sinful nature of humans entails that every concrete action of unregenerate humans is sinful, displeasing to God, deprived of any true good. Second, one can contest whether, even if the sinful nature does entail that every unregenerate human action is sinful, the act of faith of such persons is not sufficient for God graciously to grant salvation to them. We will consider each of these responses in turn. Before doing so, however, it will be helpful to reexamine the basic content of the Calvinistic (and traditional Arminian) doctrine of human depravity.

The meaning of the doctrine of human depravity is subject to varied interpretations. Calvin understood human sinful nature to mean that, independent of direct inner divine spiritual influence, humans can in no way do good. He insists that only damnable actions come from the corrupt nature of humans and that "the soul, plunged into this deadly abyss, is not only burdened with vices, but is utterly devoid of all good."[31] Calvin admits that by human standards various unbelievers have lived noble lives and have done

---

[31]John Calvin, *Institutes of the Christian Religion*, trans. Ford Battles, The Library of Christian Classics, vol. 20, ed. John McNeill (Philadelphia: The Westminster Press, 1960), 2.3.2. The title of this chapter in the *Institutes* is "Only Damnable Things Come Forth From Man's Corrupt Nature."

good things. He also acknowledges that not every person is willing to execute or actually commits every possible sin. However, Calvin rationalizes this state of affairs by asserting that God's grace pervasively restrains the heart of each human, preventing each from performing many of the evils that he or she is inclined to do. According to Calvin, such restraining grace does not bring salvation to individuals; it only tempers their evil.[32] Indeed, whatever actual good nonbelievers perform only occurs as a result of the special and direct inner action of God's grace in their lives.[33] Interestingly, then, Calvin endorses his own form of prevenient grace, but it is a grace that only restrains from some sin and aids in producing non-saving righteous acts. It is not a grace that enables persons to respond in faith to Christ. This latter form of grace requires yet a further activity by God's Spirit upon the human heart, an action administered only to those that God has predestined for salvation.[34]

Later Calvinistic writers offer a deeper analysis of human depravity, often softening the edges of Calvin's conjectures. For example, Louis Berkhof contends that due to the original sin of Adam and Eve, humans are corrupted and totally depraved. This means that every aspect of human life is plagued by sin, and there is no *spiritual* good in humans. That is, "the unrenewed sinner cannot do any act . . . which fundamentally meets with God's approval and answers to the demands of God's holy law."[35] Further, the sinner "cannot change his fundamental preference for

---

[32]Ibid, 2.3.3. Calvin writes that "it ought to occur to us that amid this corruption of nature there is some place for God's grace; not such grace as to cleanse it, but to restrain it inwardly . . . ." Further, while God cures the corrupt nature of the elect, those not selected for salvation "he merely restrains by throwing a bridle over them only that they may not break loose, inasmuch as he foresees their control to be expedient to preserve all that is." Ibid.

[33]Ibid., 2.3.4.

[34]Ibid., 2.3.6-7.

[35]Louis Berkhof, *Systematic Theology* (Grand Rapids, Michigan: Wm. B. Eerdmans Publishing Co., 1939), p. 247.

sin and self to love for God, nor even make an approach to such a change."[36] The doctrine of total depravity, however, does not mean that each human is as depraved as she possibly can be, nor that the unregenerate person practices every kind of evil. Further, it does not entail that unregenerate persons have no moral conscience, no innate awareness of God's moral expectations. Further, it does not mean that the unsaved never performs good acts or never behaves in the interest of others. For Berkhof, the key depravity of humans is that they can never perform an act whose motive is authentic love for God.[37]

While Berkhof's account echoes Calvin's views in numerous ways, it also ameliorates his harsher claims. Berkhof interprets human depravity in terms of the inability to perform acts whose motive is genuine love for God, rather than as an inability to do any good. This allows him to acknowledge the authentic goodness of some unregenerate human acts and to avoid claiming that the only reason unsaved humans do any acts of good is by a direct, non-saving, divine influence upon those persons. As I understand him, Berkhof is claiming that some good flows from human nature, even in its corrupted state, and even without direct divine spiritual aid. The catch is that no such good acts are truly motivated by love for God and, consequently, none leads to salvation in a person's life.

Challenging Total Inability. At this point, Arminians may offer one of two non-traditional interpretations of human depravity and human faith. The first is to deny that the sinful nature of humans entails that every action of unregenerate individuals is sinful and displeasing to God. Several Bible passages insinuate that this denial is accurate. For example, in Matthew 7:9-11 Jesus asks who of us would give a stone or a snake to a son if the boy were to ask for bread or fish? The answer is obvious. Jesus concludes that even though we are evil, we know how to give good gifts to our children. In other words, Jesus seems to say that even

---

[36]Ibid.
[37]Ibid., 246-247.

though we are sinners, we are capable of generating some righteous acts. Indeed, such actions on our part are analogous to how the Holy and Heavenly Father responds to our requests! In such situations, perhaps we are (unconsciously) imitators of God (Ephesians 5:1)! Or consider another example: In Romans 2:14-15, the apostle Paul asserts that when humans follow the dictates of conscience, they perform acts that conform to divine law and show that God's law is written on their hearts. Paul here is not declaring that humans are not inwardly sinful. Rather, he seems to be saying that even in our sinful condition we occasionally do good by following the dictates of conscience. Now if these scriptures indicate that sinners can sometimes perform good acts, then it may also mean that on certain occasions the act of faith, even on the part of a sinful person, is a genuinely good act, one that pleases and is accepted by God.

This interpretation does not deny that humans are sinful, that humans have a depraved nature. Instead, it simply declares that even though sin dominates a person's life, upon occasion she is capable of freely enacting genuinely good deeds. Further, this does not mean that any human ever does or even could completely avoid sin. While the fact that sinful persons can perform some good acts may lead to the theoretical possibility that some individuals could live a morally perfect life, it does not mean that such an occurrence is practically possible. The weight of the sinful nature, of the proneness to sin, may be so great that even if sinful persons occasionally do good things, the prospect of never doing evil, of living a perfect moral life, may be so astronomically slim that it is a virtual or statistical impossibility. Sin remains an inevitability, even if not a logical or causal necessity.[38]

---

[38] This understanding of the inevitability versus the necessity of sin is similar to the kinds of statistical inevitabilities found in empirical science. For example, it is impossible to track with certainty the deterioration of any given single atom, but it quite easily is possible to discern the likely behavior of a collective mass of such atoms, to such a degree that its future behavior as a collection is virtually certain.

Such an understanding of the human condition suggests a nuanced understanding of God's holy expectations. Rather than assuming, as did Calvin (and apparently Arminius and Wesley), that every unregenerate human act is evil and unacceptable to God, one may maintain that even a life full of genuinely good acts is not sufficient to fulfill the divine expectations. For the holiness of God does not merely demand some good works, or even a greater balance of good over evil. Instead, God expects a life of only good deeds with absolutely no sin. Humans stand condemned not because their every act is spiritually evil, but because God demands that none of their acts be evil. Since no human utterly avoids sin, none avoids divine condemnation. All fall short of God's glorious expectations (Romans 3:23).

The good news, the gospel, however, is that God has provided a means to salvation independent of a person completely fulfilling the moral law. God conditionally has ordained that by the free choice of the sinful person to exercise faith in Jesus Christ, that individual graciously will be granted salvation. She will be declared righteous even though in fact she has not perfectly met the demands of the moral law (Romans 3:21-24). In this case, the act of faith is a good act performed by a sinner. It is not sufficient to meet the holy demands of God, the demand to live a morally perfect life. Nevertheless, because of Christ's atonement and because of God's gracious decree, this good act will be accounted sufficient to receive a salvation that was neither deserved (by living a perfect life) nor attainable through human effort (because all in fact sin and fall short of God's expectations).

Two Calvinistic protests against this perspective may be anticipated. First, some will maintain that this proposal affirms salvation by merit. As we saw in chapter two, Augustine insisted that because Pelagius taught that faith is a natural human act, that this implies that salvation is earned by a person's faith. For Augustine, unless faith itself directly is given by God, salvation is not a gift, but something earned. In chapter three, we questioned the cogency of Augustine's claims. That faith in Christ is a free human act hardly implies that salvation is somehow earned. It remains the case that the human believer has not lived a perfect moral life and, thus, has not fulfilled God's moral expectations. Subsequently, the believer still deserves divine condemnation. But this condemnation is not forth-coming, because *graciously* God has ordained that those who exercise faith in Christ will be granted remission of sin and will receive spiritual union with Christ—i.e., salvation. Salvation is still by grace because God has accepted the atoning sacrifice of Christ in the place of our living morally perfect lives. Further, it is not even the case that faith itself is an act that the human could perform absent of divine (non-deterministic) influence. The Arminian may contend that without the inner urging of the Holy Spirit, without the inner light of the Logos, perhaps without the hearing of the Good News of Jesus Christ, the sinner could not exercise faith. God's pervasive activity is still required in this model of the human condition.

A second anticipated Calvinistic reply to this model of the human condition is that allegedly it contradicts the Bible's declaration that humans can do no genuine good. Calvin understood the apostle Paul literally to mean that persons can do no good. He got this from Paul's assertion that "there is no one righteous, not even one . . . . there is no one who seeks God . . . . there is no one who does good, not even one (Romans 3:10-12, NIV)." For this reason, Calvin asserted that the good that we see unregenerate persons do is the result of the divine restraining of evil and the divine inducing of good in persons. Berkhof, on the other hand, insinuates that Paul's words here mean that while unregenerate humans can do some good, they can do no *spiritual* good, no act genuinely pleasing to God. But it may be better to understand Paul to mean not that unregenerate humans literally never do good. Instead, he means that whatever good we do is not sufficient or salvific because in fact we also all sin and thus fall short of God's expectations. Humans do in fact keep many of God's laws, either consciously through a knowledge of the law or unconsciously through a tacit awareness of the law written in their consciences. But no one completely keeps that law and, so, all stand condemned. In such an interpretation, Paul's quotes from the

Psalms here can be seen as hyperbole, as poetic over-statement designed to emphasize a quite literal truth that no human ever lives up to God's holy and holistic expectations. This seems reasonable in light of Paul's own acknowledgment that through conscience humans sometimes can do works in conformity with God's law.[39] At any rate, one possible non-traditional Arminian response to the problem of human depravity is simply to deny that every act of corrupt humans is evil and displeasing to God.

Grace In Spite of Sin. A second augmented Arminian response would be to assert that even if unregenerate persons cannot enact genuinely good acts, God graciously ordains that some of these acts will be sufficient for receiving the saving benefits of Jesus' atonement. In other words, even if no act of unregenerate humans is truly righteous (because such acts are never motivated by a genuine love for God), this need not mean that such persons cannot freely exercise a faith sufficient to receive the blessings of divine salvation. It could be that the deity has ordained that even an act of faith whose motive is not fully based on love for God nevertheless will be sufficient to receive the benefits of Christ's saving power. Such an act of faith would not be pure; it would still be the act of a sinner. But in God's amazing grace, even such an action would be accredited as righteousness (Romans 4:3).

Here we perhaps expose an ironic aspect of the Augustin-ian/Calvinistic system—namely, the presumption that the act of faith itself must be morally pure, untainted by sinful motives or self love. In short, in order for God to grant salvation, the act of faith must be *worthy* of God's acceptance; it must *merit* the divine granting of salvation; it cannot be tainted by the sinful nature. For this reason, both Augustine and Calvin declare that God must empower the sinful soul with a genuine/saving faith. But why should we think this? Why should we believe that the act of faith

---

[39]That the scriptures often use hyperbole can hardly be denied, even by Calvinists. Few Reformed thinkers take Jesus' recommendation literally in Matthew 5:29-30.

must be morally pure? Does not such an assumption usher in its own peculiar form of works-righteousness? Are not Calvinists tacitly asserting that because God has made the act of faith truly moral, the deity is able to grant salvation? But what if the grace of God is so magnanimous that the deity accepts as sufficient for salvation even the faith of the morally impure sinner! What if the act of faith is tainted with false motives, and with failure to love God, and yet God accepts it anyway? Amazing grace indeed! It seems to me that such a scenario is the more realistic view of human faith. What Christian is willing to claim that his act of faith in Christ was or is utterly pure, motivated by a complete and untainted love for God? Is it not more realistic, and for that matter more scriptural, to believe that God accepts our faith, even though we are sinners and our acts are not pure? It seems to me the answer is, Yes.

The benefit of this second proposed Arminian reinterpretation of the human condition is that it takes seriously the traditional doctrine of human depravity. Humans may well never generate acts that are morally pure, completely satisfying in God's estimate. As Emil Brunner notes, even if an individual in principle could perform every act of the divine law, it need not follow that that person is not a sinner. Sin may well cut deeper than that, so that while individuals may be able to keep the law externally, they never fully keep it internally. They never fully live in covenant with God, nor in love with God.[40] Even if this is the case, however, this second Arminian interpretation allows for the faith that exudes from such sinful persons to be sufficient to receive the benefits of Christ's atonement. This is not because such faith deserve these benefits, but because God graciously has willed it to be so.

Again, an anticipated Calvinist response to this second augmented Arminian perspective might be to assert that this view

---

[40]Emil Brunner, *Dogmatics: vol. 2, The Christian Doctrine of Creation and Redemption,* trans. Olive Wyon (Philadelphia: Westminster Press, 1952), pp. 108-112.

makes faith a human work that merits salvation. At least the Calvinistic system makes faith a *divine* work that (in a qualified sense) merits salvation. But again this is not quite right. In the model I have proposed, faith does not merit salvation at all. Faith does not meet the righteous demands of God's law. It is only because God graciously has willed that Christ's death atones for sin and that faith in Christ will be the condition upon which the benefits of this atonement are received that faith in any way affects salvation. Further, the activity of the Spirit of God upon the individual heart may still be required in order to urge the person toward this (blemished) faith in Christ. Even if the faith itself is not utterly guileless, without a divine nudge, no human response would unfold. Further still, and perhaps most profoundly, in the model of faith proposed here, divine grace accepts an act of faith that itself is not even morally righteous. It is not utterly pure, not motivated by sheer love for God. Nevertheless, in grace, God accepts it anyway! This is not salvation by works. It is grace, through and through.

I conclude that a substantial case can be made for the Arminian doctrine of grace. This is possible either by affirming prevenient grace as traditionally taught by Arminius and Wesley, or by reinterpreting the implications of the doctrine of human depravity. In either case, it seems that a biblical case can be made for the notion that humans are free to accept or reject the gift of salvation offered in Jesus Christ; they are free to exercise faith or not exercise it.

Conclusion

Certainly there are puzzles in the scriptures. Verses can be cited both for an Arminian/open theistic perspective and for a Calvinistic outlook. However, I believe that the stronger case remains the Arminian one. The Bible assumes that humans sin, that God does not want them to sin, and that God holds them responsible for their actions. Further, while various passages point toward God's over-arching sovereignty, these verses do not necessitate the belief that God directly causes all cosmic events. Rather, room is left for divine permissive will and for genuine human freedom. Further, the Bible also makes room for belief in prevenient grace, either as traditionally taught by Arminius and Wesley, or (perhaps more persuasively) by reinterpreting the nature and the effect of the human sinful condition and the faith that such a condition allows. But even if a tenuous Biblical case can be made for the Arminian perspective, it is not abundantly clear that this system is philosophically/rationally cogent. In the next chapter, we turn to this concern.

Chapter 6

Navigating the Storm II:
Sailing with the Winds of Logic

In chapter five, I submitted the thesis that traditional Arminianism provides the most satisfying model for the divine-world relationship. However, such a claim faces several questions: (1) Does this model match the Bible's view of divine causal influence in the world?, (2) Is there room in scripture for the notion of prevenient grace?, (3) Can God be conditioned by creatures?, (4) Does the alleged relationship between time and timelessness make sense?, (5) Can a timeless and immutable God be personal and interpersonal?, (6) Is divine foreknowledge compatible with freedom?, and (7) Is divine foreknowledge useful for God's providence? In chapter five, I answered the first two questions in the affirmative. There my concern largely was one of biblical exegesis. In this sixth chapter, I will consider questions (3)-(7). Our focus mainly will be on logical coherence.

A Conditioned God?

In chapter three, we noted two key Calvinistic challenges to the Arminian model, namely that such a theory denies divine sovereignty and salvation by grace alone. Underlying these accusations was, in part, the assumption that God cannot be conditioned by creatures. If God cannot be affected by creatures, then the Arminian claim that God permissively allows creatures to act cannot be true. In order for God to permit some event, that incident must be initiated by a being other than God. But this seems to imply that the deity somehow depends on the creature to perform the act so that God might permit it. But if the deity cannot be affected by creatures, then he cannot depend on the creature to act in order to permit its action. In turn, if God cannot be affected by creatures, then the Arminian affirmation that faith is a human act that is undetermined by God also cannot be true. In such a scenario God's granting of salvation *depends* on the faith-act of the person being saved. But if God can in no way depend on another being, then such divine conditionality is not possible.

But why cannot God be affected by creatures? Several rationales may be cited in support of this conclusion. One justification stems from the doctrine of divine creation. Some reason that if God is the cause of all things other than himself, then he cannot depend on anything else. Otherwise an incoherent causal loop occurs. One may ask: How can God be caused by something that he causes? Such reasoning, however, needs clarification. In one sense, this argumentation is correct, if one is talking about causing something to exist absolutely, causing something to have being that previously had no existence whatsoever. And so, my wife and I cannot be caused absolutely to exist by our son whose existence we caused. On the other hand, it seems quite possible for something whose absolute existence is caused by another, in turn, to affect/causally influence that which brought it into being. Consequently, once our son comes into existence, he can and does causally affect both my wife and me. In like manner, prima facie, it seems possible for God (who created the very being of the created order) to be affected by the creation once it has come into existence. And so, it is not immediately clear that appeal to the doctrine of creation alone is sufficient to ground the notion that God cannot be affected by creatures.

However, other considerations may come into play. Brian Leftow has argued that when combined with the concept of divine simplicity the notion of creation disallows God from being affected by others. The doctrine of divine simplicity teaches that God's nature and attributes are the same and that "they" are a singularity. Thus, for example, God is identical to the divine knowledge. But if this is the case then it follows that if the existence of divine knowledge is causally influenced by events in the created order, then God's very existence is causally influenced by events in creation. This is impossible, however, for God is said to be the cause of created things. And if created things, in turn, are the cause of God, then somehow God "causally contributes to His own existence,"[1] which is impossible.

Leftow's argument rests on the assumption that God is a simple being, that God's nature and attributes (especially knowledge) are identical. But why should someone believe this? A central reason given by medieval and modern writers for affirming divine simplicity is that God must be independent of other beings. Allegedly, God must be simple, for a composite being depends on its parts in order to exist.[2] Unfortunately, all of this begs the question, since the point of Leftow's argument is to *establish* that deity cannot be affected by other things. And so, it will not do to argue *for* divine independence based on God's simplicity since divine simplicity itself is grounded in the alleged divine independence. Leftow's argument is not convincing.

But perhaps another consideration when annexed to the doctrine of creation requires that God be unaffected by creatures. Admittedly, it seems possible for a *temporal* being to cause the very existence of something and yet also to be influenced by that being *later*, as is the case with the generation of and subsequent rearing of a child. But is the same possible for a *timeless* being? Can a timeless God be the creator of the being of all other things and yet also somehow causally be influenced by those same things? Such a scenario is problematic, for it seems to allege that at the very eternal moment that God generates the being of

---

[1]Brian Leftow, *Time and Eternity* (Ithaca: Cornell University Press, 1991), p. 171.

[2]William Mann, "Simplicity and Immutablity in God," *International Philosophical Quarterly* 23 (September 1983), 267-276.

creatures those same entities eternally simultaneously are influencing God. Is this possible?

It seems to me that it is. Consider this analogy. Suppose that a parent immediately could be aware of the conception of his/her child. In that moment, then, the parent would be generating the being of that child and also the child's existence would be affecting the parent. Granted, normally humans do not know of an event immediately upon its happening, but only learn of it later through some medium like eye-sight or hearing, each of which requires temporal process. But if a parent could somehow know of the occurrence of an event (like conception) immediately, then it seems possible for her/him both to be the generating cause of a child and simultaneously to be affected by the existence of that offspring. There is no obvious reason why immediate knowledge is logically impossible, or why knowledge per se requires temporal process. And so, there is no conspicuous incoherence to the scenario that I have proposed. In turn, presumably this is something like a timeless God's knowledge of an entity whose being he generates in the single moment of eternity and whose existence the deity immediately is aware of in that same timeless instance.[3] Consequently, God's timelessness and the notion of creation do not require an utterly unconditional divine nature.

But perhaps there is a second rationale for denying that God can be affected by others. It springs from the declaration that God is pure actuality, that within the deity there is no potentiality. As we saw in chapter two, Aristotle, Thomas Aquinas, and perhaps Augustine each endorsed this concept of God. Obviously, if God is pure actuality, then there is no potential for God to be affected by other things. God simply is what he is with no potential to be affected by creatures. But why should one believe that God is pure act, that there is no potential in the deity? Interestingly enough, the

---

[3]For a similar view of divine knowledge and timelessness see William Alston, *Divine Nature and Human Language: Essays in Philosophical Theology* (Ithaca: Cornell University Press, 1989), pp. 123-129.

answer is related to the claim that God is Creator. Following Aquinas, various writers insist that the nature of the created universe requires the existence of an entity that is pure act, pure being, that has no potential. Consider the following argument. Many things exist in our world. And existence (*esse*) is an act. It is the act through which a thing is/exists. Now the act of existence must have a cause or explanation. It cannot emerge out of nothing or be unexplained. But what type of causes or explanations for existence might there be? There appear to be two. Either something exists because of something (some existence/act) extrinsic to it or because existence (*esse*, act) is the very nature (*essentia*) of the thing. Now all things cannot exist due to something extrinsic to them, for in this case there would be no ultimate cause or explanation for the existence of anything. And so, in order for the many things of the world to exist, there must be something whose very nature (*essentia*) is the act of existence (*esse*) itself. In short, God must be pure existence, pure act. And as pure act, there is no potential in God. Therefore, God cannot be affected by other beings.[4]

Such reasoning is a version of Aquinas' cosmological argument. It has been criticized in various ways. Some have questioned its assumption that existence needs an ultimate explanation. Others have insisted that an infinite regress of extrinsic causes is possible and thus that the argument does not *demonstrate* the existence of a necessary being.[5] Even if these criticisms are correct, however, they may not help the Arminian case for a God who is affected by creatures. For many Arminian

---

[4]This is essentially a restatement of Aquinas' cosmological arguments. See *De Ente et Essentia*, trans. A. Maurer (Toronto: Pontifical Institute of Mediaeval Studies, 1968), 4, 7, and *Summa theologica*, 1.3.4. I particularly am indebted to Thomas Weinandy's explication of Aquinas' argument in *Does God Suffer?* (Notre Dame, Indiana: University of Notre Dame Press, 2000), pp. 120-122.

[5]John Hick, *Philosophy of Religion*, 4th ed. (Englewood Cliffs, New Jersey: Prentice Hall, 1990), pp. 20-23.

theists sympathize with the conclusion of the argument, namely, that a necessary being, namely God, exists. The critical question is whether such a being must be pure act, as the Thomistic argument concludes.

I will not assess the soundness of this Thomistic reasoning. But for the sake of argument, let us assume that its conclusion is correct, namely that the ultimate cause of being must be fully actual, must be the very act of existing itself.[6] It need not follow from this that *every aspect* of God is fully actual. A variety of theists have contended that perhaps elements of God's nature are necessary while others are open, potential. For example, William Alston maintains that while God's *existence* may be necessary, the divine *knowledge* may be subject to change; it may vary depending on the specific world that God creates and the subsequent "effect" that such a world might have on God.[7] In an analogous way, perhaps components of God's being are fully actual—are being itself—while other portions are not. Indeed, perhaps the potential aspects of the divine being depend on the fully actual parts of God. In this case, the basic insights of the Thomistic argument are retained, namely that the created order requires the existence of a fully actual being. The critical difference is that in this interpretation only a portion of the divine being is fully actual, not all of it. There is nothing obviously incoherent about such a claim. One perhaps could rebut this proposal by insisting that God is simple, that he has no diverse aspects. But as noted above, short of circular reasoning, it is not clear why one must affirm divine simplicity. Consequently, my proposal coheres. And so, even if the Thomistic claim is correct that the created order demands the existence of a fully actual being, it need not follow that every aspect of the deity is fully actual. There may be potentials within God and this allows for the deity to be partially conditioned by creatures.

---

[6]My intension is not to claim that the Thomistic argument is sound, but that if it is it need not require that God be unaffected by creatures.

[7]Alston, pp. 123-129.

But perhaps there is a third rationale for believing that God cannot be affected by others. Possibly divine independence flows from the divine perfection, from God's status as the greatest possible being. As we have seen, Plato argued that a perfect being cannot change, for to change is either to get better or worse, neither of which is possible for a perfect being. And so if God is a perfect being, he cannot change. In turn, to be affected by another is to be different than one would have been if one had not been so influenced. And since God—as a perfect being—cannot be different from what he would have been if he had not created, then the deity cannot be affected by that which he in fact did create.[8]

The chief difficulty with this line of reasoning is that it fails to recognize the possibility of changes/differences that in no way affect perfection. It overlooks the potential for neutral change, change neither for the better nor for the worse. William Hasker comments:

> Plato's argument is straightforwardly fallacious, because it rests on a false dichotomy. It rests on the assumption that all change is either for the better or for the worse, an assumption that is simply false. Consider the operation of an extremely accurate watch. A short while ago, it registered the time as five minutes after six o'clock, but now it registers twelve minutes after six. Clearly, this is a change in the watch . . . . Is this a change for the better, suggesting a previous state of imperfection. Not at all . . . . Is it then a change for the worse, a decline from perfection? Again, this is clearly not the case . . . . So there are changes that are neither for the better nor for the worse, and the change in the watch is such a change. It is, in fact, an example of *a change that is consistent with and/or*

---

[8]This seems to be the core reasoning found in one of Aquinas' arguments for God's utter aseity. See my discussion of these matters in Michael Robinson, *Eternity and Freedom: A Critical Analysis of Divine Timelessness as a Solution to the Foreknowledge-Free Will Debate* (Lanham: University Press of America, 1995), pp. 219-223.

required by a constant state of excellence.[9]

In light of the failure of this third rationale, I conclude that there is no clear reason to maintain that God cannot be affected by creatures. Further, with this deduction it follows that divine sovereignty and grace are not threatened by the Arminian model of the God-World relationship.

A Timeless, Immutable, Personal, and Interpersonal God?

In addition to the question of God's conditionality, the traditional Arminian model of providence faces problems associated with claiming that God is timeless and immutable. It is not immediately clear that the ontological relationship between time and eternity that is implied by the timelessness theory makes sense. Further, one might wonder whether a timeless, immutable God can be personal or can interact with other persons. In this section we will consider each of these quandaries.

The Coherence of Divine Timelessness
The theory of divine timelessness has been the subject of considerable debate in recent years. The most promising model of this theory is offered by Brian Leftow.[10] Pulling from the insights of Anselm, Leftow proposes that the relationship between time and eternity should be understood as analogous to the relationship between space and time. As space is to time, so time is to eternity. Leftow draws seven key implications from this analogy:

---

[9]William Hasker, "A Philosophical Perspective," *The Openness of God*, Clark Pinnock et. al. (Downers Grove: InterVarsity Press, 1994), pp. 132-133. Hasker's emphasis.

[10]Leftow, *Time and Eternity*.

[1]   As space and spatial things are literally in time, time and temporal things literally do exist in eternity.

[2]   As spatially distant things exist in one and the same temporal present at once, so temporally distant things exist in one and the same eternal present at once.

[3]   As spatial objects remain spatial even though they exist in time, so temporal objects remain temporal even though they exist in eternity.

[4]   As existing at the same time does not wipe out spatial differences of here and there, so existing in the same eternity does not wipe out temporal differences of here and there, i.e., of present versus past or future.

[5]   As the temporal present contains all space without being in any way spatial, so the eternal present contains all of time without being temporal.

[6]   "X exists in space" entails "x exists in time," but not vice versa. In the same way, "x exists in time" entails "x exists in eternity," but not vice versa. (An eternal God does not necessarily exist also in time.)

[7]   As a nonspatial object (e.g., an angel) can exist with all spatial objects in one temporal present, so a nontemporal object (God) can exist with all temporal objects in one eternal present.[11]

Leftow compares divine timeless-eternity to a dimension beyond time in which all temporal events are contained.[12]

Leftow also appeals to the special theory of relativity to explicate the relationship between time and timeless-eternity. The

---

[11]Ibid., pp. 212-213.   Cf. Delmas Lewis, "Eternity, Time and Tenselessness," *Faith and Philosophy* 5 (1988), 77-78.   Bracketed numbers are mine.

[12]Ibid., pp. 183-184.

special theory of relativity teaches that space and time are relative to the speed at which an object is moving relative to other objects. As speed increases, time slows down or space contracts for that object. One of the most intriguing features of this theory is that simultaneity also varies depending on the relative speed of objects to one another. And so, under certain conditions a rocket-bound observer (moving at a very high rate of speed) could fly past an earth-bound observer, and could observe (be simultaneous with) an event that is still several hours into the earth-bound person's future. In other words, in the rocket-bound observer's frame of reference, the earth-bound person and some event x are simultaneous; but in the earth-bound person's frame of reference event x is still in the future by several hours or even days![13] The relativity of temporal frames of references offers Leftow an analogy for the relationship between time and eternity. Eternity can be understood as a unique, divine frame of reference in which all temporal events are simultaneous.

Leftow believes that this version of divine timelessness avoids the problem mentioned in chapter two concerning the relationship of time to timeless-eternity. There we noted that some philosophers complain that the theory of divine timelessness implies that all temporal events are simultaneous, that events of yesterday are simultaneous with events of tomorrow. In one sense, this is correct. All events are simultaneous *in God's eternal/timeless frame of reference*. But due to the special theory of relativity, it need not be true that all events are simultaneous *in other frames of reference*. Indeed, one can claim that even while events are actualized at diverse moments of past, present and future in various temporal frames of reference, they are all simultaneous in the divine eternal frame of reference. Leftow explains:

---

[13]See Paul Davies, *Space and Time in the Modern Universe* (Cambridge: Cambridge University Press, 1977), 29-55. It should be noted that Leftow's model depends on a specific interpretation of the special theory of relativity. See my discussion of these matters in Robinson, pp. 69-72, 89-110.

A defender of God's timelessness can assert that (in a strictly limited sense) one and the same event is present and actual in eternity though it is not yet or no longer present or actual in time. That is, it can be true at time t that an event dated at t + 1 has not yet occurred in time, and yet also correct at t to say that that very event exists in eternity . . . . We can see how this can be so by applying anew the relativity of simultaneity. If simultaneity and presentness are relative to reference frames, then if present events are actual in some way in which future events are not, this sort of actuality is itself relative to reference frames. Thus, there is a (strictly limited) sense in which the relativity of simultaneity entails a relativity of actuality . . . .[14]

It would seem, then, that a case can be made for the ontological relationship between time and timeless-eternity.

Timelessness and a Personal and Interpersonal God

Even if Leftow's theory of divine timelessness resolves the puzzle concerning the relationship of time and eternity, questions remain concerning the personal and interpersonal nature of God. Some philosophers of religion have argued that a time-less/immutable being cannot be personal. As noted in chapter two, Robert Coburn insists that a timeless God could not remember, anticipate, reflect, deliberate, decide, intend, or act intentionally, for such actions take time.[15] But it is not clear that Coburn is correct. Certainly, he is partly right. Remembering, anticipating, and deliberating take time. But it is less clear that actions like

---

[14]Leftow, pp. 231-232. Leftow's views are not uncontroversial, but I believe they are sound and I have defended them in Robinson, *Eternity and Freedom*. For similar views on divine timelessness see Eleonore Stump and Norman Kretzmann, "Eternity," *Journal of Philosophy* 78 (August 1981), 429-458.

[15]Robert Coburn, "Professor Malcolm on God," *Australasian Journal of Philosophy* 40-1 (1962-3), quoted by Nelson Pike, *God and Timelessness* (New York: Schocken Books, 1970), p. 121.

knowing or willing take time. While learning something seems to involve temporal process, knowing something seems more like an immediate state of being. While reading a sentence takes time, *understanding* the meaning of sentence seems to occur in a single instant. And so, at very least, a timeless being could know certain truths. In turn, willing something does not obviously take time. If a person can know the meaning of a sentence in a single instance, it also seems possible for a being in a single moment to *will* that something be true or will that something happen. Further, if God acts by willing that something occur, then it appears that a timeless deity could enact certain states of affairs in a singular moment simply by willing them. This is true even for events that occur over several temporal moments. It does not take any more time to understand or will the sentence "Let some world x exist for ten billion years" than it takes to understand or will the sentence "Let some world x exist for ten minutes." Each of these thoughts can be understood and willed instantaneously. Subsequently, it appears that a timeless being could know, will, and willfully act. In short, while being a different kind of person than we are, a timeless being seems capable of having key personal qualities.[16]

These insights are enhanced by considering the ontological relationship between timelessness and time proposed by Leftow. One may assert that in the singular moment of eternity God wills a host of events to occur at several temporal coordinates across time. Since all those temporal coordinates literally occur simultaneously in the eternal frame of reference, all the events divinely willed are willed and enacted in that singular eternal moment. Nevertheless, in various *temporal frames of reference*, these same events are not simultaneous; they unfold at different times. In short, a timeless person could act in the single moment of eternity and yet also affect diverse events across differing times. Unfortu-

---

[16]For similar considerations see R. L. Sturch, "The Problem of the Divine Eternity," *Religious Studies* 10 (1974), 487-493, Stump and Kretzmann, 446-447, Leftow, pp. 285-287, and Robinson, pp. 166-172.

nately, a deeper problem remains. Even if we grant that a timeless God could know, will, and willfully act, and could produce effects across diverse temporal moments, it is less clear that such a being could *interact* with other persons. To interact with another seems to require that one wait for the other individual to act and then *respond* or *react* to her. But this appears to be impossible for a timeless being. If God is timeless, all divine and creaturely actions occur simultaneously in a single eternal present. And so, there appears to be no opportunity for the deity to be affected by creatures *and then* to react to them. In short, a timeless God could not interpersonally interact.

Fortunately, these difficulties can be ameliorated if we postulate that God's eternal will is conditional, that God knows all possibilities, and that God timelessly is aware of what creatures do at each temporal moment across time. In this case, claims Leftow, one may speculate that eternally God wills a given divine response for every *possible* set of creaturely events. That is, the deity wills something like this: If x happens, then a will occur; if y happens, then b will occur, etc., for every possible circumstance. In turn, in timelessly knowing every event that in fact creatures perform throughout all times, God eternally wills (and thus enacts) a specific response to those acts. In this case, God's willing of a response to a possible event coupled with the divine knowledge of the actual occurrence of that creaturely activity combine to produce a specific divine response for that circumstance. Leftow cites the example of God sending a voice to Abraham not to slay Isaac in the event that Abraham should attempt to do so. In this case, the following three propositions eternally are true.

(1) Eternally, God wills all of His conditional intentions, among them an intention that if eternally, God knows that Abraham does act A, then eternally, God wills that event E occurs.

(2) Eternally, God knows that Abraham does A.

(3) Eternally, God wills that event E occurs.[17]

Proposition (3) logically depends on claims (1) and (2), even though the events described by all three happen simultaneously. As I have commented elsewhere on these matters: In this case,

> God's willing of conditional responses coupled with the actual actions that creatures perform in eternity is logically equivalent to God's actualizing responses to those creaturely events. God need not wait for Abraham to act to respond to Abraham's action. God may respond even as Abraham is acting, based on God's simultaneous conditional decrees that if Abraham act in a certain way, God will respond in a certain way.[18]

One might question whether this proposed scenario truly constitutes divine response. Does not response require temporal process? William Alston says no. While it may be impossible to have a response *prior* to an action to which one is reacting, there is logically nothing that forbids *simultaneous* response. Alston writes:

> Why should we suppose that the initiatory volition of the answerer must also be assigned a later date? Even with communication between human beings the fact that A's voluntary initiation of a reply to B's utterance always comes later than B's utterance is due to human limitation rather than to requirements imposed by the concept of a reply. Suppose that you emit a cry of despair and I offer consolation. As we are actually constituted I will not initiate my attempt at consolation until some finite time (however short) after your cry. But isn't that just due to our limitations? If I could be so closely tied to you as to apprehend your cry while you are in the act of producing it, and if I were able to offer my consolation (or at least do the most immediate part of this, the volition) at that very same moment of apprehension, would I not still be

---

[17]Leftow, p. 305.
[18]Robinson, p. 174.

responding to your cry? We can't actually bring this off, we can't respond that quickly, but that has no bearing on the concept of reply. I recognize that the concept prevents anything I do before X from being a reply to X, but simultaneity is ruled out only by human limitations. And if a response to X that is simultaneous with X, from the side of the respondent, is a conceptual possibility even for a human responder, we certainly can't rule out responses to human actions by a timeless deity on the grounds that none of His volitions temporally succeed any human actions.[19]

In light of Alston's and Leftow's argumentation, then, it seems possible to affirm that a timeless being indeed can engage in interpersonal interplay. God simultaneously can will a given response to a possible creaturely action, can be aware of the actual creaturely action, and thus implicitly can will the specific response to that action. A timeless deity simultaneously can be aware of prayers and respond to them, can be aware of natural circumstances and providentially react to them, etc. Further, while these events are simultaneous in the eternal frame of reference, they may be temporally diverse in various temporal frames of reference. In short, a timeless God can be personal and interpersonal.

Foreknowledge and Freedom

Beyond concerns over the conditional and timeless nature of God, a third critical tension faces the Arminian model of providence—namely, the alleged incompatibility of freedom and divine foreknowledge. As we have seen, Arminianism affirms libertarian freedom, the belief that in morally significant cases a person is able either to perform or refrain from performing some action. In turn, the traditional Arminian model affirms exhaustive divine foreknowledge. But as noted in chapters three and four a number of

---

[19]Alston, pp. 155-156.

authors across history have claimed that these two doctrines are incompatible. A particularly compelling argument against the compatibility of these doctrines is the following. Assuming that to know something is to know something that is the case, one may assert that

(1) Necessarily, if God knows that I will do A, then I will do A.

Further, supposing that God has complete foreknowledge and that God has had this knowledge sometime in the past, then one may assert that

(2) Accidentally necessarily, God knows that I will do A.

Further still, if we assume that necessity transfers from necessary propositions to propositions that are entailed by those necessary propositions, then it seems to follow that

(3) Therefore, accidentally necessarily, I will do A.

Now if we assert that

(4) If necessarily I will do A, then I will not do A freely.

Then, from (3) and (4), it deduces that
(5) I will not do A freely.

The argument appears to be valid. If its premises are true, it seems to prove that divine foreknowledge and libertarian freedom are mutually exclusive. Likewise, the traditional Arminian model seems to crumble.

Calvinists and open theists accede to the force of this incompatibility argument, the former denying that humans have libertarian freedom, the latter rejecting exhaustive divine foreknowledge. Traditional Arminians are unhappy with either of these options, preferring to deny the incompatibility of freedom and foreknowledge, and seeking logically to dismantle the argument. Several solutions have been proposed and a wide body of literature has arisen around the discussion. We cannot offer a comprehensive examination of this exchange. However, we will mention three notable replies. The first assumes that God is temporal, the third that God is timeless. The second suits either a temporal or atemporal deity.[20]

First, some writers–often called Ockhamists in honor of medieval theologian William of Ockham—deny premise (2) above. They deny that God's past beliefs about the future are accidentally necessary and contend that even though God is temporal and has beliefs in the past, the deity's past beliefs *about the future* are not accidentally necessary. Accidental necessity is a peculiar kind of necessity. The only reason an event is accidentally necessary is that it *has happened*; it is in the past. In light of this, claim Ockhamists, God's beliefs about the future can only be accidentally necessary if and when the future events divinely known actually occur. In other words, God's past beliefs about future events only become accidentally necessary when those events actualize in the future. Or to use vernacular common in the literature: God's past beliefs about the future are "soft facts" because they deal with future contingent events. They are not "hard facts" because their claims are not exclusively about the past. The Ockhamist move has the advantage of avoiding the problems associated with claiming that God is timeless. The chief weaknesses of Ockhamism are (1) the difficulty of clearly distinguishing between hard and soft facts and (2) the problem of explaining precisely how future events can affect God's past or present

---

[20]The reader may notice that I have not included a discussion of Molinism in this list of possible solutions to the foreknowledge-free will dilemma. The reason for this is that Molinism more or less *assumes* the compatibility of foreknowledge and freedom and does not attempt to show that the incompatibility argument fails. Molinism offers a view of divine knowledge that may permit a maximum level of divine control over the universe, short of direct divine causal determinism. But it does not directly show that foreknowledge and free will are compatible.

knowledge if God is temporal. The debate over these matters is extensive and I will not enter into it here, except to note that at this point I do not find the Ockhamist position persuasive.[21]   A second attempt to show that foreknowledge and freedom are compatible is to argue that the incompatibility argument confuses the causal relationship between divine foreknowledge and future contingent events. Various authors point out that there is something odd about the foreknowledge-free will argument. Imagine that some person P will perform an action A at some future time t. In turn, suppose that there are no circumstances prior to t which causally necessitate that P perform A. P at t is the determining cause of A. In other words, event A is freely enacted by P. Now imagine someone else S at t sees P doing A, but does not cause P to do A and does not even causally contribute to P doing A. In this case, it seems obvious that P still does A freely and that S's observing P does not negate P's freedom in performing A. At this point, the dilemma for the foreknowledge-free will argument arises: How can God's "observing" of P doing A possibly take away P's freedom? If God's knowledge is not the *cause* of P doing A, then how does the divine knowledge remove the freedom of P doing A?[22] The answer is unclear.   Early medieval theologian Origen was one of the first to notice and comment on this conundrum. He believed that those who challenge the compatibility of foreknowledge and freedom simply confuse the causal relationship that holds between divine foreknowledge and future events.

---

[21]For the Ockhamist view see William of Ockham, *God's Foreknowledge, and Future Contingents*, trans. Marilyn McCord Adams and Norman Kretzmann (Indianapolis: Hackett, 1983); Marilyn McCord Adams, "Is the Existence of God a 'Hard' Fact?" *The Philosophical Review* 76 (1967), 492-503; Alvin Plantinga, "On Ockham's Way Out," *Faith and Philosophy* 3 (July 1986), 235-269. For criticisms of this view see William Hasker, *God, Time, and Knowledge* (Ithaca: Cornell University Press, 1989), pp. 75-95.

[22]Here I am assuming, with Arminians and contrary to someone like Aquinas, that God's knowledge is not the cause of creaturely actions.

According to Origen, one must recognize that divine foreknowledge does not *cause* the future events that are known, rather the
events make possible God's knowledge of them.[23] Contemporary
author Bruce Reichenbach echoes Origen's sentiments when he
insists that the foreknowledge-free will argument confuses

> the order of causes (what brings something about) with the
> order of knowledge (the basis on which we know something).
> What God knows is the event itself. Thus, God will know that
> event if and only if the event occurs. That is, God will have a
> certain belief about an event occurring if and only if that event
> occurs. It is because (in a noncausal sense having to do with
> our knowledge) the event occurs that God believes it occurs.
> But then one cannot turn around and make the event depend on
> God's knowledge of the event, as the objector does when he
> says that God's foreknowledge determines, for foreknowledge
> depends on the event, and not vice versa.[24]

Advocates of the foreknowledge-free will argument are quick
to assert that appeal to causal relationships is irrelevant. The
foreknowledge-free will argument says nothing about causes. It
simply concludes that if God has foreknowledge then the actualization of the known future event is necessary! And if it is necessary,
then the event is not free in the libertarian sense. Jonathan
Edwards comments: "Whether prescience be the thing that *makes*
the event necessary or no, it alters not the case. Infallible foreknowledge may *prove* the necessity of the event foreknown, and

[23]Origen, *Contra Celsum*, trans. Henry Chadwick (Cambridge:
Cambridge University, 1953), 2.18-20.

[24]Bruce Reichenbach, "God Limits His Power," *Predestination &
Free Will: Four Views of Divine Sovereignty & Human Freedom by John
Feinberg, Norman Geisler, Bruce Reichenbach, Clark Pinnock*, ed. David
Basinger and Randall Basinger (Downers Grove: InterVarsity Press,
1986), p. 110.

yet not be the thing which *causes* the necessity."[25] In other words, no matter what causes the future event, genuine foreknowledge of the event makes it necessary and, therefore, denudes its freedom.

Edward's counter has considerable force. However, Katherin Rogers has rejuvenated discussion of these matters by arguing that causal relationships are the *critical issue* and indeed that necessity per se is irrelevant to the freedom of future events. Rogers insists that "[t]he key to freedom lies not in a literal and absolute ability to do otherwise but in *self*-generated choices which are not the inevitable products of factors, external or internal, beyond the agent's control."[26] And so, even though foreknowledge necessitates future actions of free agents, those actions are free because (1) there are no prior conditions that determine that the agent act as she does and (2) foreknowledge does not *causally* necessitate the event in question. Indeed, foreknowledge *cannot* causally necessitate a future event because foreknowledge itself is caused by (or at least made possible by) the event itself. Rogers concludes:

> The sort of necessity entailed by divine omniscience does not conflict with libertarian freedom. If I choose A at t, then God knows eternally that I choose A at t. And if God knows eternally that I choose A at t, I cannot fail to choose A at t. Necessarily I choose A at t. But it is my choice that is the source of the necessitating knowledge. In the very act of choosing I make it impossible that I could choose other than I do choose, but this would be true with or without an omniscient God. I cannot, after all, choose both A and not-A in the same

---

[25]Jonathon Edwards, *The Works of Jonathan Edwards*, vol. 1, *Freedom of the Will*, ed. Paul Ramsey (New Haven: Yale University Press, 1957), p. 263.

[26]Katherin Rogers, "Omniscience, Eternity, and Freedom," *International Philosophical Quarterly* 26 (1996), 412. Brackets are mine.

way at the same time.[27]

Another way we might express Rogers' point is to say that while it is true that "Necessarily if I am sitting, I am sitting," it need not follow that "While I am sitting, I necessarily am sitting." In other words, it is coherent to claim that "Necessarily, while I am freely sitting, I am freely sitting." Such necessity does not seem to take away freedom. In a similar manner, it is not clear that the necessity that foreknowledge implies for future events truncates the freedom of those actions.

Rogers applies her reasoning explicitly to divine timeless knowledge. In a moment we will consider how her argumentation interfaces with divine timeless knowledge. However, let us note here that Rogers' reasoning also may work for affirming the compatibility of freedom with a temporal deity's foreknowledge. It simply is not clear why the kind of necessity implied by the foreknowledge-free will argument dissolves the freedom of the future actions at issue, particularly if Rogers is correct in asserting that the critical issue is the causal history leading up to the future event and not necessity per se.[28]

A third reply to the foreknowledge-free will dilemma is to appeal to divine timelessness. As noted in chapter four, Boethius argued that the deity exists outside of time in a static eternal instant. Consequently, God experiences all temporal moments at once, in a single, unchanging eternal moment. God does not know events as they are going to happen in the future, but knows them as they are happening in the divine eternal perspective. According to Boethius, since knowledge of present events does not causally necessitate those present events, neither does God's timeless knowledge of future events causally necessitate them. Boethius

---

[27]Ibid.

[28]Rogers rejects temporal divine foreknowledge for some of the same reasons cited above against Ockhamism, namely it is hard to discern how a temporal being could have knowledge of a future event if that future event literally does not yet exist. Ibid., 401.

concluded that divine timeless foreknowledge does not negate creaturely freedom.[29]

Formally, Boethius' appeal to divine timelessness defeats the incompatibility argument. Premise (2) of the incompatibility argument above assumes that it is now necessary that God knows some future event A because God's knowledge is in the past; God's belief is now accidently necessary. But if God is not in time, not in the past, his beliefs are not in the past and so premise (2) is incorrect. It is not the case that (accidentally) necessarily God knows that A will happen. Subsequently, the incompatibility argument fails.

Appeal to divine timelessness, however, faces challenges. Even if we assume (as argued above) that divine timelessness is an intelligible concept and that a timeless being could be personal and interpersonal, some believe that timelessness does not solve the foreknowledge-freedom dilemma because it leads to its own form of determinism. Alvin Plantinga offers one example of such argumentation. He insists that even though the appeal to divine timelessness allows one to deny that God's *knowledge or beliefs* are in the past and, therefore, enables a person to assert that God's beliefs are not accidentally necessary, it remains the case that *true statements* concerning God's eternal knowledge can be stated *in time*, and these declarations allow one to assert an argument like (1)-(3) above. Plantinga essentially argues that

  (1a) Logically necessarily, if *it is true* that God knows that I will do A, then I will do A.

  (2a) Accidentally necessarily, *it is true* that God knows that I will do A.

  (3) Therefore, accidentally necessarily, it is true that I will do A.

---

[29]Boethius, *The Consolation of Philosophy*, The Loeb Classical Library, trans. I. T., revised H. F. Stewart (Cambridge Massachusetts: Harvard University Press, 1918), 5.6.

Premise (1a) makes the common assumption that truth corresponds to reality, that if a statement is true then it somehow reflects the way things are. Premise (2a) assumes that if a statement were true in the past, then one now cannot change the fact that it *was* true. In other words, if a statement were true in the past, then its past truth now is accidentally necessary. In light of this, Plantinga insists that, unlike premise (2), proposition (2a) is not falsified by an appeal to divine timelessness. This is the case because one can make true statements *in time* about God's eternal knowledge. In another words, if yesterday one could correctly say that "God eternally knows that I will do A at some future time t," then today it is accidentally necessarily true that yesterday "God eternally knows that I will do A at some future time t." From (1a) and (2a), conclusion (3) seems to follow. Consequently, according to Plantinga, appeal to divine timelessness does not defeat the argument for the incompatibility of foreknowledge and freedom.

Ingenious as Plantinga's argument is, it is not altogether convincing. Linda Zagzebski has questioned whether truth is in the past, whether truth is accidentally necessary. *Events* actualize at certain times and, so, may be accidentally necessary once they occur, but truth per se does not actualize. In other words, accidental necessity applies to occurrences or events, not to truths proper. And so, claims Zagzebski, premise (2a) is incorrect. It is not now accidentally necessary that it is *true* that God knows that some future event will occur.[30]

William Hasker offers another criticism of Plantinga's reasoning. He notes that essentially Plantinga is asserting that

> in the past the statement "God eternally knows that I will do A at some future time t" expressed the claim that God knows eternally that I will do A at some future time t, and this claim is true.

---

[30]Linda Zagzebski, *The Dilemma of Freedom and Foreknowledge* (New York: Oxford University Press, 1991), p. 45.

In turn, notes Hasker, this assertion logically is equivalent to the conjunction

> (a) In the past, the statement "God eternally knows that I will do A at some future time t" expressed the claim that God knows eternally that I will do A at some future time t, and (b) God knows eternally that I will do A at some future time t.

Hasker points out, however, that while proposition (a) may be now accidentally necessary, it is irrelevant to whether the event in question is necessary. Rather, what is germane is whether proposition (b) is now accidentally necessary. And it simply is not clear that (b) is accidentally necessary. (b) seems to depend upon the future occurrence of A. Therefore, it cannot be accidentally necessary until A happens. In other words, while in the eternal frame of reference God's knowledge of event A is concurrent with all events of the past, present, and future, in our temporal frame of reference, God's knowledge of event A is still in the future! It is simultaneous with and dependent upon the actualization of A, which is still future to us. Subsequently, God's knowledge, like event A itself, is not accidentally necessary. In our frame of reference, the divine knowledge is still future.[31] Again, Plantinga's argument fails.

A second objection to divine timelessness as a solution to the foreknowledge-free will dilemma is proposed by Linda Zagzebski. Zagzebski argues that even if divine timelessness allows one to deny that foreknowledge destroys freedom in time, it still may truncate freedom in timeless-eternity. Zagzebski writes:

> But what can be more fixed than eternity? Both ontologically and modally the realm of eternity seems to be much more like the realm of the past than of the future. It is ontologically real, like the past and unlike the future, and if *p* is some proposition about a timeless state of affairs, it is not very likely that there exists (timelessly) a potency for *not p* . . . . Ockham connected

---

[31] Hasker, *God, Time, and Knowledge*, pp. 173-176.

his doctrine of the necessity of the past with the fact that the past has lost potency for being otherwise. So the reason used by Ockham for maintaining the necessity of the past seems to apply equally well to the eternal realm . . . . It seems as if there is nothing I can do about those beliefs that are now irrevocable, and eternal beliefs seem to be just as irrevocable as past ones. If the commonsense view of time . . . leads us to think that it is now impossible that actual past events did not occur, surely what little we know about the nature of the timeless realm leads us to think that it is now impossible that actual timeless events do not occur timelessly. So just as the inalterability of God's past infallible belief about the future seems to lead to necessity in the future, by the same reasoning the inalterability of God's timeless infallible belief also seems to lead to necessity in the future.[32]

Zagzebski's point may be expressed in a couple of ways. First one might argue that *in eternity* all human events of all times are occurring simultaneously. This means, then, that while a person at t1 is contemplating doing actions x or y at some future time t2, that same person is also doing x at t2. But if this is the case, what use is there for the person at t1 to ponder whether to do x or y at t2 if she is already doing x (to the exclusion of y) at t2? In other words, in what sense is she free *in eternity* at t1 not to do x at t2? The answer appears to be that she is not free. Another way to express Zagzebski's point is to restate the foreknowledge-free will argument, this time assuming that God's knowledge is timeless. One may argue that

(1) Necessarily, if God knows that I will do A, then I will do A.

(2) Accidentally necessarily, God knows that I will do A.

(3) Therefore, accidentally necessarily, I will do A.

---

[32]Zagzebski, p. 60.

This argument is identical to the one given above and the critical premise remains (2). However, the reason for affirming (2) differs from the original argument. Instead of claiming that God's beliefs are *in the past* and thus accidentally necessary, one is asserting here that God's knowledge is *in eternity* and thus is accidentally necessary. In this case, that necessity transfers to conclusion (3). In short, accidentally necessarily I will do A.

At this point, Rogers' reasoning (from above) proves helpful for denying Zabzebski's line of reasoning concerning the incompatibility of divine eternal knowledge and freedom. If the causal history of an event is the critical issue in determining whether an event is free, then the sheer accidental necessity of the occurrence may not negate its freedom. It simply is not clear why some event at t2 is not free if it is being chosen by a person P at t2 and if no events prior to t2 determine that P perform that action. The incompatibilist is hard-pressed to show why freedom is negated in this situation. And Zagzebski's argument collapses.

A further consideration may be voiced. As we have seen in our discussion of the relationship between time and eternity, one may assert that the actualization of events is relative to frames of reference. And so, events that are simultaneously actualized in one frame of reference need not be simultaneously actualized in another frame of reference. In this case, one may argue that even if events of all temporal coordinates are actual and thus accidentally necessary in eternity, they need not be (indeed are not all) actual and accidentally necessary in various *temporal* frames of reference. In other words, even if there is a kind of determinism in eternity due to the fact that all events of all times are already actualized there, it need not follow that such determinism exists in time where events are not all actualized simultaneously. Again, Zagzebski's argument misfires.

I conclude, then, that divine foreknowledge and free will are compatible. This is the case even if God's knowledge is temporal but especially the case if we assume that God and the divine knowledge are timeless.

Providential Control and Foreknowledge

A final difficulty facing the Arminian model of divine providence concerns God's plan for and providential control over creation. As we saw in chapter three, Calvinists insist that the Arminian model does not allow God to articulate a meticulous plan for creation nor sufficiently to control nature. Arminian Jack Cottrell has responded by claiming that God's foreknowledge allows for an exhaustive providential plan and for complete divine control of the created order. According to Cottrell, via foreknowledge God can choose what future events he will permit and which ones he will not allow. Further, through foreknowledge the deity can anticipate his own responses to future creaturely actions and, thus, can know of the ultimate achievement of divine goals. Open theists, however, have counter-charged that simple foreknowledge cannot be used in this manner. In particular, it cannot be employed to decide which events to permit and which to deny. If God knows now what the future will be, there is no way to change it, to permit it or disallow it. It simply will be as God foresees it. In short, according to open theists, simple foreknowledge is useless for divine providence. In turn, if open theists are correct, it seems to follow that Cottrell's response to Calvinists fails and the Calvinistic charge returns—namely that under the Arminian system, God cannot have a meticulous plan for creation nor truly govern the flow of creation-history. How might an Arminian answer such accusations?

We may begin by conceding the basic point made by open theists that foreknowledge *per se* offers little aid for divine providence. Certainly, God cannot use knowledge of what will be to prevent or allow what will be. If God knows that x in fact will occur, the deity cannot prevent x; or if God knows that x in fact will not occur, then God cannot somehow allow it. It simply will happen or fail to happen as God foresees it. And so, Cottrell's response to Calvinism falls short. However, there may be other means by which an Arminian might construct a strong view of the divine plan and providence. Two methods come to mind. Before discussing them, however, we need to exclude from the mix one possible theory of divine control. This is the Calvinistic notion of divine foreordination. Certainly, if God decrees every event to happen in a certain way, then God retains absolute and exhaustive control of the natural order. But as we have seen, such determinism leads to intractable problems for Christian theism, including human moral insignificance, God's culpability for sin and injustice toward humans.

Middle Knowledge

For Arminians, there are more tenable mechanisms by which divine control might be exercised. The first is middle knowledge. Middle knowledge is a theory about divine knowledge and providence developed by late medieval/early enlightenment theologian Louis de Molina (1535-1600).[33] Molina proposed that there are three types of divine knowledge that play an important role in providence. First there is divine natural knowl-

---

[33]Luis De Molina, *On Divine Foreknowledge (Part IV of the Concordia)*, trans. Alfred Freddoso (Ithaca: Cornell University Press, 1988). A variety of contemporary writers endorse middle knowledge. See Alfred Freddoso, "Introduction," ibid., pp. 1-81; Alvin Plantinga, *The Nature of Necessity* (Oxford: Oxford University Press, 1974), especially chapter 9; Jonathan Kvanvig, *The Possibility of an All-Knowing God* (New York: St. Martin's Press, 1986); William Craig, *The Only Wise God* (Grand Rapids: Baker Publishing House, 1987) and *Divine Foreknowledge and Human Freedom: The Coherence of Theism: Omniscience* (Leiden: E. J. Brill, 1991), especially chapter 13; and Thomas Flint, *Divine Providence: The Molinist Account* (Ithaca: Cornell University Press, 1998). Adversaries of Molinism include Reginald Garrigou-Lagrange, *The One God*, trans. Dom. Bede Rose (St. Louis: B. Herder, 1944); Robert Adams, "Middle Knowledge and the Problem of Evil," *American Philosophical Quarterly* 14 (1977), 109-11; Hasker, *God, Time, and Knowledge,* especially chapter 2; and Zagzebski, especially chapter 5.

edge–knowledge of all logical necessities and possibilities. With this knowledge God knows all metaphysical necessities. These are propositions that are true at all times in every possible world.[34] The deity also knows every event that possibly *could* happen in every possible world. Natural knowledge is a cognizance independent of the divine will. It is information that God simply has logically prior to any divine volition. A second form of divine knowledge is free knowledge. This is God's comprehension of what in fact happens in the actual (and not merely possible) world throughout all time. It concerns contingent events, occurrences that did not (logically necessarily) have to happen, but that in fact do happen. This knowledge is based on the divine will. Actual events occur because God (efficaciously or permissively) wills them, and in willing them the deity knows of their occurrence.

Between these two forms of divine knowledge is a third, namely, middle knowledge. This is God's awareness of what *would* happen in every conceivable circumstance. Unlike natural knowledge which is an awareness of what *could* or *might* happen if a particular set of antecedent circumstance were to obtain, middle knowledge is a cognizance of what in fact *would* happen if a specific set of antecedent circumstances were to occur. An example may help. Presumably, prior to creation, through natural knowledge God would know something like this:

> (1) If offered thirty pieces of silver at time T, Judas freely might or might not betray Christ.

But through middle knowledge, the deity further would know:

> (2) If offered thirty pieces of silver at time T, Judas freely *would* betray Christ.

That is, not only would God know what Judas *could* do freely, but what in fact he freely *would do*. Like natural knowledge and

---

[34]Freddoso, p. 11.

unlike free knowledge, middle knowledge is pre-volitional. It is information that God has logically before exercising the divine will. Indeed, based on middle knowledge God makes certain wise providential choices. On the other hand, like free knowledge and unlike natural knowledge, middle knowledge deals with contingent events. Such events are not logically necessary. Rather they are conditioned by God's free decision to create a world of a certain type and by creatures' choices to act certain ways under given circumstances. Nothing internal nor external to Judas, nothing in the prior history of the world up to that point, necessitates his action.[35] Rather, it simply is the case that in those circumstances, Judas freely would choose to betray Christ.

According to Molina and his followers, through these three types of knowledge, divine providence can be explained–a providence that allows for complete divine control and yet also for human freedom and responsibility. To see this, consider the following scenario. Imagine that God is considering whether or not to create a universe. Assume that events in whatever universe God creates will be temporally related. Presumably through natural knowledge God would know something like this:

(3) If I create a universe in an initial state A at T1, then at T2 events x, y, or z will happen.

In turn, through natural knowledge, God would comprehend those events that could follow in each subsequent moment from that initial state, in times T3, T4, T5, etc. And so, God knows:

(4) If event x occurs at T2, then events a, b, or c will occur at T3.

(5) If event y occurs at T2, then events l, m, or n will occur at T3.

---

[35]Ibid., p. 16.

Etc.

In short, God would discern the entire possible history that *could* emerge from that initial universe state. Further, God would know this for every possible initial universe state. And so, God discerns every possible history for every possible initial universe.

Now admittedly, such information would be vast, but not particularly precise. God would know everything that *could* happen throughout the history of each possible universe, but the deity would not know what particular events in fact *would* happen throughout these histories. And here the importance of middle knowledge emerges. Through middle knowledge, not only would God grasp what might happen at T2 if he were to create initial universe A, but also what *would* happen if A were to obtain. And so, God would know something like this:

(6) If I create a universe in an initial state A at T1, then at T2 event x will happen.

In turn, God also would comprehend what *would* happen at T3, T4, T5, etc. That is, God would know the entire history that would flow from initial universe A. Further, God would discern the conditional histories of all possible initial universe states. God would know not only what could happen in each universe, but what would happen, if such a universe were created. Included among the conditional statements known by God for each universe are statements concerning the actions of free creatures, including, for example, the conditional acts of Judas.

Equipped with this finely tuned awareness of what would happen if he were to create a given initial universe, the deity is able to pick which universe—along with its entire history—that he wants to generate. This is where divine free knowledge comes into play. By freely choosing one initial universe, God effectively and freely wills an entire creation-history. Through the divine choice of one initial universe, God knows precisely the entire history that will actualize.

Advantages. The theory of providence that arises from this scenario grants libertarian freedom to humans, but also allows God to have complete sovereignty and enables the divine plan to be exhaustively meticulous. On the one hand, creatures remain free because nothing internal nor external to them necessitates the actions that they engage. The various conditional statements about what creatures would do simply are true because that in fact is what they freely *would* choose to do. On the other hand, the deity remains sovereign. In selecting an initial world-condition, knowing fully what all creatures (including free ones) will do throughout the history of that universe, God determines the whole history of that world. Every detail is anticipated and efficaciously or permissively willed by the deity. Nothing surprises God and he remains in complete control. While God does not choose which conditional statements about creatures are true, God does use this information to determine which antecedent *conditions* to bring about and, thus, which consequential creaturely events will actualize. If God did not create the initial state of a universe, that world and its history simply would not actualize.

The theory of middle knowledge offers several advantages to Arminianism. First it avoids the difficulties faced by Cottrell's appeal to simple divine foreknowledge. As noted above, it is doubtful that foreknowledge alone affords God the ability to control the created order. The deity cannot disallow or allow an event that in fact will happen. By the time God knows that it will happen, it is "too late" to affect it. But with middle knowledge, God knows what the future will be if he generates certain conditions. And so, God exercises complete control over the future by controlling the antecedent conditions of that conditional future.[36] A second benefit of middle knowledge is that it ties divine foreknowledge more closely to the divine will, offering an explanation for God's prescience that is independent of some sort of direct perception of the future. With middle knowledge, the deity need not "experience" the future in order to know it. Instead, by comprehending all conditional truths and by freely deciding

---

[36]Ibid., p. 35.

what conditions will obtain, God knows all that will in fact unfold from those conditions.

A third attraction of middle knowledge is that it helps ameliorate the theistic problem of evil. Why does God permit human sin? Because the conditional truths known by God through middle knowledge are pre-volitional—that is, true logically before the exercise of the divine will–they limit what God can accomplish. If God wants creatures with genuine freedom, and if in every potential world where free creatures exist they in fact would sin, then the deity cannot make a world with free creature where sin does not occur. With natural knowledge, God might discern that it is logically possible for there to be a world where genuinely free creatures never sin. But with middle knowledge, perhaps God simply knows that in every universe with genuinely free creatures those creatures in fact would sin. And so, God had no choice: either create a world *without* genuine freedom or create a world with libertarian freedom where unfortunately sin will occur. In the divine wisdom and grace, perhaps God chose to create just such a universe.

Divine Passivity. In spite of its advantages, the theory of middle knowledge faces a number of challenges. First, various Thomistic writers have charged that Molina's theory implies passivity in God and that this runs counter to the divine aseity, simplicity and pure actuality. For these writers, God's knowledge and will must be the efficient cause of all events in the universe. God must not only permit humans to act as they choose; he must also generate the very act of will within them. Molinism, however, denies this, insisting that the acts of the human will are generated by the will itself and not efficaciously caused by God. Related to the charge of passivity is the claim that Molinism denies salvation by divine grace and teaches salvation by human works. Because Molina taught that God's grace is not irresistible and that humans under the divine gracious influence can reject or accept Christ, then attaining salvation ultimately is in the hands of humans rather than under divine control.

These charges echo the accusations of various Calvinists

against Arminianism, challenges to which we already have responded in this text. As we have argued, it simply is not clear that God cannot be conditioned at least in some ways by creatures. Further, it is not obvious that the affirmation that God's call is resistible genuinely contradicts salvation by grace.[37] Similar sentiments are tendered by patrons of Molinism. For example, William Craig writes:

> I do not see why the Christian theist should wish to adopt the view that God is the determining cause of everything that occurs or that he is impassible actuality . . . . More than that . . . the admission that God's grace is resistible would not seem to imply that God is therefore not the cause of a person's conversion. All that follows is that the cause is not efficacious so long as one refuses to allow it to act. One could maintain that the final, free consent of the human will is a necessary condition of salvation without holding that man thereby causes his own salvation, in the sense of being an efficient cause.[38]

Beyond this, however, as some defenders of Molinism point out, there is a strong sense in which the doctrine of middle knowledge is quite consistent with a robust understanding of divine control, even with predestination unto salvation and damnation. For even though the theory of middle knowledge holds that God's gracious inner influence upon humans does not inwardly determine their acceptance or rejection of salvation, still the degree of inner influence exercised is decided wholly by the deity. For example, God decides how much grace both Peter and Judas receive, and the amount or quality of influence need not be equal. Further, God ultimately decides under which conditions each individual will be placed, knowing through middle knowledge whether or not those conditions will result in that person's free acceptance or rejection of Christ. Subsequently, in a very real sense, God remains utterly

---

[37]See my discussion of these matters in the first section of this chapter and in chapter three.

[38]Craig, *Divine Foreknowledge and Human Freedom*, p. 271.

in control of the salvation and damnation of persons. It very well could be that under differing conditions, under differing degrees of divine influence, for example, Peter would have rejected and Judas would have accepted Christ. And it was in God's power to exact just those conditions.[39] Even Craig concedes the validity of this reasoning, although he qualifies it by insisting that the grace offered by God is always "sufficient" unto salvation, even if in fact the person does not capitulate to that grace.[40] Apparently Craig means that for a person who rejects Christ, the grace offered always makes it such that the individual freely *could* accept Christ even though in fact she *would* not do so under those conditions.

Grounding, Truth and Knowledge. At this point, the reader may feel that some sort of sleight of hand is being played by the Molinist. In what significant way does it make any difference to say that a person could choose a beneficial alternative, but certainly would not choose that option? In either case, in a strong sense, the persons in fact *could not* make the choice. We will return to this problem in a moment. Before doing so, however, we will consider another difficulty facing the theory of middle knowledge. This is the problem of grounding. What makes conditional future contingent propositions true and how might such conditionals be known?

The Molinist is committed to the notion that neither God nor creatures determine the truth of statements about conditional future contingents. God does not determine their truth because such propositions are said to be true prior to the exercise of the divine will. Indeed, allegedly God uses the independent truth of these propositions to aid him in making wise providential choices. In turn, actually existing creatures do not bring about the truth of these conditional statements because (1) such statements are supposedly true prior to the existence of any actual creatures and (2) many of these conditional statements concern "creatures" or "possible entities" that in fact *do not and never will exist*. But if

[39]Flint, *Divine Providence*, pp. 111-120. Also, Freddoso, pp. 64-66.
[40]Craig, *Divine Foreknowledge and Human Freedom*, p. 242.

neither God nor creatures make these statements true, what does? Critics conclude that such statements are not true, for they have no metaphysical grounding.[41]

The principal response by Molinists to this charge is to endorse the correspondence principle of truth–namely, that a proposition is true if it corresponds to reality. And so, according to Molinists, what makes a proposition like "If I were a better writer, I would publish more works" true is the fact that if I were a better writer, I would publish more works. And so, propositions about conditional future contingents are true if they correspond to the way things would be; they are false if they do not correspond to the ways things would be. If the critic should protest that such propositions are not grounded in reality because there is *no present* reality to which they correspond, the proponent of middle knowledge counters that it is not clear that there must be some *present* reality grounding the truth of claims. For example, consider the present truth of statements about the past. What currently grounds the truth of the following claim?

(7) In 1492, Columbus sailed the ocean blue.

Even though this proposition is currently true, it is not immediately obvious that any *present* state of affairs funds its truth. Rather, its truth seems to be founded on the fact that in the past a specific state of affairs obtained, namely, that in 1492 Columbus sailed the ocean blue. Or again, consider the truth of claims about contingent possibilities. What grounds the truth of the following statement?

(8) President George W. Bush might run for a second term in 2004.

---

[41]This seems to be the core criticism of certain Thomistic critics of Molinism and of contemporary antagonist Robert Adams. See Garrigou-Lagrange, *The One God* and Adams, "Middle Knowledge and the Problem of Evil."

Most persons would accept such a proposition as true. But what presently grounds the truth of such a claim?[42] Nothing currently actualized seems to ground the truth of this claim. Rather, its truth seems to be based on the fact that at some future, yet unrealized, time (2004) Bush could run again for president. In a similar manner, argues the Molinist, the grounding for the truth of statements about conditional future contingents is the fact that in the future if placed in a specific set of circumstances, a given entity *would* act a certain way. No further analysis is required. (Molinist make similar claims concerning statements about the non-conditional, or absolute, contingent future, such as "In 2004, Bush will run for a second term." If this claim is true, its truth is grounded in the fact that in 2004, Bush will run for a second term.) Molinists admit that their reasoning here is controversial, but insist that it is sufficient to show that the anti-Molinist case is not iron-clad.[43]

Further, the defenders of middle knowledge point out that it is a common intuition for many to believe that at least some conditional future contingent statements are true. For example, I am fairly confident that the following conditional statement is true.

(9) If tomorrow I were offered a substantial pay-increase for the job I currently do, I would accept it.

Notice that I believe that this statement prospectively and hypothetically is true. It is true both prior to the actualization of its antecedent and even if its antecedent never obtains. Even more, from the standpoint of retrospection, it seems to make perfect sense to claim that such a statement is true. If yesterday I claimed that (9) "If tomorrow I were offered a substantial pay-increase for the job I currently do, I would accept it," and if in fact today I were offered a substantial pay-increase and agreed to take it, then it makes complete sense today to claim that the conditional statement

---

[42]This text is being written prior to 2004.
[43]Freddoso, pp. 72-73; Flint, pp. 126-135; Craig, pp. 259-261.

which I made yesterday *was* true.[44] Again, Monlinists conclude that the anti-Molinist case against the truth of future conditional statements is not irrefutable.

But even if we grant the force of this Molinist counter-argument concerning the *truth* of conditional future contingent statements, the critic can dispute whether anyone, including God, could *know* the truth-values of such statements. By what means might the deity know these truths? Typical avenues of knowledge-acquisition appear to be closed. On the one hand, analytic-style reasoning does not provide this information. For example, knowing the (conceptualized or actualized) essence of a free creatures does not yield data concerning what in fact a free person would do in any given situation, but only what she might do. This is the case because Molinism assumes that such creatures have libertarian freedom which entails that in any given condition where a choice is genuinely free the agent could choose to perform or refrain from performing the action in question. On the other hand, the information alleged to be a part of middle knowledge does not seem to result from some sort of a direct awareness or perception-like cognizance of an actualized state of affairs. While many conditional contingents actualize at some point in the concrete world, most do not. And so, the divine middle knowledge cannot simply be an awareness of what actualizes. That is, middle knowledge is not like human empirical knowledge which depends on the actualization of the events that it knows. But if analytic and experiential analogies fail, divine middle knowledge seems to have no analogy to human cognition, and arguably this should evoke concern in its defenders.

Indeed, modern proponents of the theory admit consternation with this dilemma. For this reason contemporary Molinists, Craig and Flint, reject Molina's own solution to the problem. Molina proposed that God has a "supercomprehension" regarding created essences. This is an ability to know potential created beings so well that the deity discerns not only what flows necessarily or

---

[44]Freddoso, pp. 71-74.

possibly from a potential entity, but also what would flow from its essence in any given circumstance. Molina's fellow Jesuit and contemporary, Francisco Suarez, rejected Molina's proposal on the grounds that even an infinite mind cannot know that which is unknowable. Flint and Craig concur.[45]

Perhaps the best approach for Molinists on this score is to maintain that middle knowledge is innate to the deity; it is knowledge simply and inexplicably possessed by God. Following Suarez, Craig argues that perhaps God knows all true propositions, and since some conditional future contingent propositions are true, then the deity simply innately knows their truth-value.[46] The difficulty with such a maneuver is that it leaves the theory of divine middle knowledge rationally inexplicable and, subsequently, rationally unpersuasive to its opponents. To quote Katherin Rogers: In rational discourse, one hopes to discover "some sort of causal story for any given bit of knowledge and . . . such a story ought to involve somehow relating the knowledge of a proposition to the fact upon which the truth-value of the proposition depends."[47] Craig's proposal offers no such explanation. Instead, it relegates divine middle knowledge to the realm of "Impenetrable Mysteries."[48] For many, myself included, this makes affirmation of the doctrine of middle knowledge problematic. Even if conditional future contingent propositions are true, it is difficult to understand how the deity might know their truth-value.

Middle Knowledge and Human Freedom. A third problem confronting the doctrine of middle knowledge is that it arguably negates human freedom. As noted earlier, there is something

---

[45]See Craig, *Divine Foreknowledge and Human Freedom*, p. 268; and Flint, p. 56, n. 26.

[46]Craig, *Divine Foreknowledge and Human Freedom*, p. 268.

[47]Rogers, 400. Rogers is critiquing Craig's appeal to innatism in solving the problem of divine knowledge of absolute future contingents, but she applies the same criticism to his proposals concerning middle knowledge. See ibid., 403.

[48]Ibid., 401.

strange about the Molinist's claim that God places a person in a situation where she *could* choose between two options, but where in fact there is only one choice that she actually *would* make. If there really is only one option under any given circumstance, what sense does it make to say that under those conditions she *could* make a different choice? William Hasker offers an extended argument addressing these concerns. He contends that middle knowledge and genuine freedom are incompatible.[49] The core of his argument seems to be the following. Molinists concede that human agents do not actualize the truth of the various conditional future contingent proposition known by God prior to creation. This is the case because no human agent exists prior to creation so as to actualize the truth of those claims at that time. Further, many conditional future contingent statements deal with potential events and potential agents that never exist–events that only would exist if certain conditions were to obtain, but never actually eventuate. And so, the truths known by middle knowledge are not established by actually existing human agents. Subsequently, if from all eternity the proposition

(10) If Peter were in situation A, he would deny Christ.

were true, Peter himself does not actualize the truth of this claim. It is true prior to Peter's existence; it is true if Peter never exists; and it is true even if Peter exists but is never placed in those circumstances. In like manner, if proposition (10) is true from all eternity, then the following claim apparently is false.

(11) If Peter were in situation A, he would not deny Christ.

---

[49]William Hasker, "A Refutation of Middle Knowledge," *Nous* 20 (1986), 545-557 and *God, Time, and Knowledge*, pp. 39-52. Hasker's argument is quite complex. For the sake of expedience, I am offering the much simplified version of this reasoning presented by Freddoso, pp. 75-77. For a more extensive Molinist exposition of and reply to Hasker's argument, see Flint, pp. 138-158.

Again, Peter does not make this claim false. Indeed, it appears that Peter cannot make either of these propositions true or false. They are true independently of Peter's existence and actions. On the other hand, because they endorse libertarian freedom, Molinists also wish to maintain that even though Peter cannot cause (10) to be false or (11) to be true, he has it in his power to make either of the following statements true:

(12) In situation A, Peter denies Christ.

Or

(13) In situation A, Peter does not deny Christ.

That is, Peter is free to actualize either (12) or (13).

Now the problem with the Molinists position at this point is that proposition (13) seems to entail the truth of proposition (11). That is, necessarily, if (13) "in situation A, Peter does not deny Christ," is true then (11) "if Peter were in situation A, he would not deny Christ" is true.[50]   But if proposition (11) were false from all eternity, and if Peter cannot bring about the truth of (11), then it appears that Peter cannot make (13) true either since in order to make (13) true Peter must be able to make (11) true. Further, if God ordains that situation A obtains, and if Peter cannot make (13) true, then the apostle has only one choice, namely, to actualize (12). And if he has only one choice, his choice in that instance is not free. Hasker concludes that if conditional future contingent

---

[50]Freddoso's appeal to the truth of conditional future contingents based on retrospection seems to assume the validity of such an entailment. And so, he reasons that if one should claim yesterday that "if I were in situation x, I would do a," and if in turn today in situation x, I do a, then one would naturally conclude that the proposition was true. In other words, the truth about the actualization of the events in question seems to entail the truth of the conditional proposition about those same events. See Freddoso, pp. 71-74.

propositions about creatures are true, the creaturely actions described by those conditionals are not genuinely free.

Another way to express these misgivings about middle knowledge and freedom might be to say that divine middle knowledge limits God's natural knowledge of genuine possibilities. Consider the following argument. Assume that Peter's actions are free. It seems to be the case, then, that *prior* to their actualization (by Peter), the unactualized states of affairs described in propositions (12) and (13) are compatible with each of the following possibilities:

(14) If Peter were in situation A, he might deny Christ.

Or

(15) If Peter were in situation A, he might not deny Christ.

In other words, prior to the actualization of the events described in (12) and (13), propositions (14) and (15) are both true. Peter could deny Christ or refrain from denying Christ. But upon the obtaining of the states of affairs referenced in either (12) or (13), respectively either proposition (15) or (14) is rendered false. For example, if (12) "in situation A, Peter denies Christ" obtains, then it is false that (15) "if Peter were in situation A, he might not deny Christ." This follows from the notion of accidental necessity. It is impossible for an event not to be occurring while it is occurring. And so, once (12) is true, (15) cannot be true. It is no longer possible for Peter not to deny Christ if in fact he is denying Christ. To see this, let p stand for the claim that (12) "in situation A, Peter denies Christ." Upon the occurrence of the events referenced in (12), the following statement appears to be true:

(16) Accidentally necessarily p.

Now since the following equation is valid: $p = \sim(\sim p)$, then

(17) Accidentally necessarily $\sim(\sim p)$.

is true. Further, (15) above can be restated as follows:

(15*) Possibly, ~ p.

But if (17) is true, then (15*) is false. If it is now necessary that in situation A Peter denies Christ, then it is now not possible for Peter not to deny Christ. Analogous to this argument from accidental necessity, we may argue that middle knowledge implies that certain propositions about creaturely actualizations are now *logically necessary* and that this, in turn, implies that various propositions about possibilities are false. For example, as noted above, if per hypothesis proposition (11) were false from all eternity, and if Peter cannot bring about the truth of (11), then it appears that Peter cannot make (13) true since in order to make (13) true Peter must be able to make (11) true. Further, if God ordains the occurrence of situation A, and if Peter cannot make (13) true then he has only one choice, namely, to actualize (12). In other words, the falsehood of proposition (11) and the truth of proposition (10), when combined with certain divinely ordained conditions, render proposition (12) logically necessary. In turn, if (12) is logically necessary, then (15) must be false. Again, let p stand for the claim (12) that in situation A, Peter denies Christ. To say that this proposition is logically necessary is to assert that

(18) Logically necessarily, p.

And since p = ~(~p), the following claim also is true.

(19) Logically necessarily, ~ (~p).

But if (19) is true, then (15*) is false. If it is now logically necessary that in situation A Peter denies Christ, then it is now not possible for Peter not to deny Christ.

In effect, then, the divine middle knowledge narrows the content of the divine natural knowledge of possibilities. What initially appears to be possible is not. Only those "possibilities" compatible with true conditional future propositions (contingent and necessary) are in fact possible. For Molinists to deny this would be to reject their explicit claim that through middle knowledge God knows the future in meticulous detail by choosing an initial world-condition. Molinists (by implication) are declaring that the number of genuine possible futures is reduced to only one through divine middle knowledge and through God's ordaining of a specific initial world-condition. In other words, there is not a multitude of possible futures connected to an initial world-state but in fact only one possible future. On the other hand, in claiming this, Molinists also implicitly deny human freedom. In any given conditional situation, where God has determined the antecedent conditions, there in fact is only one possible consequent. This is not compatible with genuine freedom.[51]

Conclusion. Not surprisingly, Molinists are convinced neither by the argument that God could not know conditional future contingents nor by the claim that middle knowledge is incompatible with human freedom; indeed, they offer diverse

---

[51]The reader may detect a tension in my reasoning at this point. For earlier I argued that foreknowledge need not negate human freedom, that via timeless knowledge God can know the future as it happens and, therefore, know it as certain. But does not the certainty of these events in eternity limit the number of possibilities to only that set of events that in fact actualize in eternity? In one sense the answer is yes. Obviously, while some event is (eternally) occurring, it is not possible for it not to be (eternally) occurring. But there is a critical difference between the Molinist account and the appeal to timeless eternity. The distinction is that in the Molinist system conditional future contingent events are true prior to the acts of human beings. And so, likewise, the necessity of a person's future actions (which is entailed by the truth of those conditionals) also obtains prior to his or her actions. But with divine timeless knowledge, the situation is different. Human actions are not necessary prior to there occurrence, but only at the time of there happening. That is, they are necessary once they are occurring, but not before.

counter arguments against these assertions.[52] In some ways, the jury is still out on these discourses. Suffice it to say that if Molinists make a persuasive case in such matters, then the doctrine of middle knowledge offers Arminianism a useful tool for explaining divine providence, absent of divine causal determinism. Suffice it also to say that at this time I am not persuaded by the Molinist account.

The Conditional Will-Actual Foreknowledge Model

Even if appeal to middle knowledge fails, a second mechanism for conceptualizing divine control over creation is available to traditional Arminianism. For the sake of convenience we will call this the conditional will–actual future model of providence (hereafter, simply CW-AF). Similar to our discussion of divine timeless interaction with creatures, let us suppose that humans are able to make genuinely free choices (at least in many cases) but also that (1) God knows all possibilities, (2) God formulates potential divine reactions to each of these possibilities, (3) through timeless knowledge (or perhaps temporal foreknowledge) God directly knows which possibilities in fact actualize throughout time, and (4) in light of his knowledge of (2) and (3), God also decides and knows which responses he makes throughout all times. In this situation, one can assert that God has an exhaustive plan for and ultimate control over creation, without appealing either to divine foreordination or to middle knowledge, and without denying human freedom. To see this, let us analyze the CW-AF model further.

Propositions (1) and (2) above suggest that God has an exhaustive and meticulous plan for every possible world that he might create. Proposition (1) implies that God might know something like this:

---

[52]See especially, Flint's counter to Hasker's arguments, Flint, pp. 138-158.

(5) If I create world W1 at time T1, then at T2 events A, B, or C will follow.

(6) If I create world W2 at time T1, then at T2 events D, E, or F will follow.

Etc.

In turn, for each of the possible events listed in the consequents of (5) and (6) God also will know the possible events that could flow from them. And so, for example, God would know that

(7) If A at T2, then at T3 events l, m, or n, will occur.

(8) If B at T2, then at T3 events x, y, or z will occur.

Etc.

Although impossible for a finite mind, such an analysis presumably could be played out infinitely and exhaustively by an infinite, divine mind.

In turn, proposition (2) implies that for each possibility, God could envision a potential divine response. And so, God might will conditional decrees something like this:

(9) If A at T2, then at T3 I will do α.

(10) If B at T2, then at T3 I will do β.

Etc.

God's reactions in (9) and (10) may be as unintrusive as permitting the whole set of possibilities that flow from A or B, or they may comprise a more restrictive decree that permits only one of the possibilities that could flow from A or B. For example, in the former case God might decree that

(9a) If A at T2, then at T3 either l, m, or n will be permitted.

In the latter case, God might decree that

(9b) If A at T2 then at T3 only l (but not m or n) will be permitted.

Further, in circumstances like (9b), God would have diverse options available for obtaining the occurrence of l but not m or n. In cases were the created order simply, freely, "naturally," produces l, God need only allow it to do so—permit it, sustain it in its action. On the other hand, where the created order might be inclined to produce m or n, God simply could dictate/determine that it do l. Such divine actions would truncate freedom in those instances and presumably would be rare in a universe where God intends for the created order (especially humans) to be morally free. Still these activities would be an option for divine control.

This type of divine intentionality could be delineated for every possibility of every possible created world. Presumably, through such planning God would know how the divine objectives *could be* accomplished in every possible created world. This would produce a plan that would be utterly *meticulous and particular* in the sense that it would detail every possible divine reaction for every possible creaturely event, and it would envision divine victory (as appraised by God) for every possible world. On the other hand, such a scheme would be quite *general* in the sense that through it God would not know how *in fact* he would accomplish his goals, only that eventually through one course or another he would achieve them.

It is here that the significance of proposition (3) emerges. For when combined with claims (1) and (2), proposition (3) implies that God knows not only how he *could* accomplish the divine goals, but also how he in fact does (will) achieve them. In knowing what possibilities in fact actualize for each temporal moment, God knows which divine reactions to perform at each subsequent temporal moment and, consequently, knows how the divine plan in fact is accomplished. For example, if God eternally wills that

    (9) If A at T2, then at T3 I will do α.

    (10) If B at T2, then at T3 I will do β.

And if God eternally knows that

    (11) A at T2.

Then God also knows that

    (12) At T3 I will do α.

If God and his knowledge are timeless, then the divine awareness of (9), (11), and (12) are simultaneous in the single moment of eternity. However, the truth and actualization of (12) depend on the truth and actualization of (9) and (11). (12) would not actualize without (9) and (11). In turn, a similar situation holds for a temporal deity with foreknowledge. In this case, at all times God knows (9), (11), and (12), but (12) remains logically and causally dependent upon (9) and (11). In principle, this process could be applied to a full series of divine conditional intentions and to the divine awareness of actualized events throughout all times. Consequently, through such a mechanism God would know not only how he *could* achieve the divine goals in all possible created worlds, but also how in fact he does (eternally) or will (temporally) accomplish these ends.

    Observations. Several observations may be made at this point. First, this model of divine control assumes that God can be and is affected by creatures, a point for which I argued in the first section of this chapter. Second, this paradigm allows for and assumes human libertarian freedom and responsibility. God's knowledge of future events is not the result of divine causal determinism of creaturely events. The deity's awareness of these events must be a kind of direct intuitive cognizance. Third, this model is analogous to the perspective proposed by some open theists. For example, Richard Rice contends:

> In addition to the precise range of options available to His creatures and the likely choices they will make, God is also aware of His own potential responses to each creaturely decision. He can envision a course of action appropriate to every conceivable situation (see Jer. 18:7-10). So there is no possibility of God's being caught by surprise by any development in the creaturely world. He will never find Himself at a loss to meet a situation . . . . [T]his enables God to maintain ultimate sovereignty over the world, even though His control over the actual course of events is not absolute since it allows for creaturely freedom.[53]

The chief difference between Rice's version of divine providential control and the one proposed here is that while his theory requires that God wait for time to unfold in order to know which set of creaturely events and divine reactions actually accomplish the divine goals, the CW-AF theory allows God timelessly (or in all times through temporal foreknowledge) to be aware of that set of creaturely and divine events which in fact achieve the divine ends. In other words, in Rice's version God only knows that somehow he will accomplish the overarching divine goals not how this will occur (at least not until time unfolds). In the CW-AF model, God knows both that he somehow will achieve his goals **and** how in fact he does so.[54]

A fourth observation concerning this model of providence is that while it appeals to divine knowledge of future events, it does not claim that God uses knowledge of events that occur in later

[53]Richard Rice, *God's Foreknowledge and Man's Free Will* (Minneapolis: Bethany House Publishers, 1980), p. 57.

[54]This model of providence is suggested by Brian Leftow's remarks concerning divine interaction with creatures. See Leftow, p. 305. It also is hinted at by David Hunt in "Divine Providence and Simple Foreknowledge," *Faith and Philosophy* 10 (1993), 412.

temporal instances to determine how to act in earlier temporal moments. For example, God does not decree something like the following, where T2 is earlier than T3.

(13) If event A occurs at T3, then at T2 I will do x.

In chapter seven we will consider the feasibility of God carrying out such a divine intention. But for now, let us maintain that God's conditional intentions–mentioned in proposition (2)–always involve an event that occurs *before* (in a prior temporal coordinate) the divine reaction to it. This assumption makes our model even more like Rice's perspective. Because Rice assumes that God is temporal, that God does not have foreknowledge, and that the past cannot be altered, the deity's conditional intentions presumably cannot involve God willing that an event in an earlier temporal instant occur *because of* the actualization of an event at some later temporal point. By the time the later event occurs *and* is known by God, it is too late to change events in earlier moments, events in the past. In a similar manner, the model that I have proposed assumes that God does not act in earlier temporal moments in reaction to events of later temporal instances.

Criticisms and Replies. Assuming the initial plausibility of the CW-AF model, several critical puzzles remain. First, what is the advantage of this theory over the one proposed by Rice? As already noted, the CW-AF model strongly resembles Rice's view of God's providential control, with the exception that the CW-AF model affirms either divine timeless knowledge or temporal foreknowledge. In turn, this allows God to know not only that somehow he will accomplish his goals, but also precisely how (and when) he will execute them. But why is this important? After all, in each model God's knowledge and subsequent actions depend on creaturely deeds. Therefore, in each God's knowledge is a kind of acquired knowledge–a knowledge based on the activities of others. Further, neither model offers more divine control than the other. In both, the mechanism of control essentially is the same: God envisions all possibilities, imagines potential divine responses to each possibility, "waits" for creatures to act in those instances where he has granted freedom, and "then" responds to them. Admittedly, the divine wait for creatures to act is not terribly long in timeless eternity. It is simultaneous with all other events, including God's reaction to them. Still the degree of concrete risk appears to be the same. For example: If an individual should opt to disobey rather than obey God at some time T, and if the deity should conditionally will that that person will be permitted either to obey or not obey at T, the risk is no greater if these events occur in a temporal or atemporal frame of reference. If God prefers that the individual obey him at T, the deity will still be disappointed over the action of the person. And so, what advantage does the CW-AF model offer?

Several benefits may be noted. One is that this model extends to God the greatest amount of knowledge possible over the greatest amount of time. In Rice's theory, God only knows how the divine goals are accomplished once history has unfolded. And so, God is ignorant of certain facts for great lengths of time. But in the CW-AF model God is never ignorant of these facts. If God has temporal foreknowledge, God always knows (in all times) how the divine goals will be achieved. If God is timeless, God timelessly knows (in the single moment of eternity) how the divine goals will be realized. In each case, the deity is never ignorant of these facts. This may be important if God is to be understood as the greatest possible being, which presumably includes having the greatest possible knowledge.

Another advantage of the CW-AF model is that it allows one to advocate a version of individual predestination. Arminius explained divine predestination in terms of God's conditional decree that those who believe in Christ will be saved. When combined with divine foreknowledge (or timeless knowledge) of who in fact will turn to Christ, this decree entails a complete awareness of which individuals will be saved (and not saved).[55] In the Rice-formula, God does not know the specific individuals who are saved. God only knows that those who believe will be saved. Which specific individuals will believe, or even whether any at all will turn to Christ, God cannot know until time unfolds. Now this would not be particularly important if it were not for various scriptures that at least suggest that God predestines specific individuals, as is intimated by passages such as Romans 8:29. The CW-AF models allows an Arminian to affirm an individual-specific understanding of conditional predestination.

A final and perhaps most portentous benefit of the CW-AF model of divine control is that it enables God to know of his own necessary existence and nature; and this, in turn, allows the deity to know of his own future sovereignty. As argued in chapter four, a divine being without timeless knowledge or foreknowledge could not know of his own necessary existence or necessary nature. In turn, this would hamper God from knowing of his own sovereignty into the future. But a God with timeless knowledge or complete foreknowledge would be aware that he always will exist and always will have the attributes that he has; and so, such a deity would know of his own sovereignty into the future. Now all of this leads to debilitating consequences for Rice's theory. Earlier we conceded that in Rice's model of divine control, in knowing all possibilities and in imagining potential reactions to each possibility, God could know that somehow he would achieve the divine goals. God would know this even though he could not know precisely how he would do so. We must now retract this concession. Since Rice's theory denies that God has timeless knowledge and complete foreknowledge, his model prevents God from knowing of the divine necessary existence, necessary nature, or future sovereignty. And this, in turn, prohibits God from knowing

---

[55]See James Ariminius, "A Declaration of the Sentiments of Arminius," *The Works of James Arminius*, vol. 1, trans. James Nichols, The Master Christian Library, version 6 [CD-ROM] (Albany, Oregon: AGES Software, 1997), pp. 213-214.

not only how he will accomplish the divine ends but also whether he can achieve them at all. Consequently, the CW-AF model is superior to Rice's theory not only because it enables the deity to know how he will complete the divine goals, but also because it allows God to know that he can accomplish those ends! This is a momentous advantage, indeed.

We turn to a second puzzle facing the CW-AF model. Even if the theory holds considerable advantages over Rice's formula, one may question whether it offers genuine divine control over the created order. A Calvinist might wonder if in fact such a theory is nothing more than a declaration that God accedes to whatever creatures choose to do. For example, Millard Erickson notes that the Arminian view of predestination implies that salvation is a divine capitulation to human choice.[56] There is some truth to this charge. If God creates genuinely free creatures and if the choices these beings make play a significant role in both their own salvation and in the outworking of God's plans on earth, then a certain degree of divine concession to humans is implied. Nevertheless, a couple of important factors assuage this problem. First, whatever capitulating to humans God endures is a self-chosen surrender. According to the CW-AF model, the divine will dictates whether and to whom God acquiesces. God need not surrender to anything, but he freely chooses to do so. Further, in this model, creaturely endeavors ultimately remain the product of the divine will and action. It is the divine will that sustains creaturely existence and activities at any given moment, so that without God's consent creatures would neither exist nor be able to act as they do. When the deity "capitulates," he does so freely and remains in ultimate control.

This brings us to a third and perhaps most troublesome puzzle for the CW-AF model. As noted above, this theory asserts that (2) God imagines a potential divine response for every possible creaturely state of affairs, and (3) that God's timeless knowledge

---

[56]Millard Erickson, *Christian Theology* (Grand Rapids: Baker Book House, 1988), p. 355.

or foreknowledge enables the deity to know precisely which set of possible states of affairs will actualize. In turn, allegedly (2) and (3) together allow (4) God to decide which divine reactions in fact to actualize—thus, granting to God an awareness of both how he *could* bring about the divine aims and how *in fact* he does so (or will do so). But at this point open theists (and maybe others) might complain that this model involves an unacceptable logical and perhaps causal loop. For the decisions made in proposition (4) appear already to be known in proposition (3). That is, knowledge of (4) how God *reacts* to creatures in the future is implied in (3) God's exhaustive knowledge of the future. But if this is the case, it is redundant to claim that (4) God decides how to react through knowing (2) and (3), if in knowing (3) alone, the deity already knows how in fact (4) he decides to react. It seems that by the time (4) God chooses to react to creatures, he already is (3) reacting to them or (if God has temporal foreknowledge) already is aware that he will react in that specific way! Although not articulated in the context of the CW-AF model, this seems to be the fundamental criticism offered by open theists against the utility of foreknowledge for providence. As Hasker states: "if we could foresee *everything*, then for us, as for God, it would be too late to do anything about it."[57]

How might the defender of the CW-AF model reply to this difficulty? We may begin by noting that there are different events known by the divine (timeless or temporal) foreknowledge. For the sake of simplicity, we may break down God's foreknowledge into two parts: (3a) divine knowledge of *creaturely actions* and (3b) divine knowledge of *divine reactions* to creatures. Next we may point out that the logical grounding of God's knowledge of these events varies. Presumably, the grounding of God's knowledge of creaturely affairs is the occurrence of those events, and the foundation of God's knowledge of divine reactions is the actualization of those divine deeds. In light of all this, it seems possible to assert that (4) God's decision to react a certain way depends on (2)

---

[57]Hasker, *God, Time, and Knowledge*, p. 62.

the divine conditional will and (3a) the deity's awareness of certain creaturely actions. But (4) God's decision to react does not depend on (3b) God's awareness of how he will react. Indeed, on the contrary, (3b) God's awareness of the divine reaction depends on (4) the divine decision so to react (and on the actual reaction itself). Direct contradiction is avoided if one splits divine foreknowledge (3) into its diverse parts (3a) and (3b). Whereas (4) depends on (3a), it does not depend on (3b). And interestingly enough, (3b) depends on (3a) and (4).

In timeless eternity, all of the events mentioned above would occur simultaneously. That is, (3a) God's awareness of creaturely actions would be simultaneous both with (4) the divine decision to react a certain way and with (3b) the divine cognizance of the deity's own reactions. The situation would be slightly different for divine temporal foreknowledge. In this case, God's awareness of (3a) would be simultaneous with (3b), but not necessarily simultaneous with (4). That is, (3a) God's awareness of creaturely events would be simultaneous with (3b) God's knowledge of how he will react to creature, but not necessarily simultaneous with (4) God's decision to react a certain way (or the divine *reaction* itself). Presumably, a temporal deity with foreknowledge will know at all times (3a) creaturely actions of all times and (3b) divine reactions of all times to those creaturely states of affairs, but such a God would not always *be reacting* to creaturely states of affairs in all times. Despite these differences between timeless and temporal foreknowledge, the logical and causal relationships between (3a), (3b) and (4) would be the same in each situation. (4) would depend on (3a), but not on (3b). And (3b) would depend on (4).

The detractor may wonder whether all of this is possible. Can (4) depend on (3a) if in fact (3b) is simultaneous with (3a) and if (3b) depends on (4)? That is, can (4) God's reaction to creatures depend on (3a) God's knowledge of creaturely actions if in fact (3b) God's knowledge of the divine reactions is simultaneous with (3a), and if (3b) depends on (4)? I see no reason why it cannot. First, we may note that there is no reason why (4) God's reaction cannot depend on (3a) the divine knowledge of creaturely events, even if (3a) is simultaneous with (3b) God's knowledge of his own reactions. To see this consider the following argument.

(14) If A at T1, then I will do a at T2.

(15) A at T1 and I will do a at T2.

(16) Therefore, I will do a at T2.

(16) follows from (14) and (15), even though "I will do a at T2" is conjoined to "A at T1" in (15). And this is the case whether (3a) and (3b) occur before or simultaneously with (4).

Second, we may consider whether (3b) can depend on (4). Here the matter is trickier, but not unmanageable. In timeless eternity, there seems to be no reason why (3b) cannot depend on (4). Each event (or set of events) is simultaneous with the other. And since it is possible for someone to know something while it is happening, there is no clear reason why God cannot (3b) know of the divine reaction to some creaturely event while (4) that reaction is occurring. Further, since it is possible for one event to depend on another even though each is occurring simultaneously, there again is no reason (3b) cannot depend on (4). Consequently, assuming that God's knowledge is timeless, there is no particular problem in claiming that (3b) depends on (4).

But what if God has *temporal* foreknowledge? Can (3b) depend on (4)? That is, can (3b) God's knowledge of his future reactions depend on (4) the future actualization of those reactions? Obviously, this would be impossible if future events cannot affect the past, if future events cannot affect the divine present or past knowledge. But if this were the case, there would be no sense in asking if (3b) can depend on (4) for a God *with temporal foreknowledge*, since from the start the possibility of temporal foreknowledge would be denied. On the other hand, if we grant the possibility of temporal foreknowledge, the possibility of some sort of backward causal influence of the future upon the past, then there is no clear reason to deny that (3b) can be affected by (4). Indeed, such a claim is no more problematic than claiming that the divine foreknowledge of creaturely affairs is impacted by these future creaturely events. I conclude that the scenario that I have proposed is possible. That is, it is possible for (4) to depend on (3a) even though (3a) is simultaneous with (3b) and (3b) depends on (4).

But perhaps a second concern motivates the detractor of my proposal. Conceivably the scenario I have advanced curtails the divine freedom to react (4). If God (3b) knows how he will react then it seems that when he (4) does react he cannot react any other way. If this is the detractors' concern, it essentially duplicates the foreknowledge-free will dilemma, which we already have addressed in the third section of this chapter. As noted in that section, such a concern is readily dismissed for divine timeless knowledge, and may be laid to rest—by appeal to Rogers' solution—for divine temporal foreknowledge. I refer the reader to section three of this chapter for this discussion. Subsequently, I do not think that the freedom of the divine action in (4) is threatened. I conclude that the third puzzle faced by the CW-AF model can be resolved. In turn, I deduce that the CW-AF model offers a viable mechanism for explaining the interrelationship between divine foreknowledge and God's providential care for the universe. Through this operation God would know not only how he *could* achieve the divine goals in all possible created worlds, but also how in fact he does so. The divine plan is meticulous and God remains permissively in control of all.

Conclusion

In light of these discussions, I am ready to conclude that a tailored version of traditional Arminianism provides the best model for divine providence. It avoids some key problems associated with Calvinism and open theism. Specifically, contrary to Calvinism, it finds it easier to explain how humans are responsible for transgressions, how God is just in condemning creaturely actions, and why the deity tolerates evil. In contrast to open theism, traditional Arminianism can more readily endorse God's knowledge of the divine future sovereignty, trustworthiness and ultimate victory. In turn, traditional Arminianism overcomes many of the difficulties alleged against it. A biblical case can be made for divine permissive sovereignty and prevenient grace. Further, certain important Arminian assumptions/claims appear to cohere logically. In particular, it seems to be intelligible to assert that some aspects of God's life can be affected by creatures, that the deity can be timeless and yet also personal and interpersonal, that divine foreknowledge and freedom need not cancel each other, and that an adequate model of divine sovereignty can be constructed by traditional Arminianism. But what does the Arminian model of divine providence mean for the average believer? What difference does all of this make to Christian faith and practice? To these questions we turn in the next chapter.

Chapter 7

Caring for the Crew

In the latter chapters of this book, we have come to endorse an augmented version of traditional Arminianism. Such a model of providence seems to avoid many of the debilitating problems associated with Calvinism's theological determinism. It also dodges some of the critical difficulties faced by open theism's denial of divine foreknowledge. In short, a biblical and rational case for traditional Arminianism can be made. But what are the ramifications of this theory for the practical life concerns of Christians? What are its implications for matters such as evangelism, prayer, coping with suffering, pastoral care, etc.? In the next few pages we will address these final critical questions. But before we consider these issues, let us briefly summarize the chief tenets of our nuanced Arminian paradigm.

The Voyage Thus Far

The Arminian model affirms divine sovereignty, maintaining that the deity ultimately is in control of all that happens. No event occurs that God has not permissively ordained. However, this does not mean that God determines every event that transpires. Rather, God has granted libertarian freedom to creatures, particularly to humans. Humans are able freely to determine many of their own actions. Such choices are contingent upon the human agent herself and are not determined by prior internal or external conditions. Instead, the individual chooses between at least two viable options and in many cases God merely permits the agent to act as that person freely chooses. God does not have to grant this freedom, but he does so willingly.

In turn, humans play a significant role in receiving salvation. Through the atoning work of Christ, God has made salvation possible for all persons and now extends a general call to all people to come to eternal life through faith in Christ. Each human is free to receive or to reject this divine call. While God's Spirit urges persons to accept salvation through faith in Christ, this divine influence is resistible. Those who receive this inner calling are free to receive or to reject the gracious offer of salvation. It is true that humans are sinners and that this sinful state negatively affects the human ability to respond to Christ in faith. Nevertheless, the Arminian maintains that in some way God offers a prevenient grace to all humans so that, in spite of their sin, they are able positively to respond to the divine offer of salvation. As noted in chapter five, there are at least three ways the Arminian might interpret this process. One way simply is to accept the traditional Arminian/Wesleyan explanation of prevenient grace. Here one asserts that the sinful condition makes it impossible for humans willingly to exercise faith in Christ. Subsequently, God must and does provide a pervasive grace for all humans that nullifies the impact of the sinful nature sufficiently to allow persons freely to accept (or to reject) the divine offer of salvation. Another option is to renounce the notion that human sinfulness implies that no action of sinful humans is acceptable to God. It may be that even though humans are sinful, some actions of these individuals are still good in God's eyes and therefore are positively received by God. In particular, perhaps the act of faith in Christ (even though performed by a sinful person) is a good act and is graciously received by God as if it fulfilled the righteous demands of the law. It in fact does not meet fully these righteous demands, but God accepts it as such due to the atoning work of Christ. A third possible way to understand the process whereby God accepts the faith of a sinner as a means to salvation is simply to assert that even if faith in Christ itself is not a righteous act because of the sinful condition of those who exercise it, God nevertheless graciously accepts this act as a mechanism for receiving the saving benefits of Christ's work. God does this as a sheer act of grace, in light of the atonement offered by Jesus. In each of these interpretations of the relationship between faith, sin and grace, one maintains that while humans are sinners, they freely may turn to God through faith in Christ and receive the benefits of a salvation made available through divine grace. In neither case do humans earn salvation or receive what they deserve.

The Arminian model also affirms that God knows the future. This knowledge is a perception-like awareness of creaturely events, and is not the result of a divine determinative decree. Somehow God directly is aware of the occurrence of future events. While this foreknowledge may be understood as knowledge of the future possessed by a temporal divinity, the better explanation is that this "foreknowledge" results from God's atemporal eternity. God directly knows events of the future as they happen because all times are present to the deity in the singular moment of atemporal eternity. While the notion of a timeless deity is problematic, one may contend that it essentially is coherent. Specifically, divine timelessness is compatible with the claims that God is personal and interpersonal, and with the assertion that creatures are free. One implication of this view of divine knowledge is that God, in some sense, is affected by creaturely events. God is not pure act, but has some potentialities.

While our revised Arminian model affirms divine foreknowledge, it recognizes the limited utility of this foreknowledge for divine providence. Unlike those Arminians who claim that foreknowledge allows God to decide what future events he will permit and disallow, our augmented Arminianism recognizes that simple foreknowledge does not enable God to decide whether a foreknown event will occur or not. If it is foreknown, it simply will occur. (Indeed, in an ironic way, knowledge of the future occurrence of an event implies that God already—timelessly—has permitted that event). Nevertheless, our revised Arminian model does assert that foreknowledge combined with the divine conditional will and with divine knowledge of possibilities does provide a mechanism for divine providence. Through knowledge of possibilities, God knows all events that could unfold. With the divine conditional will, the deity envisions a potential response to any and all possible situations. And with the divine foreknowledge, God knows which set of possible antecedent circumstances actualize at various temporal coordinates; and so God also knows how to respond in each subsequent temporal moment. In this scenario, God envisions a plan for accomplishing the divine goals which anticipates any and all possible routes to victory. With the divine foreknowledge and conditional will, God knows and wills a specific plan. Presuming that God is timeless, all of this occurs in the singular instance of atemporal eternity.

With this basic model of providence in mind, we are ready to consider some of its ramifications for the practical concerns of Christian life.

Petitionary Prayer

Do the petitionary prayers of believers affect God? Do such exhortations encourage or persuade God to action? That petitionary prayers influence the deity to action is clearly suggested in various scriptural passages. Jesus urges us in Matthew 7:7 to "ask and it will be given to you; seek and you will find; knock and the door will be opened to you (NIV)." The author of James informs us that often we do not have because we do not ask of God (4:2) and that "the prayer of a righteous man is powerful and effective (5:16, NIV)." The writer goes on to illustrate this latter point by commenting on the effective petitions of Elijah (5:17). Throughout the Bible examples are found of God heeding the requests of those who pray to him.

An augmented Arminian model interprets these scriptural passages at face value. It asserts that God is affected by creatures and that the deity can and does respond to petitionary prayers. These responses are genuine. They do not merely appear to be reactions to human requests. They are reactions. In other words, there is authentic divine-human interpersonal interaction. The human agent as a free person makes a request that she could have refrained from making. And God responds to the petition with an action that the deity could have kept from enacting.

Here Arminianism agrees with open theism and disagrees with Calvinism. The Calvinist recognizes the scriptural commendation of petitionary prayer, but interprets these endorsements in the light of his commitment to a static notion of God and to theological determinism. For the Calvinist, God does not literally respond to human requests, but only appears to react to us. As a static, purely actual being, God cannot be affected by creatures. God simply acts, but does not react. Further, God determines what humans do. While the deity may will that when some human A asks for x, God will bring about x, the fact remains that the deity determines that A asks for x. Hence, the divine fulfillment of a petition is not a reaction to a human agent who freely has made a request that she could have refrained from making. That the request was made was determined by God, not by the human agent (as an agent). The divine "reaction" to a petition simply is the performing of one divine act after another divine act. It is as if God picks up one tool—the individual human—and does something with it, and then picks up a second tool—for example, the physical environment—and does something else with it. There is no genuine interpersonal interaction.

Consider the admonition in the letter of James that "you do not have because you do not ask God (4:2, NIV)." The Arminian (and open theist) may maintain that sometimes God does not act because humans do not freely request such action. The Calvinist, on the other hand, must contend that God does not act because the deity has not caused some human to request such action. In the former case, the responsibility to ask is placed upon the human. In the latter case, the responsibility seems to be placed upon God. In this second situation, the moral culpability of his readers that is implied in James' admonition drops away. The letter would better read: "You have not because God has not willed that you ask of him." This surely is an aberration of the text's intended meaning. The Arminian may avoid such hermeneutical gymnastics.

The vision of petitionary prayer that emerges from the Arminian model, then, is one where God genuinely responds to the requests of human prayers. There is an authentic divine-human interpersonal dialogue. This need not imply that God only acts when humans ask, or that God always responds to the requests of believers. But it does entail that upon some occasions, divine action is a personal response to a personal request.

Certainly, puzzles remain for this Arminian interpretation of petitionary prayer. Most notably, one may wonder why a perfectly good God would choose to refrain from performing some good action because a human agent *did not* request such an action. In other words, why would God allow the divine plan and actions to depend on the feeble and often fickle petitions of humans? Would not God want to perform those deeds that are the best in any given situation, regardless of what humans request or fail to request? The Calvinist answer to this question is "yes." God would (and does) perform those actions that he deems to be the best for any and all circumstances. For this reason, human initiated requests play no real role in the divine decision to act. But as we have seen, such an answer seems to generate more problems than it solves. The Arminian maintains that in spite of this dilemma, it is still wisest to insist that God often does allow the divine actions to depend on the requests of humans. But why? Why would God do this?

Ultimately, the answer appears to be that God values personal interaction and human freedom to a degree sufficient to warrant refraining from doing certain good things in certain situations. The case with petitionary prayer is analogous to that of God's decision to rely upon the human response to the call of salvation, or to rely upon humans to make moral choices. In each circumstance, the best choice may not be the one that humans choose. Humans sometimes decide to reject Christ rather than to believe. We sometimes resolve to disobey rather than to obey. Still God allows humans freely to choose the lesser good—the evil option—in these cases. Why? God values our freedom. In a like manner, one may postulate that God does not bring about certain good events in some situations because he values our freedom to request such good events. Further, the deity values the interpersonal dialogue that is entailed in the human petition-divine response scenario. Consequently, when humans do not freely request certain divine actions, those actions do not occur.

But why would God so value freedom and interpersonal relations? The Arminian may answer that, in the divine wisdom, God has discerned that *the best* for many situations is for creatures freely to choose good rather than divinely to be forced to choose good. For example, it is better for humans freely to receive Christ than for God to cause them to accept Christ. It is better for humans freely to choose good than for God to force them to choose good. And it is better for humans freely to ask for good things than for God to coerce them to ask for good things. Now since the best is for creatures freely to do these good things, then God cannot force them to do such things. They must be able to refrain from doing them. And this means that it is possible for them to fail to do what is best. In sum, it is because God wants the best—namely, for humans freely to do good—that he willingly allows for them to refrain from doing good, willingly allows them to do evil. In turn, because God wants the best—namely, for humans freely to ask for good things, for humans to participate in the redeeming of the world—that he refrains from doing certain good things until they ask or if they do not ask.

The Problem of Evil

Our discussion of petitionary prayer quite naturally leads to an examination of the problem of evil and suffering. Why does God allow evil and suffering in our world? The problem of evil perhaps is the most intractable difficulty faced by Christian theism, one that cannot easily be answered, much less easily answered in a few pages in this chapter. Still some theistic responses are better than others. And here an Arminian explanation holds formidable advantages over Calvinism.

As noted in chapter two, a chief weapon in the theist's arsenal against the problem of evil is the appeal to human freedom. As noted in our discussion of petitionary prayer, one may postulate that in the divine wisdom, God has determined that it is better for humans freely to choose good than to be forced to choose good; it is better freely to accept Christ than to be caused to accept him, etc. A corollary of humans being able freely to choose good is that they equally be free to choose evil. This is not to say that for humans freely to do good they also must *do* evil. Rather, it is to proclaim that in order freely to do good, it must be *possible* for humans to do evil (or at least possible to refrain from doing good). And it is precisely here that an explanation for evil emerges. In God's wise choice to create a world where the best might happen—namely, where people might freely choose good—God also has had to make it *possible* for evil to happen. Indeed, if in general it is best for humans freely to choose good than to be forced to do good, then in general God must leave open to humans the opportunity to do evil. Such an explanation goes a long way toward ameliorating the problem of evil for theists.

A couple of important consequences flow from this appeal to free will. First, humans genuinely are responsible for many of the choices (good or evil) that they make, and in those cases, God justly can hold them accountable. A second ramification is that there need not be a specific divine reason for every particular human evil act. God's permitting of evil results from a general principle that it is better for humans freely to choose good than to be forced to perform good. Since the actualization of this principle in any given instance requires that the human person also be able to do evil, then as a general policy God also leaves open the possibility of humans doing evil. Often the evil that God allows persons to perform serves no further providential purpose than to make *possible* freely chosen good acts. Such evil acts need not and often do not lead to some further specific good. In short, there often may be gratuitous evil—evil human actions that lead to no specific higher good. Such events are permitted only because the *potential* for their occurrence makes it possible for humans freely to choose good. And this possibility God deems valuable.

The practical import of admitting the existence of gratuitous evil warrants further comment. It implies that in pastoral care for persons who have undergone tragedy at the hands of others, the care-giver need not assert that there must be some specific higher divine purpose underlying the victims' difficulties. To do so suggests that God hoped to accomplish some specific good consequence through their misery and that perhaps persons ought to chastise themselves for their feelings of anger and depression because such reactions to tragedy tacitly dishonor God's higher purpose in it all. The Arminian care-giver need make no such assumptions. She may suggest that God too is disappointed with the tragedy that has ensued, and shares their pain. Further, she may encourage them with the hope that *in spite* of this truly evil affair, God is with them and will help bring about good even in the midst of these unhappy circumstances.

As pointed out in chapter two, the appeal to human freedom is not readily available to the Calvinist. Implicit in the Calvinistic system is the belief that every event that happens explicitly is determined by God. That humans sin, that tragedy unfolds, that the offer of salvation is rejected by certain individuals are all determined by God's unilateral decrees. The Calvinist cannot appeal to the principle that it is better for humans freely to do good than to be coerced to do good, because in fact consistent Calvinism must insist that humans only do good (or evil) because God determines what they do. Consequently, Calvinism cannot explain moral evil in terms of human libertarian freedom. Humans perform evil acts not because the potential for evil is required in order for them freely to do good. Rather, evil happens (as does good) because God causes humans to perform it.

But if this is the case, several negative consequences follow for the Calvinist. First, there seems to be no good reason for God not to cause humans always to do good. There is no reason for "allowing" evil at all. Second, as noted in chapter two, the whole notion of human responsibility seems to be lost. It hardly seems just or reasonable for God to hold humans accountable for actions that he causes them to do. Third, the Calvinist seems forced to maintain (and often explicitly asserts) that every evil act somehow leads to some higher good. Since Calvinism cannot appeal to the value of freely chosen good over coerced good, it also cannot explain the need for *potential* evil as a requirement for significant moral acts. Subsequently, the Calvinist must contend that every evil event somehow leads to some higher (divinely intended) good. But such a notion, while perhaps incapable of being disproved, is subject to reasonable doubt. It simply is not clear that every evil event leads to some higher good, or that whatever higher good might be accomplished could not be realized without such evil occurrences. Fourth, the Calvinistic view of divine causality makes it difficult to avoid the conclusion that persons in tragedy should suppress the anger and hurt that they experience because such pain reflects a lack of appreciation for God's higher purpose. The grieving process, while perhaps natural, ultimately is dishonorable to God. A fifth difficulty is that since human responsibility is negated by Calvinism and since God is the determining cause of all human actions, then God is responsible for evil human activities. For many, none of these consequences is acceptable. On the other hand, the Arminian perspective goes a long way toward making sense of God's tolerance of human moral evil.

Thus far, we have offered an explanation of human moral evil, but another form of evil needs explication. This is *natural* evil. Why does God allow evil that is independent of human moral choices? For example, why does the deity allow a rock to fall upon a railroad track eventually causing a passenger train to derail, killing many innocent people in the process? Why does God allow a tornado to crash into a church packed with Sunday morning worshipers, killing dozens and maiming many others? Why allow earthquakes that overtake thousands without warning? While appeal to human freedom seems to help explain human moral evil, it less obviously aids in elucidating natural evil.

Diverse answers are available to the Arminian, but the

strongest seems to be to claim that the *possibility* of natural evil is necessary in order for there to be moral freedom. In order for humans to make moral choices, they must exist in an environment where they can casually bring about good and evil. And so, nature must manifest certain predictable patterns where the consequences of one's actions can be anticipated and where one can consciously choose to enact some event knowing that it will bring about an intended goal (good or evil). John Hick expresses this well when he says:

> Suppose that, contrary to fact, this world were a paradise from which all possibility of pain and suffering were excluded. The consequences would be very far-reaching. For example, no one could ever injure anyone else: the murderer's knife would turn to paper or the bullets to thin air; the bank safe, robbed of a million dollars, would miraculously become filled with another million dollars . . . . No one would ever be injured by accident: the mountain climber, steeple jack, or playing child falling from a height would float unharmed to the ground; the reckless driver would never meet with disaster. There would be no need to work, since no harm could result from avoiding work; there would be no call to be concerned for others in time of need or danger, for in such a world there could be no real needs or dangers . . . . One can at least begin to imagine such a world–and it is evident that in it our present ethical concepts would have no meaning. If, for example, the notion of harming someone is an essential element in the concept of a wrong action, in a hedonistic paradise there could be no wrong actions–nor therefore any right actions in distinction from wrong. Courage and fortitude would have no point in an environment in which there is, by definition, no danger or difficulty. Generosity, kindness, the *agape* aspect of love, prudence, unselfishness, and other ethical notions that presuppose life in an objective environment could not even be formed. Consequently, such a world, however well it might promote pleasure, would be very ill adapted for the develop-

ment of the moral qualities of human personality.[1]

The Arminian may contend that while no particular natural evil event is required for human moral freedom, the general possibility of natural evil is required in order for humans morally to be free. While no doubt there are problems with this explication, its general contours seem to give a plausible explanation of natural evil.

Like its explanation of moral evil, the Arminian explanation of natural evil is not readily available to Calvinists. Since Calvinists deny libertarian freedom, contending that God determines every human (and cosmic) event, there seems to be no clear reason why even the *possibility* of natural evil is required. Presumably God determines every natural event, including those that bring about great human and animal suffering. But why would God do this? One answer for Calvinism might be that God uses such natural calamities to punish people or to send them some kind of message—perhaps a warning to repent. But such an explanation fails for Calvinism. First, as we argued in chapter two, the whole idea of punishing persons who have been internally coerced to perform some act seems to be unfair. Second, not only sinners but many innocent persons suffer in natural disasters. Third, while sending a message via natural evil might be one way a sovereign being could get creatures to reconsider their actions, a more direct mechanism of changing human actions is available to the deity of Calvinism—a means that avoids producing misery in either the guilty or the innocent. This mechanism simply is to determine that creatures only do good and, therefore, do not ever need to be compelled by nature to repent. In short, Calvinism cannot offer a convincing explanation for natural evil.

As was the case with moral evil, the Arminian may insist that there are many natural evil events that are not directly willed by God. The deity simply has ordained a world where genuine moral freedom exists and one of the requirements of such a universe is

---

[1]John Hick, *Philosophy of Religion* (Englewood Cliffs: Prentice Hall, 1990), p. 46.

that natural evil must be possible so that moral evil may be possible. Of course, the Arminian may maintain that upon occasion God does intervene, preventing some natural evil events from happening. And this may lead one to puzzle over why God does not intervene more often. Still the Arminian is better equipped to explain the existence of natural evil in general than is the Calvinist.

Many of the claims made here in behalf of traditional Arminianism concerning the problem of evil equally could be made about open theism. In a variety of ways, the perspectives of these two models are identical. But one exception may be noted. As argued especially in chapter four, it is unclear that the deity affirmed by open theism can know of his own future moral character and sovereignty. And if this is so, then God could not know of his own future victory over sin, or of his own impeccable good nature. In other words, not only would the deity not know specifically when he will bring about ultimate victory over evil, but God may not know *that* he will bring about such a victory nor even that he will retain the good moral character that he currently possesses. These problems do not arise for traditional Arminianism. In this latter model of providence, God knows that he ever will be morally perfect, that he can bring about victory over evil, and in fact how he will do this. All of this is possible through the divine foreknowledge or atemporal knowledge.

Evangelism

Among the goals of the Church is that of spreading the good news about Jesus Christ. Historically, Christians have felt compelled to bear witness concerning Christ and the salvation that is available through him. On this, Calvinists, Arminians, and open theists agree. However, the mind-set out of which each approaches this undertaking varies. While the Calvinist exposes others to the gospel, she believes that her efforts are of no avail for those whom God has not preordained to salvation. And while her endeavors may be used by God to draw those preordained to salvation, those same actions have no affect on persons who are not so predestined. Further, in a very real sense, her efforts are of little ultimate consequence because it finally is God's will that determines who will be saved and how they will be saved. Nothing that the human evangelist does ultimately can bring about or prevent this from happening.

The mental perspective of the Arminian (and open theist) is different. While recognizing the futility of evangelism without the inner working of the Spirit of God upon the human heart, Arminians presume that God desires for all persons to be saved and that the deity already is active within the hearts of unbelievers, attempting to bring them into a saving relationship with him. It is not a select few that will receive divine spiritual urging to turn to Christ; rather, it is all of humanity, including any and all who are evangelized. Consequently, there is no fruitless evangelism from the perspective of God's will. God is an evangelistic God, longing for all to be saved, and working toward the goal of calling all to his side. If evangelism fails to produce converts it is not because God secretly wills that such persons not come to him. The rejection of the offer of salvation results from the refusal of the human heart, not from the refusal of God to call persons to him. Therefore, Arminians (and open theists) can rest assured that their evangelistic efforts are sanctioned by the will of God.

But why evangelize? What function does this ministry play in leading others to salvation? While Arminians recognize the ineffectiveness of evangelism without the spiritual testimony of the Holy Spirit, they see evangelism as playing a vital role in bringing people to a right relationship with God. There long has been debate among theologians concerning whether evangelism is essential to the conversion of unbelievers to Christ. Some Christians maintain that salvation is only available to those who hear the gospel in this earthly existence. Others contend that salvation may be accessible to persons through general revelation. They insist that belief in and submission to God as he is revealed in nature and in human conscience is a tacit belief in and submission to Christ who made atonement for sin and who is the means of reconciliation with God. Still others assert that while persons must directly hear the gospel message and must consciously submit to Christ, this opportunity will be given to them after death, in a post-mortem evangelism. We will not attempt to unravel the details of this discussion here.[2] However, while each of these views significantly differs from the others, they all share some common assumptions. Each agrees that Christ is the fullest revelation of God and is the means through which persons can obtain atonement for sin and renewed fellowship with God. Consequently, all agree that knowledge of Christ now is the best way to come to know God and to attain fellowship with the deity in this life. Further, in the case of those who affirm the possibility of salvation via general revelation, they often acknowledge that hearing of Christ makes it more likely that a person will turn to God in this life.

All of this places considerable responsibility upon Christians to tell the good news of Jesus. Our efforts matter. God has chosen to allow us freely to contribute to the divine mission of reconciling people to him (2 Corinthians 5:18-19). For this reason the Church is urged to bear witness about Christ to all the world and to make disciples of all nations (Acts 1:8, Matt. 28:19-20). However, apparently it is possible for Christians to refuse to share this message and for them to be held accountable for their obstinacy.[3]

---

[2]For a review of these and other views see John Sanders, et. al., *What About Those Who Have Never Heard: Three Views on the Destiny of the Unevangelized* (Downers Grove: InterVarsity Press, 1995).

[3]Throughout scripture it is assumed that believers can refrain from sharing their knowledge of God with others and that God, in some sense, holds them accountable for this refusal. A classic text confirming this idea is Ezekiel 3:16-19, where the Lord calls Ezekiel to be a watchmen for Israel and asserts that if the prophet does not warn them to turn from wickedness, then Ezekiel will be held accountable for their blood. Echoes of this idea are found in Acts 18:6 and 20:26 where the apostle Paul is said to have fulfilled his responsibility of sharing the good news of Christ and thus was innocent of the blood of those who reject Christ. A similar

This is not to say that the salvation of others is exclusively in our hands. Obviously, God is free to bring individuals to him by means other than evangelism, if he so chooses. But it is to say that God's gracious gift of allowing Christians to participate in his salvific mission comes with responsibility, an obligation we are to take seriously.

Divine Guidance

A common assumption of Christians is that God can and often does direct people in the choices that they make, particularly persons who seek his advice. This guidance is given in a general way through scripture. Various Biblical passages allude to this function of scripture, such as Psalm 119:105 ("Your word is a lamp to my feet and a light for my path" [NIV]) and 2 Timothy 3:16 ("All Scripture is God-breathed and is useful for teaching, rebuking, correcting, and training in righteousness . . . [NIV]"). However, the Bible also indicates that God sometimes guides through the presences of the Holy Spirit in the lives of believers. And at times, this leading is quite specific. Luke 4:1 indicates that Jesus was full of the Holy Spirit and was led by the Spirit into the desert. John 14:26 speaks of the Holy Spirit as a Counselor who will teach and remind believers of Christ's teachings. Throughout the book of Acts, the early church is shown to be filled with and led by the Holy Spirit. Often this leading is toward quite specific tasks (Acts 2:4; 4:31; 8:29; 9:31; 10:19; etc).

Presumably, God's guidance is grounded in the divine wisdom and knowledge. In some sense, through that wisdom and knowledge, God discerns what is best for each person's life and attempts to lead individuals along an appropriate path. But questions surface. How exhaustive and detailed is the divine plan for

---

comment is made in 1 Timothy 4:16. Another example of one who at least attempted to avoid sharing God's message with unbelievers is Jonah.

individuals? Does God conceive a single plan for each person's life that circumscribes an entire possible life-history for that person? If so, is this proposed life-history re-calibrated each time an individual makes a choice that does not fit with God's original "best" plan for her life, so that as time passes God continually re-envisions a best path for the remainder of that person's life? Or is God's plan more general than all of this? Does the divine plan picture a multitude of possible life-histories, each roughly morally equal, each having positive and negative aspects to it, and each being fully desirable by God? Or perhaps God's plan is even less specific than this. Suppose that God's basic plan is that a person live a Christ-like life, a life of moral righteousness and interpersonal relationships with the deity and with others. While occasionally God may have very specific plans for an individual and may directly intervene to move the person along in that specific direction, maybe normally he has no concrete vision of the best path for that person. In this case, many avenues are equally available as long as an individual lives according to certain cardinal life-principles.

Divine Guidance and Calvinism

Our three models of providence offer different perspectives on these issues. We begin with Calvinism. Calvinism asserts that the divine will determines the whole course of cosmic events. God wills a certain world history and that history evolves as the deity ordains it. Entailed in this cosmic plan are the life-histories of every human being. Subsequently, every event that occurs in the world and in human life is preordained by God. This is not to say that Calvinism rejects the notion of believers seeking divine guidance or of God fulfilling his ordained plan by inwardly, spiritually directing persons toward certain actions. Calvinists grant that the deity occasionally guides persons through the Holy Spirit and that this guidance often results from individuals requesting such divine direction. When this happens, however, these events too were preordained by God. That is, God decreed that humans make such requests and that God's Spirit direct those persons.

The Calvinist probably also will want to hold that God preordains a world history that he deems to be the best, including the myriad of individual life-histories entailed in that cosmic history. It hardly would make sense to suggest that God does not decree the world that he deems to be best, that the deity deliberately selects the second best world or third best, etc. Of course, all of this can be understood in more than one way. On the one hand, to say that God chooses the best possible world may mean that there is only one best possible cosmic history, one best possible sequence of cosmic and individual events, and the deity chooses to ordain that one world-narrative. On the other hand, to say that God chooses the best possible world might mean that out of a set of equally morally valuable possible worlds, God chooses to actualize one of them. In selecting one of them, God chooses not *the best* possible world, but *a best* possible world.

The ramifications for Calvinism of these two interpretations of God ordaining the best possible world are as follows. On the one hand, if one presumes that there is only one best possible world, and that our world is that world, then every event that occurs in our world–including every human event–plays an important (perhaps even necessary) role in the obtaining of the "best" created order. In short, everything that happens in our world contributes to the whole cosmos being the best cosmos. On the other hand, if one assumes that God has chosen one among several equally morally valuable possible worlds, then one need not conclude that every event that happens–including human events—directly contributes to this being "a best" possible world. Some events simply may be morally neutral, contributing neither to the goodness nor evilness of the world. In either case, whether one thinks that there is only one best possible world or a set of equally morally valuable possible worlds, it remains true for Calvinism that every event that actualizes in our world is a product of the divine will. Indeed, for the Calvinist it makes no sense to speak of God "re-calibrating" a best possible life-history for the remainder of a person's life due to that individual failing to make a choice congruent with the deity's original plan for her. Everything that happens, in fact, fulfills God's plan for that person, and nothing that agent does can be incongruent with God's preordained plan for her life.

In light of these commitments, certain puzzles emerge for the Calvinist system. First, it is not abundantly clear that our world is the best possible world or even among a set of best possible worlds. For our world to be the single best world seems to require that there be no unnecessary evil events. That is, there can be no evil events that could have been avoided in order to make this a better world. But the suggestion that there are no unnecessary evil events in our world seems preposterous. Surely, the burden of proof lies with those who would contend otherwise. On the other hand, for our world to be a member of the set of best possible worlds seems to require that there be no other possible world where the balance of good over evil is greater. Somehow in each of the best possible worlds there can be no greater balance of good over evil than is found in our actual world. Or in yet other words, although it is possible for there to be a world different from ours that morally is as valuable as ours, there cannot be any world *better* than this one. But again, such a claim is implausible. Surely we can imagine some evil event (indeed many such events) that could have failed to occur in such a way that our world would have been a better place. Again, the burden of proof seems to lie with those who say otherwise. Indeed, we may take this a step further. As pointed out in our discussion of evil, it is very difficult for Calvinists to explain why God allows *any* evil in the world, since Calvinism denies human libertarian freedom. The dilemma only deepens when one tries to justify God's permitting the actual amount of evil that occurs in our world. It simply is not clear that any evil is required in a world where God determines all that happens, much less that the immense amount of evil in our world is needed. In sum, the Calvinist system makes little sense whether one assumes that there is a single best possible world or a multitude of possible morally equal valuable worlds.

On a more practical note, a second problem with the Calvinist system is that it makes it difficult to understand why persons need to seek God's will at all. As already observed, whatever happens, in fact, is God's will. Indeed, whatever happens is important, perhaps necessary, for the obtaining of the best possible created world. Thus, there seems to be no reason to seek God's will since the divine volition certainly will actualize anyway. Ironically, whether a person seeks or does not seek the divine will is itself decided by God. A typical Calvinistic response to this second difficulty is to evoke a distinction between God's revealed will and secret will. Allegedly, God has published his revealed will in scripture, calling all persons to live according to certain moral/behavioral principles, commending those who live by these precepts, condemning those who do not. Among the revealed principles is the maxim that persons should seek the divine revealed will. Subsequently, humans are obligated to follow God's revealed will, and are condemned for not doing so. Supposedly this is the case *even though humans cannot do other than that which God secretly has willed for their lives, which may include the deity willing that they not seek his revealed will!*

The appeal to the revealed versus the secret will of God only muddies the water at this point. For one thing, as already noted in chapter two and elsewhere, it is difficult to understand how humans can be held responsible for actions that they inwardly are coerced to perform, how God can be just in condemning them for such actions, and how the deity can avoid being culpable for the evil that he predetermines will happen. If God secretly wills that persons not obey his revealed will, and those persons cannot help but do what God secretly wills, then it makes no sense for God to condemn them for failing to do what he has ordained that they do. Another problem is that this appeal to two divine "wills" suggests an unresolved tension in the divine mind. If God's secret will results in that which is best, this implies that when God's revealed will is contrary to what God (secretly) has decreed, then the divine revealed will calls for that which is less than the best. On the other hand, if the divine revealed will unveils what truly would be the best, then when God's secret will contradicts the revealed will the former is contrary to that which is best. In either case, God ends up "willing" something less than the best. The upshot of this discussion is that Calvinists find it difficult to give a plausible account of how humans are to evoke divine guidance. God causes all things, so that whatever happens is by divine guidance, and there is no way to step outside of that divinely ordained sequence of events. Seek God's will or not, our acts are guided/caused by God.

Arminianism and Divine Knowledge of the Best Life-Course

The situation is considerably different for Arminianism. Arminianism affirms libertarian freedom for humans and denies that God determines every event of the universe. This being the case, the Arminian can disclaim that everything that happens is precisely what God intends. As pointed out above in our discussion of evil, because the deity desires for humans freely to love and to engage in moral actions, he must allow at least the possibility of evil actions. In turn, this implies that there often may be evil events that lead to no specific higher good. Often God allows evil for no greater reason than to make possible genuinely free good acts. Subsequently, the Arminian is not forced into making the implausible claims that whatever happens is what is best or that all evil events lead to higher goods. Rather, the Arminian may maintain that evil events are necessarily *possible* in order for God to make possible that which he perceives to be best—namely, that moral agents freely love and behave righteously. The Arminian also can make sense of seeking divine guidance. Since humans are free, since not every event that happens is what God intends, there are diverse pathways for people to take. Consequently, for individuals to know the best course often requires that they seek divine direction.

At this point, however, puzzles emerge for the Arminian system. As we will argue in this section, the advent of freedom seems to diminish God's ability to discern precisely what the best course of action for the long term will be for any given individual.

Further, as we will attempt to show in the next section, freedom also makes it difficult for the deity to use foreknowledge to guide persons toward specific courses of action. In chapter six, we endorsed the notion that God knows all possibilities, knows the divine conditional will for all possibilities, and knows the actual future. But none of these forms of cognition, in a universe of genuine libertarian freedom, allows the deity fully to know the specific best course for an individual's life.

Knowledge Of Possibilities. To see this, let us first consider the divine knowledge of possibilities. Like the Calvinist, the Arminian can maintain that in an ultimate sense God *knows* what is best. Plausibly, through knowledge of all possibilities and through knowledge of the relative moral value of all possibilities, the deity knows what is the best possible cosmic history and the best possible life-history of each person. Or if there are several possible cosmic histories of equal moral value and several corresponding possible individual life-histories, God knows this too. Indeed, we can go so far as to postulate that such a world or worlds likely would involve creatures always freely choosing love and righteousness over evil.

But since Arminianism rejects determinism and affirms libertarian freedom, knowledge of the best possible world or worlds is not identical to an awareness of the actual world. Our world is not the best possible world or even one of the best. Furthermore, the divine knowledge of the best possible world or worlds is not sufficient grounding for the deity to be cognizant of what will be the specific best course for an individual to take in this actual world. Since the events that take place in our world are substantially different than those that would take place in the best possible world(s), then the best paths for individuals to take in the actual world are significantly different than those in the best possible world(s). For example, suppose that in the best (or a best) possible world, Tom freely chooses to accept a job freely offered by Susan. Presumably, Susan offers the job and Tom accepts it because this is what is best or because it is within a set of best possible worlds. But suppose that in the actual world Susan never offers Tom a job because she has developed an unrighteous hatred of Tom, or because she was bribed by a coworker to offer the job to someone less qualified. In this case, the opportunities that are available to Tom in the best possible world(s) are not presented to Tom in the actual world. Consequently, the best life-history for Tom in the actual world will be different than the best life-history (or histories) for Tom in the best possible world(s). In short, while knowledge of possibilities gives God an abstract knowledge of the best possible world or worlds, it does not describe what the specific best path for an individual might be in this actual, less than best, world.

At this point, one might speculate that through knowledge of possibilities, at any given moment in the history of this world, God could "re-calibrate" what would be the best possible remaining world-history (or histories) for our universe, including what would be the corresponding best life-histories of various individuals in this cosmos. Again, one would assume that such a best remaining world-history would involve creatures always freely choosing good over evil. But again such knowledge would not be a cognizance of the actual events that will unfold in the future of our world, nor an awareness of what will be the best paths for individuals to take in the actual future. Since many of the events that will take place in the actual future will be significantly different than those that would take place in the best possible future, then the best paths for individuals to take in the remaining actual world-narrative will be notably dissimilar to those in the best possible remaining-world or worlds. Again, knowledge of all possibilities does not grant to God a knowledge of what in fact will be the best path for persons to take in this actual world.

Knowledge Of The Divine Conditional Will. But what about knowledge of the divine conditional will? Does such information allow the deity to know what is the specific best course for an individual to take in this world of free creatures? The answer appears to be no. Certainly, the deity could use knowledge of the divine will to know the best course for a person, if God deprived individuals of freedom, if the deity only permitted human agents to enact one of several possible acts in each possible circumstance. For example, God could will that Susan will offer Tom a job and that Tom will accept it. God could do this by, for example, causing Susan not to hate Tom or by causing Susan not to be tempted by a bribe offered to her. Sadly, such a maneuver would negate freedom. And if God were to exercise such a conditional will in all instances, universal determinism would ensue. Such an approach is unacceptable to the Arminian.[4]

But perhaps God could control events in a more subtle way, and in controlling them could provide a more detailed analysis of the single best course for persons to take in this world. While not directly causing individuals to choose only one option in a given circumstance, perhaps God can manipulate events around people in such a way that those individuals end up only making one choice–namely, the one divinely intended. For example, (1) suppose that God does not directly cause Susan not to hate Tom, but rather simply lays a heavy dose of subjective guilt upon her, making her aware of the injustice of her decision, until she at last capitulates and offers Tom the job. (2) Or consider another scenario: Suppose that God finagles the circumstances in such a way that Susan's boss finds out her intentions and strongly urges her to hire Tom or face being dismissed. (3) Or here is yet another possibility: God might make it so that Susan falls seriously ill through the period that the decision to offer the job is being made, so that someone else in fact offers Tom the job.

Unfortunately, each of these scenarios is defective in one way or another. The first and second fail to recognize that if Susan truly is free she could still hate Tom and refuse to offer him a job in spite of divine conscience-pricking or in spite of her boss's

---

[4]As noted in chapter five, the Arminian can endorse the notion that God occasionally directly causes human agents to act. And so, upon occasion the deity could exercise the kind of determining pressure envisioned above. However, the issue here is how God might know what is the single best course for a person's life *when free choices are being made*.

cajoling to do otherwise. On the other hand, if (1) and (2) imply that Susan *must* offer Tom the job, that God's inner-pressuring or the boss's demands are irresistible, then this entails that Susan does not *freely* offer Tom the job. But this is of little help to the Arminian who wants to explain divine guidance in a freedom-filled future. The third scenario blunders because while it insures that the job is offered to Tom it does not generate a situation in which *Susan* offers the job to Tom. And this may be important for various reason. For one, it effectively removes a moral opportunity from Susan; she is not given the chance to do what is right. If God routinely would manipulate events in this way, it would undermine the divine project of creating a world where creatures freely do what is right. In the case of Susan, it may be best that she freely offer Tom the job, but such an option is denied to Susan in the third scenario. Further, there is no clear way for God, through divine knowledge of possibilities and of the divine conditional will, to know that Susan in fact would not offer Tom the job if given the opportunity. If we assume that Susan is free, then even if she is prone to hate Tom and not offer him the job, it is still possible for her to overcome her evil propensities and act nobly. If God knows all possibilities, he will know this possibility. In turn, if Susan is free with regard to offering a job to Tom, then God cannot use knowledge of the divine conditional will to discern whether Susan will offer the job to Tom or not. Presumably in order for Susan to be free God must will that under these specific conditions Susan will be permitted either to offer the job to Tom or not offer it. In sum, there is no clear way that knowledge of the divine conditional will, in a world where genuine freedom abides, can aid God in ascertaining a definite best course for a person's life. Wherever future acts truly are free, multiple possibilities are implied and multiple possible acts conditionally are willed by God. In turn, these diverse possible events lead to their own varied possible life-histories.

Divine Foreknowledge. But what about simple divine foreknowledge? Does God's knowledge of the actual future enable the deity to know the best specific path for an individual in this world? I think that the answer is "yes," but only in a limited number of instances. To see this, we may begin by pointing out that knowledge of the actual future is not knowledge of the best possible world or worlds. In a theological system that grants genuine libertarian freedom, the actual world–past, present, and much of the future–is not the best possible world or even among the best possible worlds. Humans do not always choose what is best; consequently, knowledge of future human actions is not knowledge of what is best.

At first glance, one might suspect that simple foreknowledge could play an indirect role in God discerning the best actual course for someone's life. For example, suppose that God could know that if world condition X obtains (wherein Susan offers a job to Tom at T2), it would be best for Tom to accept that job. In turn, suppose that through simple foreknowledge God knows that in fact world condition X will obtain. And so, God also is able to know that the best practical course for Tom will be to accept the job. In turn, God could advise Tom toward accepting the future job-opening. Such a scenario seems plausible. However, appearances are deceiving.

The problem with this proposal is that it is questionable that simple foreknowledge would allow God to know that if world condition X were to obtain it would be best for Tom to take the job. In order to know that taking the job is the actual best option for Tom, God needs to know more than merely that a certain set of conditions X will obtain *prior* to Tom's possible decision to accept the job. The deity also needs to know of the events that follow *after* Tom's decision to accept the job. For example, God might need to know that after hiring Tom Susan will not become irate with herself for hiring him and decide to fire him. Or another example, God might need to know that after Tom accepts the job some terrorist will not come in and gun him down. In general, God needs to know that there will be no events that will occur after Tom accepts the job that will make Tom's situation worse than if he had rejected the job.

Now the difficulty is that, at least in many instances, simple foreknowledge would not allow God to know this; it would not allow the deity to know that there will be no events that will occur after Tom accepts the job that will make Tom's situation worse than if he had rejected the job. Consider the following scenario. Assume that a multitude of possible worlds could emerge both from Tom's decision to accept the job and from his decision to reject the job. This seems to be a reasonable assumption, at least for many decision-situations that are faced in life. In turn, let TW stand for all those possible worlds that could unfold if Tom takes the job, and let RW stand for all those possible worlds that might emerge if Tom rejects the job. Assume that each of the worlds in these sets contains the same history up to the point where Tom must choose for or against the job. Now among those worlds in TW, we may envision three basic types of worlds, based on their relationship to worlds in RW. First, there will be that set of possible TW worlds each of which is *better than all* possible RW worlds. We will call this set TW-Better worlds. Second, there will be that collection of possible TW worlds each of which is *worse than all* possible RW worlds. We will call this group TW-Worse worlds. Finally, 'between' these two sets there will be that collection of possible TW worlds wherein each is *better than some* RW worlds *and worse than other* RW worlds. We will call this set TW-Mixed worlds.

Now presumably, through knowledge of possibilities, the deity could know all of these possible worlds. In turn, through simple foreknowledge, God could know which of these possible worlds in fact will be actualized. But the problem for divine guidance is that if the actual world that God foreknows falls among the TW-Mixed worlds–that is, among the possible worlds that are better than some RW worlds and worse than other RW worlds–then the deity could not know (through simple foreknowledge) whether Tom's taking the job will be better than or worse than Tom not taking the job. Simple foreknowledge would only tell God the actual set of events that will follow after Tom takes the job; it would not tell what set of events *would* follow *if* Tom were to reject the job. In short, in those situations where the actual future is a member of TW-Mixed worlds, God could not know through simple foreknowledge (nor through knowledge of possibilities) whether it would be better for Tom to take the job or to reject it.[5]

The situation is different in the case of TW-Better worlds. If the actual world that God foreknows is a member of TW-Better worlds–that is, a member of those possible worlds each of which is better than all RW worlds–then the deity could know that it would be better for Tom to take the job than to reject it. In this case, God would know that no possible world emerging from Tom's rejection of the job–that is, no RW world—would be better than the world that actually will unfold after Tom accepts the job. Subsequently, the deity could know that it is better for Tom to take the job than to reject it. In these circumstances (and as far as I can tell, only in these circumstances), simple foreknowledge could aid the deity in discerning what the best actual course will be for Tom's life.

But a question arises: how often would the actual future of someone's life, as foreseen by God, fall among that set of worlds each of which is better than all the possible worlds that could have emerged from some other choice? Ultimately, we cannot know the answer. However, there is reason to suspect that the number of cases where this happens is fewer than, perhaps considerably fewer than, those times when the actual future falls among those possible worlds that are mixed–that is, among those worlds that are better than some possible worlds and worse than other possible worlds that could emerge from an earlier choice. Much of the anguish of human decision-making is that often we can imagine both benefits and disadvantages to any choice that we are considering; and it is not always clear that one choice is better than another. Further, we often assume that even should the "wrong" choice be made, something even better could emerge from it in the long run. In

---

[5]Obviously, middle knowledge would be very helpful to God at this point, but since in chapter six we have offered reasons for rejecting this form of knowledge, such a solution is not available to the Arminian.

light of this, it seems reasonable to assume that the number of Mixed possible worlds tends to be greater than–maybe far greater than–the number of Better possible worlds that might emerge from many (or even most) of our choices. And if this is the case, it reduces the overall utility of divine simple foreknowledge for discerning the single best course for a person in life. While simple foreknowledge could aid God in knowing the best actual course for someone's life (at least in a narrow band of instances), there are many scenarios where simple foreknowledge would not assist the deity in knowing the best actual course for someone's life.

I conclude that unlike knowledge of possibilities and knowledge of the divine conditional will, simple foreknowledge could aid God in knowing the best actual course for a person's life, although only in a narrow set of instances. But even if this is the case, a deeper problem awaits the adherent of simple divine foreknowledge: it is doubtful that the deity could use such knowledge to guide a person toward that best life-course. We turn to this issue in the next section.

Simple Foreknowledge and Specific Advice

Even if God somehow could know the best specific path for someone to take in life, it is not at all clear that simple foreknowledge would help the deity effectively to advise a petitioner about that path. First of all, we must concede the open theist's point that foreknowledge *of a specific event* makes it impossible for God to help someone bring about or avoid *that* future event. For example, suppose that God is aware that at some future time Tom will accept a job from Susan and based on this knowledge the deity advises Tom to plan on accepting that job in the future. In turn, suppose that as events unfold, Tom recalls God's advice and accepts the job. The problem with this conjecture is that it generates a circular causal loop. It alleges that a future event partially is caused by God's advice. That is, a contributing factor in Tom's decision to accept the job is that God has advised him to do so. But allegedly also God's advice causally is grounded on the occurrence of the future event. That is, God is able to know how to advise Tom because the divine knowledge was affected by the occurrence of Tom's future actions. In short, a circular causal influence is asserted: God's advice is causally dependent upon an event whose occurrence causally depends on God offering the advice. Such a scenario appears to be impossible. Consequently, divine foreknowledge of a specific event does not enable God to guide persons toward *accomplishing* that specific event. A similar case can be made against God attempting to help someone *avoid* a specific foreknown event. For example, suppose that God somehow discerns that it would be best for Susan to offer Tom a job and for Tom to take it. But if God knows that Susan in fact will not offer Tom the job and that Tom will not take it, then it will do little good to inform Tom that the best path is for him to take the job. Tom's failure to get the job cannot be avoided, in spite of divine advice to seek it.

A related difficulty arises for the scenario that we envisioned in the last section, where we claimed that, in a select set of circumstances, simple foreknowledge could aid God in knowing the best actual life-course for someone. The conundrum is this. Even in those instances where simple foreknowledge could help God *know* the best actual course for someone's life, the deity could not *use* such information to guide a petitioner toward accomplishing the goal in question. Consider the example of Tom again. According to our earlier argumentation, in certain specific instances, God could use simple foreknowledge to know that it would be best for Tom to accept a future job offer rather than to reject it. God could know this if he foreknew that the events that actually will unfold after Tom takes the job are among that set of possible worlds each of which is better than any possible world that could emerge if Tom were to reject the job. *But to know that such events unfold entails an awareness of the fact that Tom will take the job.* And if this is the case, an intractable causal loop emerges. To advise Tom about whether or not to take the job, God must know that taking the job is a part of the best course for Tom's life. But to know that taking the job is a part of the best course for Tom's life (in this actual world), God must already know that Tom takes the job. In turn, if God already knows that Tom takes the job, then it is impossible for the deity to advise him to take it (or not take it). Such a scenario implies that God would be offering advice that is causally influenced by knowledge of a future event that in turn was causally influenced by God's advice. But such a causal loop appears to be impossible. It seems, then, that even if simple foreknowledge could aid God in *knowing* the best single course for a person's life, the deity could not *use* such information to guide persons toward that best course.

At first glance, the implications of these conclusions appear to be enormous for the traditional Arminian position. Typically theologians who endorse divine foreknowledge assume that God knows *every future event*. But if this is the case, it appears that God cannot guide anyone toward avoiding or accomplishing any future action. On the one hand, foreknown events cannot be avoided since they are certain to happen. On the other hand, divine advice cannot guide toward the completion of foreknown events because this would entail an impossible causal loop. In short, simple foreknowledge seems to make divine guidance impossible.

But perhaps simple foreknowledge could aid God in advising in a more indirect way. Granted, God cannot use knowledge of a specific event to help persons avoid or accomplish that specific event, but perhaps the deity can use knowledge of events surrounding a specific event to provide guidance. For example, suppose that God knows that Susan will offer Tom a job at some future date, in which case God can advise Tom ahead of time to accept the job when it is offered. Or consider another example, suppose that the deity knows that tomorrow a certain plane is going to crash and with this information God today warns a scheduled passenger not to catch the flight. In principle, such examples could be expanded to include any given future event. Using an awareness of circumstances surrounding some possible future event the deity could give advice ahead of time designed to set a person or persons on a course toward either avoiding or accomplishing that potential future action. A general description of this model might be the following: Presume that through the divine wisdom God knows that in circumstance X at some future time T2, it would be best for some agent A to perform (or refrain from performing) some act B. Through divine foreknowledge, God knows at an earlier time T1 that circumstance X will obtain at T2. Consequently, God can advise agent A at T1 to perform (or refrain from performing) act B at T2.

Such a proposal faces numerous difficulties. The first problem is that the paradigm seems to work only if God does not know about the explicit future event about which he is giving advice. As already noted, knowledge of a specific event seems to make it impossible for the deity to guide others toward either avoiding or accomplishing the event. And since traditional Arminianism endorses complete divine simple foreknowledge—endorses that there are no future events about which God is ignorant, then there seems to be no future events for which the deity can offer advice. The advocate of foreknowledge, however, is not without rejoinder.

One could argue that God's foreknowledge is limited, that the deity only knows parts of the future. Although he does not endorse the idea, David Hunt sees this as a fallback position for those who affirm simple divine foreknowledge as a means to providential control. Perhaps God possesses an optimal combination of partial foreknowledge and partial providential control, wherein the deity only knows enough about the future to allow the fullest possible divine providential control. This could result from an external limitation of the divine knowledge–God simply does not know certain future affairs. Or it could issue from an internal limitation of the deity's knowledge–God chooses to know only limited things about the future so as to optimize his providential governance.[6]

While Hunt's suggestion is intriguing, I will not pursue it here. Two problems haunt his fallback proposal. First, it minimizes the divine knowledge. As Hunt admits, many theists

---

[6]David Hunt, "Divine Providence and Simple Foreknowledge," *Faith and Philosophy* 10 (1993), 404-405.

want God to have more knowledge than this model allows.[7] Second, one puzzles over precisely how God's foreknowledge might be so restricted. If externally limited, why does God know some future contingent events but not others? If internally limited, how does the deity close his mind to certain facts about the future in order to give advice and exercise providential care? Indeed, how does God know which facts not to know? The answers to these questions are not clear.

Even if one does not endorse limited foreknowledge, other replies may be available to those who hope to endorse the utility of simple foreknowledge for divine guidance. Hunt believes that two central principles support arguments against the utility of foreknowledge for divine providence. The first is a metaphysical principle which Hunt articulates as follows:

> It is impossible that a decision depend on a belief which depends on a future event which depends on the original decision.[8]

In the context of divine guidance, we may restate this principle as:

> It is impossible that advice depend on a belief which depends on a future event which depends on the original advice.

We already have discussed this principle in terms of an impossible "causal loop." It appears to be impossible for the deity to use knowledge of a specific future event to advise someone to accomplish that event.

Hunt names the second principle the Doxastic Principle. Here the issue involves the relationship between beliefs and the act of deciding to bring about the state of affairs referenced by those beliefs. Hunt expresses this principle as follows:

---

[7]Ibid., 404.
[8]Ibid., 398.

> It is impossible to hold the belief that p while deciding to bring it about that p.[9]

In other words, it is impossible for God simultaneously to know that some future event will occur and to decide to bring about that event (or to decide causally to contribute to conditions that will bring about that event). In the context of divine guidance, this principle would read something like this.

> It is impossible to know that p while deciding to contribute causally through advising to conditions that will bring about that p.

Hunt argues that neither of these principles defeats the utility of simple foreknowledge for divine providential guidance when that foreknowledge is of conditions *surrounding* an event that God wishes to influence and not of the event itself.[10] Concerning the metaphysical principle, Hunt observes that this precept "depends on how foreknowledge is *used*, not on how much is *possessed*."[11] As long as the deity does not attempt to use knowledge of the actual event about which he is advising and instead uses knowledge of events surrounding it, the metaphysical principle is not violated. In other words, even if God knows that some event E will occur at T2, so long as he does not use this awareness in formulating his advice about event E, no impossible causal loop emerges. And if no causal loop occurs, there is no clear reason why foreknowledge could not be used to guide persons toward certain ends.

Regarding the doxastic principle, Hunt admits that the maxim generates problems for divine guidance, even when God's advice

---

[9]Ibid., 399.

[10]Hunt's argument specifically deals with the utility of foreknowledge for divine providential *control* rather than for divine guidance. Nevertheless, his basic insights apply equally to divine guidance.

[11]Ibid., 405.

is not based on the future event about which the deity is offering advice. This is because the doxastic principle concerns not simply how knowledge is *used*, but also the specific *content* of that knowledge. In this case, if the doxastic principle is true, then if God knows that some event E will happen it makes it impossible for the deity to decide to contribute causally (through the divine advising) to conditions that will bring about E. For example, according to the doxastic principle, it would be impossible for God *to decide* to advise Tom to take the future job offer if in fact God already knows that Tom will take it. Since the content of God's foreknowledge is all future events, there is no event about which God can decide to offer advice.

Hunt, however, dismisses the difficulties that are produced by the doxastic principle because he contends that the principle is false. According to Hunt, there simply is no clear reason why one could not decide to act in a way that would causally contribute to the occurrence of an event that one knows will happen. Hunt offers the example of a woman named Sally who has been told by a fortune-teller that she will marry Chester. Sally whole-heartedly believes the truth of the sooth-sayer's prediction, but chooses to flip a coin to decide between Chester and his rival Lester. If the coin shows tails, Chester will be selected. If the coin shows heads, Lester will be the man. Hunt writes:

> It is clear that Sally's belief *need not* abort the decision-process that she has initiated. She flips the coin, believing that it will come up tails (as entailed by her choice of decision-procedure together with her credence in the fortune-teller's prediction). Note that, if the coin *were* to come up heads, she would decide in favor of Lester. Thus the decision-procedure is not merely "idling." This is perfectly compatible with Sally holding a (corrigible) belief about the outcome of that procedure.[12]

By analogy, there is no clear reason to deny to God the ability *to*

---

[12]Ibid., 410-411.

decide to contribute to the occurrence of an event (by offering advice) even while the deity fully believes that the event will obtain.

Hunt's argument is attractive. Unfortunately, I believe that it fails. I have no particular qualms with his reply to the doxastic principle. The primary problem lies with his defense against the metaphysical principle. That defense implies that an impossible causal loop *could* occur. It asserts that God offers advice based on knowledge that is grounded in conditions that causally could be influenced by the divine advice. For example, per our earlier conjectures, God might know that Susan will offer Tom a job at T2 and thus the deity might be able to advise Tom at T1 to accept the offer when it is given. But in such a situation God's advice in turn causally *could* influence Susan's decision to offer Tom the job. For instance, Susan may learn of Tom's claim that God advised him to take the job, and while she hates Tom, she may offer the position to him because she fears potential divine retribution. Or again, due to the divine advice, Tom might work hard toward preparing for the future job, and because of his efforts Susan may be impressed by his resume and subsequently offer him the position. In each case, God's advice is a part of a causal chain of events which influences Susan's decision. But if such a series of events were to unfold, an impossible causal loop would emerge. God's advice would be grounded on an event that causally is influenced (or at least could be influenced) by that same divine advice.

Of course, one might reply (in Hunt's defense) that perhaps the deity only advises based on foreknown events whose occurrence in no way is influenced by that divine advice. In this case, no causal loop ensues and the metaphysical dilemma is avoided. But such a response faces a considerable difficulty. One must puzzle over precisely why those foreknown future events are not causally influenced by God's earlier acts. It could be that the foreknown events are sufficiently distant in space-time from God's earlier advisory actions to make causal connections between them physically impossible. Such physical impossibilities are recognized in contemporary physics, when two events are at space-time coordinates that are temporally-spatially farther from one another than can be traveled by the speed of light. But such absolute physically impossible causal connections would not help divine guidance as we have construed it, since per hypothesis such counsel involves the causal convergence of the foreknown conditions with the future actions of the advisee. But if these two sets of events converge, then in principle the divine advice also could influence causally the conditions surrounding the future actions of the advisee. Consequently, if God's advice is grounded in a future event that is not influenced causally by his earlier advice, it cannot be because such influence physically is impossible.

But what then keeps these future conditions from being influenced causally by God's earlier advice? The answer appears to be that the causal disconnection between God's advice and those future events merely is contingent. In principle, the two sets of events *could be* connected causally. In other words, the foreknown future events happen to be unaffected causally by the divine advice, but in principle they physically *could be* affected. For example, even if Susan's decision to offer Tom the job were disconnected causally from God's earlier advice to Tom, this would be a matter of coincidence. In principle, her decision *could be* causally affected by the earlier divine advice. And herein lies the problem. For arguably the metaphysical principle makes even these counterfactual causal loops impossible. One may argue that there is no possible world in which God's advice can be based on Susan's decision to offer Tom the job and wherein also Susan's decision causally is influenced by the divine advice offered to Tom. But it appears that Hunt's appeal to foreknowledge as a tool for divine providence (and divine guidance) allows the possibility of just such a counterfactual world. In light of this, I believe that Hunt's defense of the utility of simple foreknowledge for divine guidance fails. In turn, the overall case for the usefulness of simple foreknowledge for specific divine guidance seems to falter.

I conclude that even if simple foreknowledge could aid God

in knowing the single best practical course for a person's life, it would not allow the deity to guide someone toward that best pathway.   Further, it must be kept in mind, in light of our discussion in the previous section, that simple foreknowledge would only aid God in knowing the single best life-course in a limited–perhaps severely limited–number of circumstances. And this, in turn, enfeebles the practical ability of God to direct persons toward a definitive future path.

Arminianism and General Divine Guidance

Does this, then, imply that Arminianism must reject the concept of divine guidance? I think not, because much room is left for the Arminian to endorse a more general form of divine guidance. While the deity may not always be able to anticipate the exact best course for the actual world and for individuals in it, God still could be cognizant of the best possible *general* courses of cosmic and individual action.   And the deity could direct persons along these general courses.   Through knowledge of possibilities, God could know every life-history that *could* unfold for the world and for persons in it.   In turn, through an awareness of the divine conditional will the deity could set parameters around these possible world- and life-histories.   While for the sake of freedom God must conditionally will *some* multiple courses for the world and for individuals, the deity need not permit multiple options *in all circumstances*.   There may well be limits to the kinds of actions and kinds of histories that God will permit, so that in many instances the deity will not permit certain events to develop, even if this means curtailing freedom in those instances.   So long as there are some (and a sufficient number of) cases in which humans can choose between multiple possible courses of action, human moral freedom can be sustained.[13] By setting limitations, God could exclude certain possibilities from the set of possible world histories and individual histories, without completely eradicating human freedom. In turn, the deity could guide individuals toward some of the better life-histories within these boundaries.

It is important to notice that the breadth of the divinely imposed parameters could vary greatly. The boundaries could be very broad. For example, God could declare that the earth will not be destroyed prior to 2020, but besides this pretty much anything goes. On the other hand, the boundaries could be quite narrow. For example, the deity could decree that a specific set of nations will grow out of definite groups of people, between certain dates, and will develop certain key technologies that could threaten the world, but that they will not be allowed to destroy the world before 2020, etc. Similar scenarios hold at the individual level. God broadly could decree that Tom will live until 2020, but besides this pretty much anything goes for Tom's life. Or the deity more narrowly could declare that Tom will live until 2020, and that between the years 2010-2020 he will live in Smallville, at 1000 Beaker Lane, and will be employed at Rich Bank, Inc., etc. Obviously, the more narrow the boundaries, the less freedom will obtain. Indeed, there will come a point where the benefits of specific divine boundary-setting will be *outweighed* by the

---

[13]The Arminian need not be committed to absolute freedom. Human freedom always is bounded by various parameters; and in some sense, these borders may be understood as having been established by God's conditional will. For example, certainly, human acts are limited by the laws of physics. None of us can jump to the moon. But this does not imply a complete destruction of moral freedom. In like manner, the divine conditional will may confine human actions in others ways, without abolishing moral freedom. For example, God might have willed not to allow the earth to be destroyed up to this point in world history. While such a conditional will limits human actions, it does not truncate all human freedom. Or consider another example: the deity may have determined not to permit Jesus to be killed prior to Calvary, in spite of the intents and attempts of some to do so.

subsequent disadvantages of cramping moral freedom. Still there is a wide range of potential divine boundary-setting which will allow at least some moral freedom. And this is all that the Arminian needs in order to affirm that God can offer general guidance to those who seek divine counsel.

Observe that God's advice remains general. Often the best possible courses of action that fall within the parameters of God's conditional will will not unfold. This is the case because of human freedom. Often humans will not heed the divine advice nor follow the general moral maxims that are expressed in scripture. Subsequently, as time passes, God's advice about and vision of the best possible courses often will change over time in order to fit the emerging circumstances of cosmic and human life. Nevertheless, as those conditions change and as the counsel alters, one can rest assured that through the divine knowledge of possibilities and through the divine conditional will, God knows how to work toward ultimate good in an individual's life. In other words, in all things God is working toward good (Romans 8:28), and no matter what conditions evolve to frustrate the best paths, the deity can still accomplish ultimate good in a person's life. Indeed, through knowledge of the divine conditional will God knows that by *some* pathway he will bring good into a person's life, even though the deity may not be certain (through the conditional will) which specific path will unfold. Even if death should ensue, God is able to bring about ultimate good for individuals who place faith in him (Romans 8:35, 37) . This seems to be the overarching tone of scripture and fits well with actual lived experience. Many stumbling blocks and evil events cross the paths of Christians—even the paths of those earnestly seeking the divine will. And in those instances, often the wisest attitude for the Christian is to admit that such occurrences are evil, but also to maintain a persistent, even stubborn, faith that through such circumstances God is working to bring positive results and ultimate victory for the individual believer.

Notice that no appeal to simple foreknowledge is being made here. God's advice/guidance is grounded on the divine conditional will, not on explicit knowledge of future events. Evoking knowledge of future events potentially would generate impossible causal loops in the divine-human counseling dialogue. And so, to avoid such a conundrum, the Arminian may deny God's use of foreknowledge for divine counsel, and affirm the use of a sufficiently broad/general conditional will.

It may be helpful to flesh out these ideas with an example or two. At time T1 God might advise Tom to take a job at some later time T2 if it is offered by Susan, and such advice would be based on the parameters set by the divine conditional will. Again, these boundaries could be broad or narrow. God could urge Tom to take the job *when* Susan offers it and the deity narrowly could decide that Susan will offer the job even if it means negating her freedom. On the other hand, God could urge Tom to take the job *if* Susan offers it and the deity more broadly could decide that Susan will be permitted to offer the job if she so chooses. In each case *freedom* is maintained, at least at some level. In the first case, Tom remains free to accept or reject the divine advice. In the second scenario, both Susan and Tom are free. Susan is free not to offer the job and Tom is free to reject the job *if* offered. In turn, in each case, God's *advice* is subject to potential frustration. In the first case, Tom could reject the divine advice. In the second situation, both Susan and Tom could take different roads than the deity hopes they will. As a result of all this, the divine advice would be subject to change. If at T2, Tom does not accept the job or Susan simply does not offer the job, then God's vision and advice for the remainder of Tom's life will alter. New pathways may need to be imagined or new roads for getting "back on the path" may need to be envisioned. Still in an ultimate sense, through the conditional will, God may well know that he can bring about good for Tom. Even if Susan never offers the job or Tom never accepts it, the divine conditional will could make the deity aware of other possible life-histories for Tom, and the deity could continue leading him toward these goals.

Possible Problems

Admittedly, puzzles emerge for the proposal that has been presented here; but these difficulties are not insurmountable. First, one might ponder how this position differs from the open theist's view. Open theists maintain that due to human freedom, God does not guide persons toward definite future goals but only toward general purposes, or that if the deity does direct persons toward specific goals, the divine advice is subject to change. John Sanders emphasizes the former position, contending that

> for most of us there is not . . . specific guidance. The will of God for our lives is not a list of activities regarding vocation, marriage, and the like. Rather, it is God's desire that we become a lover of God and others as exemplified in God's way in Jesus . . . . The way of Jesus is a way of life not concerned about blueprints but about being the kind of person God desires.[14]

David Basinger stresses more the notion that when God gives specific advice about the best path, that advice concerns only the immediate future and is subject to alteration as time passes. And so, Basinger notes: "since God does not necessarily know exactly what will happen in the future, it is always possible that even that which God in his unparalleled wisdom believes to be the best course of action at any given time may not produce the anticipated results in the long run."[15] The proposal for divine guidance that I have submitted in this section incorporates perspectives similar to both Sanders' and Basinger's views. On the one hand, if the divine conditional will specifies only general boundaries around possible individual and world histories, then something like

---

[14]John Sanders, *The God Who Risks: A Theology of Providence* (Downers Grove: InterVarsity Press, 1998), p. 200.

[15]David Basinger, "Practical Implications," *The Openness of God: A Biblical Challenge to the Traditional Understanding of God* (Downers Grove: InterVarsity Press, 1994), p. 165.

Sander's perspective is implied by my model. On the other hand, if God's conditional will articulates more specific boundaries, then something more like Basinger's proposal is implied. In all cases (Sanders', Basinger's and mine), events can occur that are outside of the deity's best wishes, events that require God to alter the advice given as time passes. Further, in all cases, foreknowledge plays no direct role in the bestowing of divine counsel. Neither my model nor those endorsed by open theists advocate the use of divine foreknowledge in God's giving of advice, affirming instead that the deity furnishes guidance based on knowledge of possibilities and knowledge of a more or less general conditional will. Consequently, one might wonder what benefit this "traditional" Arminian model might have over open theists' interpretations of divine guidance.

In point of fact, there is little difference between the Arminian model of divine *guidance* that I have proposed here and the open theist's view. As just noted, this is because the utility of simple foreknowledge for divine guidance largely has been rejected in both models. However, there is one significant exception. As argued in chapter six, the Arminian model does offer advantages over open theism with regards to divine providential *control*. Specifically, it allows the deity to know both that he *can* bring ultimate victory and *how* he does so. Each of these cognitive states is made possible by the divine (temporal or atemporal) foreknowledge. In a similar manner, the Arminian model of divine *guidance* can affirm that through the divine foreknowledge God is able to know that he can and, indeed, that he does (through timeless knowledge) or will (through temporal foreknowledge) maintain the boundaries set by the divine conditional will. Without divine foreknowledge, the open theist cannot make such a claim. In other words, like open theists, Arminians (who follow the model that I am proposing) may maintain that the divine advice is general, but unlike open theists they also may contend that the deity can be and is aware of the definite boundaries that surround possible future human and cosmic behavior, boundaries set by the divine will.[16]

This brings us to a second problem facing my proposed model of divine guidance. My model suggests that God's advice changes as time passes–alters in light of the changing circumstances of various human lives. But how can the notion of "changing" divine advice fit into a conceptualization of God as atemporal? After all, the notion of divine timelessness implies that God does not change. And so, how can the divine advice change? To answer this question, we may begin by pointing out that the Arminian model of providence need not necessarily affirm divine atemporality. While in fact I do affirm divine timelessness, I have left open the possibility of an Arminian endorsement of a temporal and foreknowing deity. If God is temporal, there is no clear tension with claiming that the divine advice changes as time unfolds. Consequently, affirmation of a temporal deity is a position to which the Arminian could fallback, if needed. Nevertheless, I do not think that such a retreat is required. My reasoning is as follows.

To say that God's advice changes over time does not imply that it changes in eternity. It simply means that God directs one thing at temporal moment T1 and another thing at a later temporal moment T3, but because both temporal moments are simultaneous in the singular moment of eternity, God's advice does not change in eternity. It always differs at two distinct temporal points in eternity. But does this then imply that God's advice contradicts itself? Not necessarily. In the model proposed above, the deity's advice at any given temporal moment will be based only on events that have occurred in temporal moments prior to the moment in question. For example, at T1 God may direct Tom to take a job if offered by Susan at T2. This advice will be based on the divine knowledge of possibilities and on God's awareness of the divine conditional will *as these are informed by events that have occurred up to T1*. On the other hand, at T3 God may encourage Tom to

---

[16]For more details, see my discussion of these points in chapter six.

take some action contrary to his continued employment at Susan's company. God may do this in light of the fact that at T2 Susan does not offer Tom the job or that at T2 Tom does not accept the job. Again, God's advice at T3 will be based on an awareness of all possibilities and on a knowledge of the divine conditional will as these are informed by events that have happened up to T3. No contradiction of guidance occurs because in each case the advice is grounded on different information and varied circumstances. Still in eternity, the deity's advice at T1 and at T3 are occurring simultaneously, and they differ because each is grounded in different sets of information. We might express this situation in terms of God's eternal conditional will. From eternity, God has willed that at each temporal moment any divine advice given will be grounded on the deity's knowledge of possibilities and awareness of the divine conditional will as these are informed by events that unveil up to the temporal moment in question. The divine rationale for such an approach might be that it allows for the emergence of genuinely free creaturely activities and for divine-human interaction within time.

I conclude that an Arminian model of divine guidance coherently can be constructed wherein God's advice is understood as often general and subject to change. This is the case even though God possesses full foreknowledge. While such a model of divine guidance is quite similar to open theism's view, the Arminian paradigm offers the advantage over the former system of allowing God to know both that he can and does maintain the boundaries that his conditional will sets for potential creaturely life-histories. In turn, the Arminian model offers several advantages over the Calvinistic understanding of divine guidance. Among other benefits, it allows one to admit that not everything that happens in our world contributes to that which is best and it permits one to make sense of the notion of seeking divine counsel.

Caring for the Crew

Conclusions

The Arminian model of divine providence possesses considerable advantages over its rivals. These benefits are both theoretical and practical. As argued in earlier chapters, an augmented version of Arminianism more readily than Calvinism can explain how humans are responsible for their sins, how God is just in condemning humans for their sins, and why the deity tolerates evil. Contrary to open theism, the Arminian model more easily endorses divine knowledge of God's own future sovereignty, faithfulness and ultimate triumph. As argued in this seventh chapter, the Arminian model also affords advantages over Calvinism and open theism in the realm of practical concerns. Specifically, against Calvinism, it enables one to make sense of concepts like petitionary prayer, the problem of evil, evangelism, and divine guidance. Against open theism, because the Arminian model allows God to know of the divine future sovereignty and trustworthiness, it also enhances the deity's ability to deal with evil and to offer divine guidance. It allows God to know both that he can and will overcome evil and that he can and will accomplish his overarching providential plans.

Epilogue

Safe at Port?

In this text, I have endorsed an augmented version of the traditional Arminian model of divine providence. According to such a paradigm, God utterly is sovereign. Nothing happens that he does not grant. Nevertheless, the deity has bestowed freedom upon humans, enabling them to love or hate, obey or disobey. Part of this freedom entails humans playing an essential role in the reception of their own salvation. While people are sinful and thus unable to fulfill the divine righteous demands, God has provided a means to righteousness through the atoning work of Christ. By placing faith in Christ, one may receive the saving benefits of Christ's work and be restored to fellowship with God. While divine inner spiritual aid is needed for a person to exercise faith in Christ and while the precise nature of this divine help is subject to varied interpretations by the Arminian, faith is a human act—one that an individual can freely choose to enact or refrain from performing. Consequently, our faith plays an important role in our salvation, and this itself is possible because of God's grace.

In this Arminian model of providence, God knows the future. This foreknowledge is a kind of direct awareness of the occurrence of future events and is not the consequence of the deity causally determining the future. This does not imply that God uses simple foreknowledge to decide whether a foreknown event will occur or not. If God knows that an event will unfold, then it simply will occur as God foresees it. Still this revised Arminian model does endorse the notion that foreknowledge, when combined with the divine conditional will and with God's knowledge of all possibilities, allows the deity to control the future. Through knowledge of possibilities, God knows all events that could evolve. With the divine conditional will, the deity envisions a potential response to any and all possible situations. And with the divine foreknowledge, God discerns which set of possible *antecedent* circumstances will actualize at various temporal moments. As a result of all this, God knows how to respond in each subsequent temporal moment. While a temporal interpretation of the deity is possible for the Arminian, I have preferred to conceptualize God as timeless. I have done this, in part, because I believe that it best explains the divine foreknowledge.

Along the way, it has been necessary to defend the Arminian model against various criticisms. I have attempted to show that an adequate Arminian interpretation can be offered both of the Bible's view of divine causal influence in the world and of divine grace (chapter 5). Further, I have insisted that it is coherent to suppose that God can be influenced by creatures, that God can be timeless, personal and interpersonal, and that divine foreknowledge and freedom are compatible (chapter 6). Finally, I have contended that such a modified Arminian model of providence is superior both to Calvinism and to open theism regarding the practical concerns of the Christian life (chapter 7).

This book, thus, comes to an end, but the voyage continues. An inevitability of the human condition seems to be that certainty evades us, at least on this side of death. Perhaps such ignorance itself is a part of the divine plan and is a summons to exercise faith. I do not presume, here, to have given the definitive answers concerning the God-World relationship. But I do offer a proposal and hope that others will enter the dialogue with me. In the end, the storms of providence still rail and the questions still echo on the wind. Onward we sail, seeking that safe-harbor. But our journey is not without hope, for we steer by the example of a great Captain who has gone before us and who is with us now. And perhaps that is the very best that anyone can do.

Bibliography

Adams, Marilyn McCord. "Is the Existence of God a 'Hard' Fact?" *The Philosophical Review* 76 (1967): 492-503.

Adams, Robert. "Middle Knowledge and the Problem of Evil." *American Philosophical Quarterly* 14 (1977): 109-11.

Alston, William . *Divine Nature and Human Language: Essays in Philosophical Theology.* Ithaca: Cornell University Press, 1989.

Ante-Nicene Fathers, vols. 1-5. Ed. Alexander Roberts and James Donaldson. Revised A. Cleveland Coxe. Peabody, Massachusetts: Hendrickson Publishing, Inc., 1994.

Ariminius, James. *The Works of James Arminius*, vols. 1-3. Trans. James Nichols. The Master Christian Library, version 6 [CD-ROM]. Albany, Oregon: AGES Software, 1997.

Augustine, *Augustin: Anti-Pelagian Writings.* Nicene and Post-Nicene Fathers, vol. 5. Ed. Philip Schaff. Peabody, Massachusetts: Hendrickson Publishing, Inc., 1995.

_____. *City of God.* Trans. Marcus Dods. Great Books of the Western World, vol. 18. Ed. Robert Hutchins. Chicago: Encyclopaedia Britannica, Inc., 1952.

_____. *Confessions.* Trans. Edward Pusey. Great Books of the Western World, vol. 18. Ed. Robert Hutchins. Chicago: Encyclopaedia Britannica, Inc., 1952.

_____. *On Christian Doctrine.* Trans. J. F. Shaw. Great Books of the Western World, vol. 18. Ed. Robert Hutchins Chicago: Encyclopaedia Britannica, 1952.

_____. *On Free Will. Augustine: Earlier Writings*, vol. 6. Trans. J. H. S. Burleigh. Philadelphia: The Westminster Press, 1953.

_____. *On the Holy Trinity, Doctrinal Treatises, Moral Treatises.* Nicene and Post-Nicene Fathers, vol. 3. Ed. Philip

Schaff. Peabody, Massachusetts: Hendrickson Publishing, Inc., 1995.

Aquinas, Thomas. *De Ente et Essentia*. Trans. A. Maurer. Toronto: Pontifical Institute of Mediaeval Studies, 1968.

_____. *Summa theologica*. Trans. Fathers of the English Dominican Province. Revised by Daniel J. Sullivan. Great Books of the Western World, vol 19. Ed. Robert Hutchins. Chicago: Encyclopaedia Britannica, Inc., 1952.

Aristotle, *Metaphysics*. Trans. W. D. Ross. Great Books of the Western World, vol. 8. Ed. Robert Hutchins Chicago: Encyclopaedia Britannica, 1952.

Basinger, David. *The Case for Freewill Theism*. Downers Grove: InterVarsity Press, 1996.

Berkhof, Louis. *Systematic Theology*. Grand Rapids: Wm. B. Eerdmans Publishing Company, 1939, 1962.

Berkouwer, G. C. *The Providence of God*. Grand Rapids: Wm. B. Eerdmans Publishing Company, 1952.

Bertocci, Peter. *Free Will, Responsibility and Grace*. New York: Abingdon Press, 1957.

Boethius. *The Consolation of Philosophy*. The Loeb Classical Library. Trans. I. T. Revised H. F. Stewart. Cambridge Massachusetts: Harvard University Press, 1918.

Boyd, Gregory. *God of the Possible: A Biblical Introduction to the Open View of God*. Grand Rapids: Baker Books, 2000.

Brunner, Emil. *Dogmatics, vol. 1: The Christian Doctrine of God*. Trans. Olive Wyon. Philadelphia: The Westminster Press, 1949.

Brunner, Emil. *Dogmatics, vol. 2: The Christian Doctrine of Creation and Redemption*. Trans. Olive Wyon. Philadelphia: Westminster Press, 1952.

Campbell, C. A. "Libertarianism," Raziel Abelson, et. al. *Ethics for Modern Life*, 4th edition. New York: St. Martin's Press, 1991.

Calvin, John. *Institutes of the Christian Religion*. Trans. Ford Lewis Battles. Ed. John T. McNeill. Philadelphia: Westminster, 1960.

Clark, Gordon. *Biblical Predestination*. Nutley: Presbyterian and Reformed, 1969.

Coburn, Robert "Professor Malcolm on God," *Australasian Journal of Philosophy* 40-1 (1962-3): 143-62.

Cottrell, Jack. *What the Bible Says About God the Ruler*. Joplin, Missouri: College Press Publishing Company, 1984.

Creeds of the Churches: A Reader in Christian Doctrine from the Bible to the Present. 3rd edition. Ed. John Leith. Atlanta, Georgia: John Knox Press, 1982.

Craig, William. *Divine Foreknowledge and Human Freedom: The Coherence of Theism: Omniscience*. Leiden: E. J. Brill, 1991.

_____. *The Only Wise God*. Grand Rapids: Baker Publishing House, 1987.

Cyprian. *Epistle 64*. Trans. Ernest Wallis. Ante-Nicene Fathers, vol. 5. Ed. Alexander Roberts and James Donaldson. Revised A. Cleveland Coxe. Peabody, Massachusetts: Hendrickson Publishing, Inc., 1994.

Davies, Paul. *Space and Time in the Modern Universe*. Cambridge: Cambridge University Press, 1977.

Eichrodt, Walther. *Theology of the Old Testament*, vol. 1. Trans. J. A. Baker. Old Testament Library. Philadelphia: The Westminster Press, 1961.

Edwards, Jonathan. *Freedom of the Will*. Ed. Paul Ramsey. New Haven: Yale University Press, 1966, 1957.

Erasmus. *Discourse on Free Will*. Trans. Ernst Winter. New York: Continuum Publishing Company, 1961.

Erickson, Millard. *Christian Theology*. Grand Rapids: Baker Book House, 1988.

Fitzmyer, Joseph A. *The Anchor Bible*, vol. 33. *Romans: A New Translation with Introduction and Commentary*. New York: Doubleday, 1993.

Flint, Thomas. *Divine Providence: The Molinist Account* (Ithaca: Cornell University Press, 1998.

Garrigou-Lagrange, Reginald. *The One God*. Trans. Dom. Bede Rose. St. Louis: B. Herder, 1944.

George, Timothy. *Theology of the Reformers*. Nashville:

Broadman Press, 1988.

Gilson, Etienne. *The Christian Philosophy of St. Thomas Aquinas.* New York: Random House, 1956.

González, Justo. *A History of Christian Thought*, vol. 2, *From Augustine to the Eve of the Reformation.* Nashville: Abingdon Press, 1971.

_____. *A History of Christian Thought*, vol. 3: *From the Protestant Reformation to the Twentieth Century.* Nashville: Abingdon Press, 1975.

Grounds, Vernon. "God's Universal Salvific Grace." *Grace Unlimited.* Ed. Clark Pinnock. Eugene, Oregon: WIPF and Stock Publishers, 1999.

Hasker, William. "A Refutation of Middle Knowledge." *Nous* 20 (1986), 545-557

_____. *The Emergent Self.* Ithaca: Cornell University Press, 1999.

_____. *God, Time, and Knowledge.* Ithaca: Cornell University Press, 1989.

_____. *Metaphysics: Constructing a World View.* Downers Grove: InterVarsity Press, 1983.

HelmPaul. *The Providence of God.* Downers Grove: InterVarsity Press, 1994.

Hick, John. *Philosophy of Religion*, 4th ed. Englewood Cliffs, New Jersey: Prentice Hall, 1990.

The Holy Bible: The New International Version. New York Bible Society, 1978.

The Holy Bible: Revised Standard Version. Ed. Herbert May and Bruce Metzger. New York: Oxford University Press, 1962.

Hunt, David. "Divine Providence and Simple Foreknowledge," *Faith and Philosophy* 10 (1993): 394-414.

Leftow, Brian. *Time and Eternity.* Ithaca: Cornell University Press, 1991.

Kenny, Anthony. *Aquinas: A Collection of Critical Essays.* Ed. A. Kenny. New York: Doubleday, 1969.

Kvanvig, Jonathan. *The Possibility of an All-Knowing God.* New York: St. Martin's Press, 1986.

Lewis,C. S. *Mere Christianity.* New York: The MacMillan Company, 1960.

Lewis, Delmas. "Eternity, Time and Tenselessness." *Faith and Philosophy* 5 (1988): 72-86.

Luther, Martin. *The Bondage of the Will.* Trans. J. I. Packer and O. R. Johnston. Grand Rapids, Michigan: Revell, Baker Bookhouse Co., 1957.

Mann, William. "Simplicity and Immutablity in God." *International Philosophical Quarterly* 23 (September 1983): 267-276.

McBeth, H. Leon. *The Baptist Heritage: Four Centuries of Baptist Witness.* Nashville: Broadman Press, 1987.

de Molina, Luis. *On Divine Foreknowledge, Part IV of the Concordia.* Trans. Alfred Freddoso. Ithaca: Cornell University Press, 1988.

Nash, Ronald. *The Concept of God: An Exploration of Contemporary Difficulties with the Attributes of God.* Grand Rapids: Academie Books, Zondervan Publishing House, 1983.

Neve, J. L. and Heick, O. W. *A History of Christian Thought,* vol. 1. Philadelphia: Fortress Press, 1946.

Ockham, William. *Predestination, God's Foreknowledge, and Future Contingents.* 2nd ed. Trans. Marilyn McCord Adams and Norman Kretzmann. Indianapolis: Hackett, 1983.

Origen, *Contra Celsum.* Trans. Henry Chadwick. Cambridge: Cambridge University, 1953.

Osborne, Grant. *The Hermeneutical Spiral: A Comprehensive Introduction to Biblical Interpretation.* Downers Grove: InterVarsity Press, 1991.

Pelagius. *The Christian Life and Other Essays.* Trans. Ford Battles. Pittsburgh: Pittsburgh, 1977, 1972.

Pelikan, Jaroslav. *The Christian Tradition: A History of the Development of Doctrine,* vol. 1: The Emergence of the Catholic Tradition (100-600). Chicago: The University of Chicago Press, 1971.

Peterson, Michael. *Evil and the Christian God.* Grand Rapids: Baker Book House, 1982.

Pike, Nelson. *God and Timelessness.* New York: Schocken Books, 1970.

Pinnock, Clark, ed. *A Case for Arminianism: The Grace of God, The Will of Man.* Grand Rapids: Academie Books, Zondervan Publishing House, 1989.

_____, et. al. *The Openness of God: A Biblical Challenge to the Traditional Understanding of God.* Downers Grove: InterVarsity Press, 1994.

Plantinga, Alvin. "On Ockham's Way Out." *Faith and Philosophy* 3 (July 1986): 235-269.

_____. *The Nature of Necessity.* Oxford: Oxford University Press, 1974.

Plato, *Republic.* Trans. G. M. A. Grube. Revised C. D. C. Reeve. Indianapolis: Hackett Publishing Company, 1992.

_____. Trans. Benjamin Jowett. Great Books of the Western World, vol. 7. Ed. Robert Hutchins. Chicago: Encyclopaedia Britannica, 1952.

Prior, Arthur N. "The Formalities of Omniscience." *Philosophy* 37 (1962): 114-129.

Reichenbach, Bruce. "God Limits His Power." *Predestination & Free Will: Four Views of Divine Sovereignty & Human Freedom by John Feinberg, Norman Geisler, Bruce Reichenbach, Clark Pinnock.* Ed. David Basinger and Randall Basinger. Downers Grove: InterVarsity Press, 1986.

Rice, Richard. *God's Foreknowlege & Man's Free Will.* Minneapolis: Bethany House Publishers, 1980, 1985.

Robinson, Michael. *Eternity and Freedom: A Critical Analysis of Divine Timelessness as a Solution to the Foreknowledge-Free Will Debate.* Lanham, New York: University Press of America, Inc., 1995.

_____. "Is Faith in Christ a Sinful Act?" *The Asbury Theological Journal* 57-58 (Fall 2002, Spring 2003).

_____. "Why Divine Foreknowledge?" *Religious Studies* 36 (2000): 251-275.

Rogers, Charles. *The Concept of Prevenient Grace in the Theology of John Wesley.* Ph.D. dissertation, Duke

University, 1967.

Rogers, Katherin. "Omniscience, Eternity, and Freedom." *International Philosophical Quarterly* 26 (1996): 399-412.

Ross, James. "Creation." *Journal of Philosophy* 77 (1980): 614-629.

_____. "Creation II," *The Existence and Nature of God*. Ed. Alfred Freddoso. Notre Dame: University of Notre Dame Press, 1983.

Royster, Mark. *John Wesley's Doctrine of Prevenient Grace in Missiological Perspective.* D.Miss. dissertation, Asbury Theological Seminary, 1989.

Sanders, John. *The God Who Risks: A Theology of Providence.* Downers Grove: InterVarsity Press, 1998.

_____, et. al. *What About Those Who Have Never Heard: Three Views on the Destiny of the Unevangelized.* Downers Grove: InterVarsity Press, 1995.

Schaff, Philip. *Creeds of Christendom*, vol. 3. New York: Harper & Brothers, 1877.

Shedd, William. *Dogmatic Theology.* Grand Rapids: Zondervan, 1969, 1888.

Stek, John H. "What Says the Scripture?" *Portraits of Creation: Biblical and Scientific Perspectives on the World's Formation.* Ed. Howard J. Van Till. Grand Rapids: William B. Eerdmans Publishing Company, 1990.

Stump, Eleonore and Kretzmann, Norman. "Eternity." *Journal of Philosophy* 78 (August 1981), 429-458.

Sturch, R. L. "The Problem of the Divine Eternity." *Religious Studies* 10 (1974): 487-493.

Strong, Augustus. *Systematic Theology.* Valley Forge: Judson Press, 1907.

Swinburne, Richard. *The Christian God.* Oxford: Clarendon Press, 1994.

_____. *The Coherence of Theism.* Oxford: Clarendon Press, 1977, 1993.

Taylor, Richard. "Libertarianism: Defense of Free Will." *Introduction to Philosophy: Classical and Contemporary*

Readings, 2nd edition. Ed. Louis Pojman. United States: Wadsworth, 2000.

Thiessen, Henry. *Lectures in Systematic Theology*. Grand Rapids, Michigan: Wm. B. Eerdmans Publishing Company, 1949.

Van Doornik, G. M., Et. Al. *A Handbook of the Catholic Faith: The Triptych of the Kingdom*. Garden City, New York: Image Books, 1956.

Ware, Bruce. *God's Lesser Glory: The Diminished God of Open Theism*. Wheaton, Illinois: Crossway Books, 2000.

Weinandy, Thomas. *Does God Suffer?* Notre Dame, Indiana: University of Notre Dame Press, 2000.

Wesley, John. *The Complete Works of John Wesley*, 14 vols. 3d ed. (1872). The Master Christian Library, version 6 [CD-ROM]. Albany, Oregon: AGES Software, 1997.

Wiley, Orton and Culbertson, Paul. *Introduction to Christian Theology*. Kansas City, Missouri: Beacon Hill Press, 1957.

Wolterstorff, Nicholas. "God Everlasting." *God and the Good*. Ed. Clifton Orlebeke and Lewis Smedes. Grand Rapids: Eerdmans, 1975.

Wright, R. K. McGregor. *No Place for Sovereignty: What's Wrong with Freewill Theism?* Downers Grove: InterVarsity Press, 1996.

Yates, John. *The Timelessness of God*. Lanham: University Press of America, 1990.

Zagzebski, Linda. *The Dilemma of Freedom and Foreknowledge*. New York: Oxford University Press, 1991.

Index